**THE LAST DAYS
IN AMERICA**

THE LAST DAYS IN AMERICA

written by
Bob Fraley

Christian Life Services
P.O. Box 22134
Phoenix, Arizona 85028

ISBN O-9612999-0-8
Library of Congress Catalog Card Number 83-073401

Published by
Christian Life Services
P.O. Box 22134
Phoenix, Arizona 85028
Printed in the United States of America

ACKNOWLEDGMENTS

The author deeply appreciates the help of the following people. My wife Barbara for her many years of continued support and the concept of the book cover design, Mary Prether for typing and proof reading, Pat O'Shell for editing and proof reading, Arlene Strandburg for editing and proof reading, our Thursday night Bible study group, our children and several Christian friends for prayer support and encouragement.

CONTENTS

INTRODUCTION

The End of an Age

Did you know that an age of peace is coming soon? The Bible refers to 1000 years of peace on earth—a time when the Prince of Peace, Jesus Christ, will reign. But before that happens, this present age will have to come to an end.

The Ages of Time

From the era of Adam to Abraham, the time span has been calculated to be approximately 2000 years. From the time the Jewish Nation began, to the beginning of the Church Age and the time of the Gentiles, was about 2000 years. From the beginning of the Church Age to the present time is nearing 2000 years.

From Adam →	Nearly 2000 Years →	To Abraham, Founder of the Jewish Nation →	Nearly 2000 Years →	To the Church Age and Time of the Gentiles →	Nearly 2000 Years →	To The Present Day

Man has been on earth about 6000 years. Though scientists attempt to pre-date man long before Adam, only God knows the exact time of his origin, because the effects of the flood made it impossible for man's wisdom to test and determine the chronology of what took place before the flood.

Six is the biblical number stamped upon all things that are human. Six is the "number of man," meaning "secular completeness." The numeral six in the Bible is associated with all that relates to man and his labor.

According to the Bible, the life of human beings on earth has spanned nearly 6000 years. When we add the 1000-year period of the millenium, the total length of time man on this earth will equal 7000 years.

Throughout Scripture the number seven denotes perfection or completeness. For example, God took seven days to complete His creation. It appears 7000 will be the number of years that will complete God's time for man to be on earth. For 6000 years, man rules the earth, and for 1000 years, Christ will rule the earth.

God has dealt differently with man in these separate 2000-year periods of time. That there have been three distinct periods has special meaning since, biblically, the number three denotes divine perfection.

The Last Days

All the signs of prophetic understanding point to the fact that we are now in the last days of this current age—the Church Age, a time that will be marked by great tribulation on a worldwide basis. This book focuses on this all-important and timely subject—important because most of us who are living now will be involved in it.

One of the major prophetic signs of the end of this age is the return of the Jewish people to Palestine and the development of a nation after 1900 years of dispersion throughout the world. Both the Old and New Testaments speak repeatedly of these signs. Nearly 2000 years ago Jesus stated that Jerusalem would be trampled down by the Gentiles until the end of this age. Since 70 A.D. Jerusalem has been trampled down by Gentiles. Then, in 1967, Israel regained control of its city—a clear indication that we are, indeed, nearing the end of this age.

We recognize that we are living in unusual times in the light of history. Prior to World War II, one could scarcely have imagined or visualized that there would ever be a nuclear age, a space age or a computer age such as we are now experiencing. Obviously, all the things taking place on earth at this time are no accident. Everything is happening for a purpose. God has not been caught off guard. He has known all along just what was to take place, and when and how.

All of these things are coming to pass to enable people all over the world to acknowledge that Jesus is real, and that He is the only answer to peace with God and among ourselves. Unfortunately, it takes hard times to make many of us give serious thought to God, and to seek to know Him.

How can we prepare for the days that are just ahead of us? The first step is to establish a right relationship with God. He alone controls the future. The second step is to be on guard, and not become victims of our deceitful times. We need to be aware of what is going on and know how to line up with our God at the end of this age, and trust in Him to bring us through victoriously.

The lessons in this book are designed to help you discover the truth surrounding THE LAST DAYS IN AMERICA. Each chapter deals with a separate topic. However, the chapters flow together to form a complete unit, designed to help you better understand this vital subject.

Chapter 1
GOD'S PROPHETIC TIMETABLE

The major element which opens the door to knowing God's prophetic timetable is His dealings with the Jewish race. In this chapter we establish, through a study of God's Word, why this is so and where we are today in this timetable.

THE JEWISH RACE

4000 B.C. ⟶ to ⟶ 2000 B.C. (Genesis 1 through 11)

Genesis chapters one through 11 provide us with the history of man during the first 2000-year period, including the creation, man's fall, Noah and the ark, the flood, the Tower of Babel and more. Many scholars trace the beginning of man in the Bible to the year around 4000 B.C.

2000 B.C. ⟶ to ⟶ 1825 B.C.

Beginning with Genesis chapter 12 the emphasis shifts. From the history of man in general it focuses on the story of a single individual, Abraham, and his descendants. God will not destroy His creation. Instead, He begins to work through

1

one man of His choice, and one nation of His choice, for the renewing of the world. Genesis takes the story of Abraham and his descendants on through Isaac and Jacob to the death of Joseph in Egypt.

It was around 2000 B.C. that God called Abraham, who lived in Ur of Mesopotamia, and asked him to pack his belongings, take his family, and leave that country. In obedient faith, Abraham obeyed and followed God's leading. It was about 75 years later that he arrived in a land subsequently called Palestine.

Because Abraham so willingly accepted what God asked him to do, God was pleased with his obedience and said He would enter into an *everlasting covenant* with Abraham. This everlasting covenant is one of the richest truths in Scripture and has lasted through the centuries.

> The Lord had said to Abram, "Leave your country, your people and your father's household and go to the land I will show you. I will make you into a great nation and I will bless you; I will make your name great, and you will be a blessing. I will bless those who bless you, and whoever curses you I will curse; and all peoples on earth will be blessed through you." (Genesis 12:1-3)

> He took him outside and said, "Look at the heavens and count the stars — if indeed you can count them." Then He said to him, "So shall your offspring be." Abram believed the Lord, and he credited it to him as righteousness. (Genesis 15:5,6)

> On that day the Lord made a covenant with Abram and said, "To your descendants I give this land, from the river of Egypt to the great river, the Euphrates." (Genesis 15:18)

> When Abram was ninety-nine years old, the Lord appeared to him and said, "I am God Almighty; walk before me and be blameless. I will confirm my covenant between me and you and will greatly increase your numbers." Abram fell facedown, and God said to him, "As for me, this is my covenant with you: You will be the father of many nations. No longer will you be called Abram; your name will be Abraham, for I have

made you a father of many nations. I will make you very fruitful; I will make nations of you, and kings will come from you. I will establish my *covenant as an everlasting covenant* between me and you *and your descendants after you* for generations to come, to be your God and the God of your descendants after you. *The whole land of Canaan,* where you are now an alien, I will give you as an *everlasting possession to you and your descendants* after you; and I will be their God." (Genesis 17:1-8.)

The words of God emphasized in italics are important for us to remember as we travel through the history of Abraham's descendants, the Jewish race.

And Abraham said to God, "If only Ishmael might live under your blessing." Then God said, "Yes, but your wife Sarah will bear you a son, and you will call him Isaac. I will establish *my covenant with him as an everlasting covenant for his descendants after him.* And as for Ishmael . . . I will make him into a great nation. But my covenant I will establish with Isaac, whom Sara will bear to you by this time next year." (Genesis 17:18-21.)

> **1825 B.C. —— to —— 1750 B.C.**

It was around 1825 B.C. when God reaffirmed to Isaac the covenant made to Abraham.

The Lord appeared to Isaac and said, "Do not go down to Egypt; live in the land where I tell you to live. Stay in this land for a while, and I will be with you and will bless you. *For to you and your descendants I will give all these lands and will confirm the oath I swore to your father, Abraham.* I will make your descendants as numerous as the stars in the sky and will give them all these lands, and through your offspring all nations on earth will be blessed, *because Abraham obeyed me* and kept my requirements, my commands, my decrees and my laws." (Genesis 26:2-5.)

God made an everlasting covenant with Abraham and because God is faithful, it was fulfilled. Keep in mind one crucial fact as we examine Abraham's descendants. God has worked through the Jewish people, not because they have always been obedient and committed to Him, but because of God's spoken promise to Abraham. The Jewish people are Abraham's descendants; that is why they are special to God. The proof of this is in the fact that the entire written Word of God, the Bible, deals with the history of these people.

The lineage of Abraham began with Isaac, who married Rebekah. They had two sons, Jacob and Esau. God chose to continue the lineage of Abraham through Jacob and reaffirmed the covenant with him.

1750 B.C. ⟶ to ⟶ 1700 B.C.

The covenant was reaffirmed to Jacob.

And God said to him, "I am God Almighty, be fruitful and increase in number. A nation and a community of nations will come from you, and kings will come from your body. *The land* I gave to Abraham and Isaac I also give to you, and *I will give this land to your descendants after you.* (Genesis 35:11, 12.)

God changed Jacob's name to Israel. To this day the land where Abraham's descendants live is known as Israel, and the people are called Israelites.

God said to him, "Your name is Jacob, but you will no longer be called Jacob; your name will be Israel." So He named him Israel. (Genesis 35:10.)

1700 B.C. ⟶ to ⟶ 1660 B.C.

Jacob, whose name was changed to Israel, had 12 sons. His youngest son was named Joseph. His older brothers, who were jealous of Joseph, sold him into slavery to a caravan going to Egypt. The brothers told their father Joseph had been killed.

Over the years God blessed Joseph in Egypt, and because of his wisdom and ability to interpret Pharaoh's dreams,

Joseph rose to the high position as governor of Egypt. Chapters 35 through 50 of Genesis tell the exciting story of Joseph.

It was about 1660 B.C. when Jacob, with his sons and their families, had to move to Egypt due to a famine in their homeland of Canaan (Palestine). They were reunited with Joseph who was able to care for them because of his position.

> ... the sons of Israel entered Egypt with Jacob, each with his family ... The descendants of Jacob numbered seventy in all; Joseph was already in Egypt. (Exodus 1:1-5)

1660 B.C. ⟶ to ⟶ 1260 B.C.

Over the next 400 years the Israelites, now living in Egypt, multiplied and grew to the size of a nation numbering about 3½ million people. God had told Abraham his descendants would live in a strange land for 400 years.

> Then the Lord said to him, (Abraham) "Know for certain that your descendants will be strangers in a country not their own, and they will be enslaved and mistreated four hundred years." (Genesis 15:13.)

As the years passed and the Israelites grew to be a nation of many people, the new leaders of Egypt knew nothing about Joseph, and this large group of Israelites worried them.

> Now Joseph and all his brothers and all that generation died, but the Israelites were fruitful and multiplied greatly and became exceedingly numerous, so that the land was filled with them.

> Then a new king, who did not know about Joseph, came to power in Egypt. "Look," he said to his people, "the Israelites have become much too numerous for us. Come, we must deal shrewdly with them or they will become even more numerous and, if war breaks out, will join our enemies, fight against us and leave the country."

> So they put slave masters over them to oppress them with forced labor, and they built Pithom and Rameses as stone

cities for Pharaoh, but the more they were oppressed, the more they multiplied and spread; so the Egyptians came to dread the Israelites and worked them ruthlessly. They made their lives bitter with hard labor in brick and mortar and with all kinds of work in the fields; in all their hard labor the Egyptians used them ruthlessly. (Exodus 1:6-14)

It was after 400 years of captivity, much of the time being severely abused, that God heard the cry of the Israelites and raised up Moses to lead them out of Egypt and back to the land God had promised to Abraham, Isaac and Jacob. This occurred around 1260 B.C.

In the third month after the Israelites left Egypt — on the very day — they came to the Desert of Sinai . . . Then Moses went up to God, and the Lord called to him from the mountain and said, "This is what you are to say to the house of Jacob and what you are to tell the people of Israel: 'You yourselves have seen what I did to Egypt, and how I carried you on eagles' wings and brought you to myself. Now if you obey me fully and keep my covenant, then out of all nations you will be my treasured possession. Although the whole earth is mine, you will be for me a kingdom of priests and a holy nation.' These are the words you are to speak to the Israelites." (Exodus 19: 1, 3-6)

God reaffirmed to Moses the covenant made with Abraham.

Then the Lord said to Moses, "Leave this place, you and the people you brought up out of Egypt, and go up to the land (Canaan) I promised on oath to Abraham, Isaac and Jacob, saying, 'I will give it to your descendants.'" (Exodus 33:1)

The book of Leviticus records the laws God gave to Moses to govern Israel.

1260 B.C. ⟶ to ⟶ 1220 B.C.

The Israelites were required by God to wander in the desert for 40 years for their unbelief and unfaithfulness. The book of Numbers records an account of the 40 years along with the census taken of all the Israelite people.

The Lord said to Moses, "Send men to explore the land of Canaan, which I am giving to the Israelites. From each ancestral tribe (from the twelve sons of Jacob) send one of its leaders." (Numbers 13: 1,2. Words in parentheses are the author's.)

These tribal leaders explored Canaan for 40 days and all but two, Joshua and Caleb, reported on their return that though the land was flowing with milk and honey, they could never defeat the giants in the land. God was angered because of their disbelief, and so decreed a punishment for their unfaithfulness.

God said, "Your children will be shepherds here for forty years, suffering for your unfaithfulness, until the last of your bodies lies in the desert. For forty years—one year for each of the forty days you explored the land—you will suffer for your sins and know what it is like to have me against you." (Numbers 14: 33,34)

A principle taught in this example is that although God's grace is a free gift to us, we, as members of His family, are accountable to Him for our actions.

The book of Deuteronomy records the message of Moses to the Israelites the day before they enter the promised land of Canaan. Moses restates the laws of God, many of which were recorded in the book of Leviticus.

Joshua was chosen to lead the Israelites into the land promised to Abraham.

After the death of Moses the servant of the Lord, the Lord said to Joshua, son of Nun, Moses' aide: "Moses my servant is dead. Now then, you and all these people, get ready to cross the Jordan River into the land I am about to give to them—to the Israelites." (Joshua 1:1, 2)

The book of Joshua records their conquest in acquiring this land, promised to Abraham, as God led and fulfilled His covenant. This land became the land of Palestine, the home of the Israelites—the Hebrew nation—the descendants of

Abraham. God renewed His covenant to Joshua in Joshua 24: 25, 26

1220 B.C. ——→ to ——→ 1040 B.C.

For nearly 200 years God ruled the tribes of Israel through judges. As long as the people were faithful, serving and worshipping Him, they had peace. But whenever they began to disobey Him and worship false idols, God would use neighboring nations to attack and inflict punishment until the people would cry out and repent. As they did so, God would raise up a judge to direct and lead them. There are 15 judges mentioned in Scripture. The more familiar ones are Deborah, Gideon, Samson and Samuel.

1040 B.C. ——→ to ——→ 1000 B.C.

Soon the people became discontented with God's method of ruling through judges, and demanded a king, like the nations around them. They thought a king would solve their problems. They failed to acknowledge that their difficulties were being caused by their own disobedience.

The last judge of Israel, Samuel, was furious with the people for wanting a king. But God gave in, and granted them their desire, though He warned it would cause the people much grief.

> But when they said, "Give us a king to lead us," this displeased Samuel; so he prayed to the Lord. And the Lord told him: "Listen to all that the people are saying to you; it is not you they have rejected as their king, but me ... now listen to them; but warn them solemnly and let them know what the king who will reign over them will do." But the people refused to listen to Samuel. "No!" they said. "We want a king over us. Then we will be like all the other nations, with a king to lead us and to go out before us and fight our battles." (I Samuel 8:6-9; 19-20)

Saul was chosen as the first king of Israel, and ruled for about 40 years.

1000 B.C.

David followed Saul as king of Israel and Israel subdued all her enemies.

Solomon succeeded David as the next king. During his reign Israel reached the apex of her glory.

> King Solomon was greater in riches and wisdom than all the other kings of the earth. The whole world sought audience with Solomon to hear the wisdom God had put in his heart. Year after year, everyone who came brought a gift—articles of silver and gold, rubies, weapons and spices, and horses and mules. (Kings 10: 23-25)

However, God became displeased with Solomon and his lifestyle. Solomon had love affairs with many foreign women, and followed their gods. (I Kings 11:1-13) God's anger with Solomon caused Him to divide the nation of Israel into two kingdoms. The northern kingdom (ten tribes) continued to be called Israel and the southern kingdom was called Judah.

> About that time Jeroboam was going out of Jerusalem, and Ahijah, the prophet of Shiloh, met him on the way, wearing a new cloak. The two of them were alone out in the country, and Ahijah took hold of a new cloak he was wearing and tore it into twelve pieces. Then he said to Jeroboam, "Take ten pieces for yourself, for this is what the Lord, the God of Israel, says: 'See, I am going to tear the kingdom out of Solomon's hand and give you ten tribes. But for the sake of my servant David and the city of Jerusalem, which I have chosen out of all the tribes of Israel, he will have one tribe. I will do this because they have forsaken me and worshipped Ashtoreth the goddess of the Sidonians, Chemosh the God of the Moabites and Molech the God of the Ammonites, and have not walked in my ways, or done what is right in my eyes, nor kept my statutes and laws as David, Solomon's father, did.' " (I Kings 11:29-33)

Many kings followed and ruled in both Israel and Judah. Their history is recorded in Scripture.

850 B.C. ──► God Begins To Send Prophets

The two kingdoms lived side by side for over 200 years. But then they began to worship false idols again and live unrighteously. So God began to raise up prophets to speak against their unbelief and apostasy. The prophets brought a warning of God's judgments. There were 16 writing prophets in all and they spoke out from 850 B.C. to about 425 B.C. The writings of the prophet Isaiah is the first in the Bible.

722 B.C.

Though the people were warned by the prophets, they did not listen. The northern tribes of Israel came under God's judgment first. They fell captive to the Assyrians in 722 B.C. As kingdoms come and go, Assyria fell to the Babylonian empire, subjecting the ten tribes to the rule of Babylon.

606 B.C., 597 B.C., 586 B.C.

The southern kingdom of Judah also came under judgment and was destroyed and taken captive during three Babylonian invasions in 606 B.C., 597 B.C. and 586 B.C. During the first siege, the prophet Daniel was taken captive and during the second, the prophet Ezekiel was captured. Both were used extensively to prophesy events that were to become part of the history of Abraham's descendants, the Jewish people.

All the tribes of Israel were together again, held captive by the Babylonians for 70 years. The prophet Jeremiah had foretold of the captivity and the length of time they would be held captive.

Therefore, the Lord Almighty says this: "Because you have not listened to my words, I will summon all the peoples of the north and my servant Nebuchadnezzar, king of Babylon," declares the Lord, "and I will bring them against this land and its inhabitants and against all the surrounding nations. I will completely destroy them and make them an object of horror and scorn, and an everlasting ruin. I will banish from them the sounds of joy and gladness, the voices of bride and bridegroom, the sound of millstones and the light of the lamp. This whole country will become a desolate wasteland, and these nations will serve the king of Babylon *seventy years*." (Jeremiah 25:8-11.)

Also, in Jeremiah 29: 10:

This is what the Lord says: "When *seventy years* are completed for Babylon, I will come to you and fulfill my gracious promise to bring you back to this place."

The time period of 70 years had a special purpose in God's plan. It was the number of years required for Israel to fulfill the Law of the Sabbath which they had been ignoring. The Law of the Sabbath required them to rest the land every seventh year and they had not observed that law since Saul became king. So, they owed the Lord for 490 years from the time they went into captivity, which would equal seventy years of rest.

539 B.C.

In 539 B.C. the Babylonian empire fell to the Media-Persian empire. Cyrus, a Persian ruler, allowed the Israelites to return to their homeland in 536 B.C., 70 years after their captivity had begun.

In the first year of Cyrus, king of Persia, in order to fulfill the word of the Lord spoken by Jeremiah, the Lord moved the heart of Cyrus king of Persia to make a proclamation throughout his realm and put it in writing: "This is what Cyrus king of Persia says: 'The Lord, the God of heaven, has given me all the kingdoms of the earth and he has appointed me to build a temple for him at Jerusalem in Judah. Anyone of his people among you—may his God be with him, and let him go up to Jerusalem in Judah and build the temple of the Lord, the God of Israel, the God who is in Jerusalem.' " (Ezra 1:1-3)

Isaiah had foretold of the event nearly 300 years before it happened, identifying Cyrus by name as the one who would allow the rebuilding of Jerusalem.

> I will raise up Cyrus in my righteousness: I will make all his ways straight. He will rebuild my city and set my exiles free, but not for a price or reward," says the Lord Almighty. (Isaiah 45:13)

Though the Israelites were allowed to return to Palestine to live, they did not regain political control until May 14, 1948. This fact has much prophetic significance which we will examine later.

During this first restoration, the Israelites anticipated Israel would return to the glory she enjoyed while Solomon was king. They did not understand that when Abraham was promised a king, a land and a people, the king was to be the Messiah. So God used the prophet Daniel to prophesy of those man-developed empires which would rule over Israel. He called them *beast*. The prophetic meaning of the word beast is a world government with awesome power. Daniel named four beast (empires): the Babylonian, Media-Persian, Grecian and Roman. He did not prophesy of those rulers who would rule the land after 70 A.D. because the Jewish people were dispersed throughout the world at that time and did not return to Palestine (the second restoration) until recent years.

Daniel also foretold the number of years until Jesus, the Messiah, would be born. (Daniel 9:24, 25) Jesus was born when Daniel stated He would be.

In all, Jesus fulfilled no less than 513 Old Testament prophecies.

70 A.D.

Abraham's descendants (the Children of Israel) rejected their own king, the Messiah, Jesus of Nazareth, born in Bethlehem. Again, God had to discipline them. God allowed the Roman army to swoop down on Jerusalem and destroy it and the temple in 70 A.D. The Jewish people were then dispersed throughout the world, scattered throughout more than 100 countries, for nearly 1900 years.

> When the dragon (Satan) had been hurled to the earth, he pursued the woman (the nation of Israel) who gave birth to the male child (Jesus). The woman (Israelites) was given the two wings of a great eagle, so that she might fly (be dispersed) to take the place prepared for her in the desert (refuge among the nations of the world) where she would be taken care of for a time, times and a half-time, out of the serpent's reach. (Revelation 12:13-15. Words in parentheses are the author's.)

In these verses, John, the writer of Revelation, tells of Satan's activities against Israel after Christ is caught up to God and His throne. Though Satan had previously been cast out of the heavens (Isaiah 14:12 and Luke 10:18), from these words of Scripture we can establish that Satan had not been thrown down to earth in the defeated manner John is discussing here. This event happened after Christ (the male child) so completely and perfectly defeated Satan with the shedding of His blood on the cross.

After Satan had been hurled to the earth he pursued Israel who gave birth to Jesus. But as John states, Israel was given the two wings of the great eagle that she might fly (be dispersed) into safety for a period of "a time, times and a half-time."

A modern interpretation of this scriptural phrase "a time, times, and a half-time" has come to mean 3½ years. However, this phrase was used differently by the Jewish scribes to signify *an unknown period of troublesome time.* The meaning used by the Jewish scribes more accurately describes recorded history. A period of troublesome time has been the lot of the Jewish people and the land of Palestine since 70 A.D.

Though the Jewish people were dispersed among many nations, God has been faithful to them. He kept His promise to Abraham and protected them, their nationality and their heritage. We have full evidence of this today. They are the only people in history to be without a country of their own for so long—having been dispersed among the nations of the world for nearly 1900 years. Yet they have kept their identity.

| 70 A.D. ⟶ to ⟶ 1500 A.D. |

From 70 A.D. until 614 A.D. the Romans ruled the land of Palestine. The Persians conquered Palestine in 614 A.D. and ruled it until about 700 A.D. when Mohammedanism spread from Spain to India. The Mohammedan Arabs took control around 700 A.D. and maintained control of the Holy Land until 1600, except for brief periods of time during the crusades directed by the Roman Church during the period of the Dark Ages.

| 1500 ⟶ to ⟶ 1800 |

During this period, Palestine fell into disuse. There were only 1500 Jewish people in the entire land.

| 1800 A.D. ⟶ to ⟶ 1897 A.D. |

During the 1800s the population began to slowly increase. By 1865, Jerusalem had a population of 18,000. About one half of the inhabitants were Jewish.

Then, in the late 1800s, the Jewish people began to suffer persecution in many of the lands where they had been living. God used the persecution to cause people to think about returning to their own national homeland. This concept was intensified through the distribution of a pamphlet called "The Jewish State," written by Theodore Herzl in 1897.

| 1897 ⟶ to ⟶ May 14, 1948 |

The desire of the Jewish people all over the world to return to Palestine became their dream around the turn of the century. By 1914 there were 90,000 Jews in Palestine. God was moving to bring about the second restoration of Abraham's descendants just as the Old Testament prophets had written.

The next major event occurred in November of 1917 when an English statesman, Arthur Balfour, wrote the Jewish Federation a 117-word letter stating that England would make a declaration to help the Jewish people return to Palestine. England was able to fulfill that commitment after World War I when they gained control of Palestine from the Turkish government.

The reason behind England's generous commitment to help the Jewish people return to Palestine involves the hand of the Lord. It all began with a Jewish scientist, Chaim Weizmann. The August, 1982 issue of *Gospel Truth* magazine reported: "Weizmann was a brilliant research chemist, and became the first president of the modern state of Israel. However, he was born in Russian Poland. He lectured in the University of Geneva in biochemistry, and in 1904 at Manchester, England. The thrilling thing in this romantic story is than when World War I broke out in 1914, God had raised up Weizmann in Poland, brought him over to England, and when it looked as though Britain might not be able to terminate the war victoriously, Weizmann worked in the British admiralty laboratories from 1916 to 1918 on acetone—a colorless, flammable, volatile liquid. In that capacity, he performed a notable service for the British government during the latter years of World War I by discovering and developing a method for synthesizing acetone (a substance essential to the manufacture of a smokeless powder called cordite). The discovery of this secret gave him national recognition. In 1917 Prime Minister David Lloyd George offered him a reward for this spectacular achievement. Weizmann chose that the British government provide a national, geographical home for the Jewish people. In November, 1917, Britain issued the celebrated Balfour Declaration in which it formally announced its favorable attitude towards the establishment in Palestine of a national home for Jews."

The Second Restoration

The next 30 years saw the Jewish population in Israel mushroom to 710,000. It appears God used the same method to detach the Jewish people from their homes among the Gentile nations that He used to wean them from Egypt in the days of Moses.

In Egypt, it was persecution from the hands of Pharaoh. In the 1920s, 30s and early 40s it was persecution from Nazi Germany and the communist movement in Russia.

It was 30 years to the month from the Balfour Declaration that a United Nations mandate returned the land of Palestine to the Jewish people, in November, 1947. I do not believe the period of 30 years was just happenstance. Thirty years has always denoted maturity in God's dealings with the Jewish people. There are many examples in Scripture—the most significant being that Jesus was 30 years old when He began His ministry.

On May 14, 1948 the United Nations mandate became effective and Abraham's descendants once again possessed Israel. This was the first time they controlled this land since Nebuchadnezzar first besieged it in 606 B.C.

Other than the second coming of Jesus, which is yet to occur, this second restoration of Israel is one of the greatest fulfillments of Bible prophecy. It is the key required to understand God's prophetic timetable. It is a sign that we are in the last days and "the time of the church age" is drawing to a close.

Several Old Testament writers prophesied about the *second restoration*.

In that day the Lord will reach out his hand a *second time* to reclaim the remnant that is left of his people from Assyria, from lower Egypt, from Upper Egypt, from Cush, from Elam,

from Babylonia, from Hamath and from the islands of the sea
(a phrase used to mean many nations). (Isaiah 11: 11,12.
Words in parentheses are the author's.)

By the words of Isaiah we know he cannot be referring to
the first restoration. Not only does he specifically say
"second," but also mentions the Israelites returning from
many nations, which was not the case of the first restoration
when they returned from the one nation of Babylon.

Other Scriptures read:

"However, the days are coming," declares the Lord, "when
man will no longer say; 'as surely as the Lord lives, who
brought the Israelites up out of Egypt', but they will say, 'as
surely as the Lord lives who brought the Israelites up out of
the land of the north and out of the countries where he had
banished them.' For I will restore them to the land I gave
their forefathers." (Jeremiah 16: 14,15)

This is what the Lord, the God of Israel, says: "Write in a
book all the words I have spoken to you. The days are
coming," declares the Lord, "when I will bring my people
Israel and Judah back from captivity and restore them to the
land I gave their forefathers to *possess*," says the Lord.
(Jeremiah 30: 2,3.)

This prophecy has much meaning because Jeremiah makes
reference to the fact the second restoration includes both
Israel (people from the ten northern tribes) and Judah
(people of the two southern tribes). We can know Jeremiah
is prophesying about the second restoration because he says
they will be restored to the land to *possess* it. The Israelites
did not *possess* the land of Palestine after their first restoration
when they returned from Babylonian captivity. Since 606 B.C.
they have not *possessed* the land until May 14, 1948.

The Hebrew word Jeremiah uses for *possess* in this verse
is Yarash (Yaw-rash) and means to occupy—by driving out
previous tenants, if necessary, and possessing in their place.
It can be defined as to seize, cast out, destroy, dispossess,

drive out, get, take and so forth. It is the same word used in Deuteronomy 28: 63 for *possess,* which is referring to the land the Israelites took under the leadership of Joshua. That type of action did not take place during the first restoration. So, Jeremiah must be referring to the second restoration where the Israelites have been in the process of possessing the land since 1948.

Ezekiel writes:

Therefore say: "This is what the Sovereign Lord says: 'Although I sent them far away among the nations and scattered them among the countries, yet for a little while I have been a sanctuary for them in the countries where they have gone.'"

Therefore say: "This is what the Sovereign Lord says: 'I will gather you from the nations and bring you back from the countries where you have been scattered, and I will give you back the land of Israel again.'" (Ezekiel 11: 16,17)

One of the more popular prophecies about the second return of the Jewish people is described by Ezekiel in chapter 37, verses one through 12.

The hand of the Lord was upon me, and he brought me out by the Spirit of the Lord and set me in the middle of a valley; it was full of bones. He led me back and forth among them, and I saw a great many bones on the floor of the valley, bones that were very dry. He asked me, "Son of man, can these bones live?" I said, "O Sovereign Lord, you alone know."

The dry bones Ezekiel saw were the Jewish people. They were as dead, because they were not fulfilling their purpose as Abraham's descendants — a nation unto God and a blessing to the world. They were as dead people because they had been scattered throughout the earth.

Ezekiel continues:

Then he said to me, "Prophesy to these bones and say to them, 'Dry bones, hear the word of the Lord!' This is what the Sovereign Lord says to these bones: 'I will make breath enter you, and you will come to life. I will attach tendons to you and make flesh come upon you and cover you with skin; I will put breath in you, and you will come to life. Then you will know that I am the Lord.' "

So I prophesied as I was commanded. And, as I was prophesying there was a noise, a rattling sound, and the bones came together, bone to bone. I looked, and tendons and flesh appeared on them and skin covered them, but there was no breath in them.

Through the message of Herzl's pamphlet and the Balfour Declaration in England (1917) the Jewish people began to return to Israel en masse... to look alive... to take the form of a nation once again.

Then he said to me, "Prophesy to the breath, prophesy, son of man, and say to it, 'This is what the Sovereign Lord says: "Come from the four winds, O breath and breathe into these slain, that they may live." ' So I prophesied as he commanded me, and breath entered them; they came to life and stood up on their feet—a vast army. (On May 14, 1948 Israel came to life as a nation once again.)

Then he said to me: "Son of man, these bones are the whole house of Israel. They say, 'Our bones are dried up and our hope is gone; we are cut off.' Therefore, prophesy and say to them: 'This is what the Sovereign Lord says: "O my people, I am going to open your graves and bring you up from them; I will bring you back to the land of Israel." ' (Ezekiel 37:1-12. Words in parentheses are the author's.)

This is what the Sovereign Lord says: "I will take the Israelites out of the nations where they have gone. I will gather them from all around and bring them back into their own land. I will make them one nation in the land, on the mountain of Israel." (Ezekiel 37:21,22)

The land of Israel is again the home of the Israelites— Abraham's descendants. They are alive! This prophecy is history.

Though Israel has been restored as a nation, the Jews have yet to return to God as a part of His holy people, which is also going to happen according to prophecy.

They will no longer defile themselves with their idols and vile images or with any of their offenses, for I will save them from all of their sinful backsliding, and I will cleanse them. They will be my people, and I will be their God. (Ezekiel 37:23)

Israel's Enemies Identified

In chapters 37-39 Ezekiel prophesies about some of the events which will cause the Israelites to return to God. These passages are a study within themselves. However, it appears that Russia is clearly identified by her ancestry, Meshech, (the founders of Moscow) and Tubal (the founders of Tobolsk), and by the title "Gog," "chief prince," which is the Hebrew word *ROSH* still used in modern Hebrew for Russia. Throughout these chapters Gog (Russia) is the power from the north, which God will cause to attack Israel. He also identifies Russia's allies: Persia (Iran), Ethiopia (East Africa), Libya (North Africa), Gomer (East Germany), Togarmah (Turkey), and all his bands which include the surrounding Arab nations—Iraq, Yemen, Saudi Arabia, Syria, Afghanistan and Jordan.

The word of the Lord came to me: "Son of man, set your face against Gog (Russia), of the land of Magog . . . 'This is what the Sovereign Lord says: I am against you, O Gog, Chief Prince of Meshech (the founders of Moscow) and Tubal (the founders of Tobolsk). I will turn you around, put hooks in your jaws and bring you out with your whole army.' (Ezekiel 38:1-4a. Words in parentheses are the author's.)

" 'In future years you will invade a land that has recovered from war, whose people were gathered from many nations to the mountains of Israel, which had long been desolate. They had been brought out from the nations, and now all of them live in safety.' (This attack occurs after the second restoration of Israel which happened in recent years.) (Ezekiel 38:8b. Words in parentheses are the author's.)

"Prophesy and say to Gog (Russia): 'This is what the Sovereign Lord says: In that day, when my people Israel are living in safety, will you not take notice of it? You will come from your place in the far north . . . You will advance against my people Israel like a cloud that covers the land . . . (Ezekiel 38:14-16a. Words in parentheses are the author's.)

" 'This is what will happen that day: When Gog (Russia) attacks the land of Israel, my hot anger will be aroused, declares the Sovereign Lord. In my zeal and fiery wrath, I declare that at that time there shall be a great earthquake in the land of Israel. I will execute judgment upon him (Russia) with plague and bloodshed; I will pour down torrents of rain, hailstones and burning sulfur on him and on his troops and on the many nations with him. And I will show my greatness and my holiness, and I will make myself known in the sight of many nations. Then they will know that I am the Lord.' (Ezekiel 38:18,19,22,23. Words in parentheses are the author's.)

"Son of man, prophesy against Gog (Russia) and say: 'This is what the Sovereign Lord says: I am against you, O Gog . . . I will bring you from the far north and send you against the mountains of Israel . . . on the mountains of Israel you will fall, you and all your troops and the nations with you. I will make known my holy name among my people Israel.' " (Ezekiel 39: 1,2,4,7. Words in parentheses are the author's.)

By the hand of the Lord, Israel will defeat the Russian army. The devastation is going to be so great that the weapons left behind by the Russian army will provide fuel for Israel for seven years. (Ezekiel 38:9)

It will be this great victory, obviously brought about by the hand of the Lord, that will turn the hearts of the Jewish people back to a true commitment to God—one which most do not presently have.

From that day forward the house of Israel will know that I am the Lord their God and nations will know that the people of Israel went into exile for their sin, because they were unfaithful to me. So I hid my face from them and handed them over to their enemies, and they all fell by the sword. I dealt with them according to their uncleanness and their offenses, and I have brought them back from the nations and have gathered them from the countries of their enemies, I will show myself holy through them in the sight of many nations. Then they will know that I am the Lord their God, for though I sent them into exile among the nations, I will gather them to their own land, not leaving any behind. I will no longer hide my face from them, for I will pour out my Spirit on the house of Israel, declares the Sovereign Lord. (Ezekiel 39:22-24, 27-29)

From 70 A.D. until recent years, the Lord hid His face from Abraham's descendants. These words of Ezekiel are historical fact.

But God's faithfulness has prevailed. Because of God's promise to Abraham, the Jews are His chosen people, and He has had to discipline them as a father disciplines a child.

The Lord did not set his affection on you and choose you (speaking of the Israelites) because you were more numerous than other people, for you were the fewest of all people. But it was because the Lord loves you and *kept the oath He swore to your forefathers* (Abraham, Isaac and Jacob) that He brought you out with a mighty hand and redeemed you from the land of slavery, from the power of Pharaoh, king of Egypt. Know, therefore, that the Lord your God is God; He is the faithful God, keeping His covenant of love to a thousand generations of those who love Him and keep His commands. (Deuteronomy 7:7-9. Words in parentheses are the author's.)

God has been faithful and kept His covenant made with Abraham over these past 4000 years.

Why have the Jews had to suffer so much? There is a principle of accountability taught throughout Scripture for all who follow the Lord. Moses gave this warning to the Israelites just before they were about to enter and possess the promised land of Canaan.

If you do not carefully follow all of the words of this law, which are written in this book, and do not revere this glorious and awesome name—the Lord your God—just as it pleased the Lord to make you prosper and increase in numbers, so it will please him to ruin and destroy you. You will be uprooted from the land you are entering to possess. Then the Lord will scatter you among the nations, from one end of the earth to the other. There you will worship other gods—gods of wood and stone—which neither you nor your fathers have known. Among those nations you will find no repose, no resting place for the sole of your foot. There the Lord will give you an anxious mind, eyes weary with longing, and a despairing heart. You will live in constant suspense, filled with dread both day and night, never sure of your life. In the morning you will say, "If only it were evening!" and in the evening, "If only it were morning!"—because of the terror that will fill your hearts and the sights that your eyes will see. (Deuteronomy 28:58,63-67)

The Jews are the only people who can truly say that the God of the universe is their God. Yet they forsook Him, and followed after the deceitfulness of their own hearts. So we can see why they have been so afflicted throughout the centuries. Even today, most Jewish people don't follow the God of Abraham, Isaac and Jacob.

The Jewish people have experienced times of dreadful persecution. Often they have been weary, not knowing what is going to happen next. Their defeats have come because of sin and unfaithfulness.

Hear this word the Lord has spoken against you, O people of Israel—against the whole family I brought up out of Egypt: "You only have I chosen of all the families of the earth; therefore, I will punish you for all your sins." (Amos 3:1,2)

God has proven over and over to mankind both His mercy and faithfulness, through His dealings with Abraham's family, the Jewish people. Their second restoration—regaining control of the land of Palestine—and the events that have followed since that day in 1948 have been almost unbelievable.

The weapons and methods may be different than those used in the days of Joshua, but the miraculous way in which the Israelites have defeated those who have opposed them since 1948 has *not* changed.

Conflicts in Israel

It was on May 14, 1948 that the United Nations' mandate ended and at noon the next day, the Jews in Palestine declared themselves a nation. Within hours, Arab forces began dropping bombs determined to rid the land of its 710,000 Jews. However, God had different plans as was prophesied, and the Israelites gained the upper hand in this first conflict with the Arabs. An armistice followed, even though the Arabs still had control of Old Jerusalem and the old temple wall.

The next conflict occurred in 1956, when President Gamal Abdel Nasser of Egypt called for a holy war against Israel. Egypt, equipped with Soviet weapons, moved into the Sinai and began the second round of fighting against this new nation of Israel. However, this second conflict was again brief, with the Israelites teaching the Arabs a dramatic lesson.

By 1958, ten years after the establishment of the new Jewish state, major progress had been made in several areas.

1. The Jewish population rose to 1.8 million. Most people were employed and self-sufficient.
2. There was agricultural self-sufficiency. Productivity was up 600%; there was a 400% increase in irrigated areas.
3. 150,000 new dwellings had been completed.
4. Nearly 100% of the second generation youth were attending school; school population had gone to 550,000 from 130,000; 10,000 were enrolled in the nation's four universities.
5. Other areas of progress included: national insurance, several welfare and health services, roads, water, electricity, sanitary facilities, irrigation and participation in free elections.

The Six Day War

In 1967, the third conflict broke out as Arab resentment exploded, beginning what came to be known as the Six Day War. The Arabs launched an all-out attack this time, but the Israelites retaliated with lightning speed, soundly defeating them.

The war started on June 4. On June 5, Israel bombed the airfields of Egypt, Syria, Jordan and Iraq, destroying 452 planes in three hours. The same day their ground forces moved against Egyptian forces at four different points in the Sinai.

On June 6, Israel counterattacked against Jordanian troops in Jerusalem and took everything except the Old City. On June 7, Israel gained possession of the Old City of Jerusalem for the first time since 70 A.D., and a quarter of a million Jews streamed into the Old City, headed for the Wailing Wall. The site where Solomon had built the temple for the Lord was back in Jewish hands.

On June 9, Israel drove the Syrians from the Golan Heights, penetrated the Sinai to the Suez Canal and took the Gaza strip. On June 10 all parties agreed to a cease-fire.

A 20-Day Conflict

The fourth conflict started on October 6, 1973, which was Yom Kippur, the most holy day for the Jews—their Day of Atonement. It looked extremely bad at first. In the south, Egyptian aircraft and artillery bombarded the Sinai and 70,000 of their troops and 1,000 tanks crossed the Suez Canal. In the north, 40,000 Syrian troops with 800 tanks attacked the Golan Heights. Within a few days Israel stopped all advances on both fronts and began to penetrate enemy lines with amazing military conquest, moving to within 62 miles of Cairo, Egypt, with nearly 12,000 troops and 200 tanks on the West side of the Suez. The Arab nations were again facing defeat and within 20 days from the war's beginning, October 25, 1973, a ceasefire was proclaimed.

The War In Lebanon

The most recent conflict at the time of this writing began on June 6, 1982, when the State of Israel launched a massive thrust into Lebanon aimed at rolling back PLO (Palestine Liberation Organization) terrorist gunners from the northern border of Israel. This conflict between Israel and the PLO in Lebanon revealed exactly how close Russia was to unleashing an all-out, massive invasion of Israel.

The most incredible and amazing story out of the Lebanon War (1982) is that Russia was set to back a PLO front invasion of Israel, probably in August 1982, and had an enormous cache of arms under the town of Sidon in Lebanon for an army of one million men. The PLO had no more than 25,000 men. Intelligence indicates Russia was ready to lead its Arab allies to settle the Israel question in one massive invasion by adding many soldiers!

Jewish Press, August 13, 1982 reported: "Prime Minister of Israel, Menachem Begin, speaks—What did we find in Lebanon? First of all, arms . . . It will take hundreds of trucks, working day and night, months to transport to Israel all of the arms we found in Lebanon. There was enough equipment for ten, perhaps hundreds of thousands of soldiers. It became clear to us that we had entered Lebanon at possibly the very last moment. These arms were not intended for terrorists alone. This is a familiar strategy of the Soviet Union . . . It seems that Lebanon was the center of powerful international intrigue against Israel, Jordan and perhaps even Saudi Arabia and the Gulf states, by an organization serving the Soviet Union."

Gospel Truth, February, 1983 stated: "Moscow has a master plan for destroying Israel. It has now been uncovered by Israel intelligence. It corresponds with Ezekiel, chapters 38 and 39. The Israelis marvel that Ezekiel, in 650 B.C., knew the secret plan to smash Israel in the latter years (Ezekiel 38:8). We too marvel that the Russian invasion was ready by a hair's breadth in 1982! How near can we be to the end?"

Many incredible reports have again come from the battlegrounds of this war just like the previous wars that have occurred since the descendants of Abraham repossessed the land of Palestine in 1948.

One of the most exciting reports was the shooting down of 86 Soviet built MIG fighters by the Israeli air force without a single loss. *Business Week,* September 20, 1982 reported: "The latest air war was lopsided, too, but this time in Israel's favor. When Syria sent up 60 Soviet built MIG fighters to defend its SAM batteries, 90 U.S. made Israelite jets pounced and shot down 36 MIGS without a single loss. On the following day, Syria dispatched 50 more MIGS to challenge the Israeli air force—and not one of those jets returned to base, the Israelis claim."

Present-Day Signposts

Around 650 B.C., a fellow Israeli prophet by the name of Ezekiel, at the command of the Lord, foretold of a battle in the latter days led by Gog (modern Russia). We now see current events leading up to this.

> You will come from your place in the far north, you and many nations with you . . . you will advance against my people Israel like a cloud that covers the land. In days to come, O Gog (Russia), I will bring you against my land, so that the nations may know me when I show myself holy through you before their eyes. (Ezekiel 38:15,16. Words in parentheses are the author's.)

Bible scholars, together with Bible-believing Orthodox Jewish rabbis, concur in the view that a federation of nations under the leadership of the Union of Soviet Socialist Republic listed in Ezekiel 38: 5,6 will attempt to destroy the modern state of Israel.

Since the June, 1982 Lebanon War, the Soviets have completely rebuilt the Syrian military. The Syrian ground and air arsenal of June 1982 is already bigger and better than before Syria lost one-third of its air force in battles against Israel. The Soviets have completed replacement of Syrian losses in tanks, planes, artillery, surface-to-air missiles and other weapons and equipment.

It appears a major Russian assault against Israel is imminent.

God's prophetic timetable, the history of Abraham's descendants, shows us without a doubt that we are in the final countdown of this age, the last days. Sometimes we neglect to remember the important part the Jewish people have played in God's plan for man. Because of God's faithfulness in keeping His promise to Abraham, the Jewish people have been a tremendous blessing. They gave us all of the Scriptures. They are the race Jesus, God Himself in the flesh, chose to use to come to earth in the form of man. Nearly all of God's Word centers on these people. They began the early church and from them came the early Christian leaders.

Their ending is also foretold by the prophet Ezekiel. Speaking of things to come after their second restoration, he says:

> My servant David will be king over them, and they will all have one shepherd. They will follow my laws and be careful to keep my decrees. (We know this has not yet happened.) They will live in the land I gave to my servant Jacob, (Remember, Jacob was the father of the 12 sons who formed the twelve tribes) the land where your fathers lived...I will make a covenant of peace with them; it will be an everlasting covenant. I will establish them and increase their numbers, and I will put my sanctuary among them forever. My dwelling place will be with them; I will be their God, and they will be my people. Then the nations will know that I, the Lord, make Israel holy. (Ezekiel 37:24-28. Words in parentheses are the author's.)

That the Jewish people will someday acknowledge and accept Jesus is made known by Zechariah, another Old

Testament prophet. Speaking of the end-times he says:

> On that day, when all the nations of the earth are gathered
> against her, I will make Jerusalem an immovable rock for all
> the nations...on that day I will set out to destroy all the
> nations that attack Jerusalem. And I will pour out on the
> house of David and the inhabitants of Jerusalem a spirit of
> grace and supplication. They will look on me, the one they
> have pierced, (what they did to Jesus at the crucifixion) and
> mourn for him as one grieves for a first born son. (Zechariah
> 12:3,9,10. Words in parentheses are the author's.)

We have reviewed the story of Abraham's descendants so
there can be no doubt as to the prophetic times in which we
now live. However, the main message of this book is not just
to establish God's prophetic timetable. We cannot stop and
camp, and just observe the Jewish people fulfill end-time
Scriptures. God recorded some crucial scriptural guidelines
for Christians during this same period of time.

Chapter 2

THE CHURCH IN REVIEW

The Church: Abraham's Second Family

Did you know Abraham had two families? And the promises God made to the first, which we discussed in the previous chapter, are also made to the second.

> ... He (Abraham) is the father of all who believe. It was not through law that Abraham and his offspring received the promise that he would be heir of the world, but through the righteousness that comes by faith. Therefore, the promise comes by faith, so that it may be by grace and may be guaranteed to all Abraham's offspring—not only to those who are of the law (Israelites), but also to those who are of the faith (Christians) of Abraham. He is the father of us all. As it is written: "I have made you a father of many nations." He is our father in the sight of God, in whom he believed. (Romans 4:11, 13, 16, 17. Words in parentheses are the author's.)

> The Scriptures foresaw that God would justify the Gentiles by faith, and announced the gospel in advance to Abraham: "All nations will be blessed through you." So those who have faith are blessed along with Abraham, the man of faith. He

redeemed us in order that the blessing given to Abraham might come to the Gentiles through Christ Jesus, so that by faith we might receive the promise of the Spirit. If you belong to Christ, then you are Abraham's seed, and heirs according to the promise. (Galatians 3:8, 14, 29)

Abraham's second family (called the church, the Body of Christ, Christians, the called out, etc.) differs from his first family. The first family consists of Abraham's descendants through natural physical birth, the Israelites. The second family is made up of his descendants through spiritual rebirth, brought about when people accept Jesus as Savior. The history of the church is the history of Abraham's spiritual family and is called the Spiritual Dispensation.

To gain a clear understanding of the last days, a working knowledge of the history of the church is essential. Church history covers all or part of three periods of world history, which can be broken down into three distinct periods: the Ancient Period, Medieval Period and Modern Period.

Ancient Period ⟶ Beginning of Time to 476 A.D.

The Ancient Period covers the historical rules of the Egyptian, Assyrian, Babylonian, Persian, Greek and Roman Empires. It was toward the end of this period during the rule of the Roman Empire that the "Church" had its beginning. Some of the key events which occurred in the history of the church during this time include:

• Life and death of Jesus
• Pentecost (church established)
• The teaching and writings of the apostles
• Paul's missionary journeys
• Persecution of Christians
• Christians living in the catacombs
• Martyrs
• Christianization of the Roman Empire
• The falling away

Medieval Period ⟶ 476 A.D. to 1492 A.D.

Key historical events affecting the church include:
- Growth and power of the papacy
- Development and growth of Mohammedanism
- The Crusades
- The Inquisition
- The years before the Reformation

Modern Period ⟶ 1492 to Present Day

Key historical events include:
- Discovery of America
- The Renaissance (Revival of Learning)
- The Reformation
- Counter-Reformation Wars
- Circulation of the open Bible
- Christian freedom from government rules
- Migration of Christians to America
- World-wide missions
- Growing brotherhood

Holy Spirit Versus Evil Spirit

There is an important biblical concept that must be understood if we truly want to comprehend the history of this spiritual family, the church. It is the battle between the Holy Spirit (God) and the evil spirit (Satan) working through individual people. This differs from the Old Testament.

In the 2000-year history of the Jewish race, Abraham's first family, God worked through a race, a nation. The Holy Spirit was not poured out on every person, but only a select few. Throughout the nearly 2000-year history of the church, God has poured out His Spirit on every individual who has become a Christian. He literally comes and indwells them. Each person becomes a temple for the living God.

This is why people who are not Christians often cannot understand those who are. It is not that Christians are better within themselves, but that with the very power of God living in and influencing them, they think and act differently.

On the opposite side of the scale, however, is God's enemy, Satan, doing all he can to war against Christians. He is out to tear down and destroy any Godly influence coming through their lives. That is the history of the church. It is a spiritual warfare of good and evil, light versus darkness, as it is expressed through the lives of individuals. This truth is stated frequently in the Scriptures.

Spirit Poured Out

Let's examine first the concept of the Holy Spirit being poured out. Jesus said:

> "If you love me, you will obey what I command. And I will ask the Father, and He will give you another Counselor to be with you forever—the Spirit of Truth. The world cannot accept him, because it neither sees him nor knows him. But you know him, for he lives with you and will be in you. (John 14:15, 16)

> But I tell you the truth: It is for your good that I am going away. Unless I go away, the Counselor (Holy Spirit) will not come to you; but if I go, I will send him to you. (John 16:7)

On the day of Pentecost, the day the church began, the Holy Spirit was poured out on all who became Christians, exactly as Jesus had promised. It has been so ever since. The following passage refers to the people who were present—about 120 in all, including the apostles.

> When the day of Pentecost came, they were all in one place... all of them were filled with the Holy Spirit. (Acts 2:1,4)

On that same day Peter stood up and preached. Part of his message stated:

> "God has raised this Jesus to life, and we are all witnesses of the fact. Exalted to the right hand of God, he has received

from the Father, the *promised Holy Spirit* and has poured out what you now see and hear. Therefore, let all Israel be assured of this: God has made this Jesus, whom you crucified, both Lord and Christ." When the people heard this, they were cut to the heart and said to Peter and the other apostles, "Brother what shall we do?" Peter replied, "Repent and be baptized, every one of you, in the name of Jesus Christ so that your sins may be forgiven. *And you will receive the gift of the Holy Spirit.* The promise is for you and your children, and for all who are far off—for all whom the Lord our God will call." (Acts 2:32,33,36,37-39.)

And then years later, Paul, writing to the Christians in Corinth, said:

Do you not know that your body is a temple of the Holy Spirit, who is in you, whom you have received from God? You are not your own; you were bought at a price. Therefore, honor God with your body. (I Corinthians 6:19)

There it is—the Holy Spirit promised by Jesus, and the fulfillment. This has been the experience of everyone who has believed and accepted Jesus, since the day the church began.

Satan Cast Out of Heaven

There are many areas in the spiritual realm that man does not understand. Though Satan had previously lost his position in heaven (Isaiah 14:12 and Luke 10:18), the Old Testament book of Job tells us that Satan was permitted to approach God and evidently had some place there, according to verse 8 of Revelation chapter 12.

At about the same time the Holy Spirit was poured out on the people, Satan and his angels lost their place in heaven. They were hurled down to earth, filled with fury, and began to make war on all those who become Christians and testify of Jesus.

The importance of this basic concept (Satan being hurled to earth and the Holy Spirit being poured out on all of God's people) cannot be overemphasized if we are to fully understand the stormy history of the church and its last days. We examined those Scriptures which teach that the Holy Spirit was poured out. Now we will review those which teach Satan was cast out of heaven at about the same time. These two events established the conditions of the church's spiritual warfare. The following verse refers to Israel:

> She gave birth to a son, a male child, who will rule all the nations with an iron scepter. And her child was snatched up to God and to His throne. (Revelation 12:5)

Of course, the son Israel gave birth to was Jesus, who will rule all the nations. He was resurrected, then taken to heaven to sit at the right hand of God.

After Jesus ascended into heaven and sat down by the Father, the following Scriptures describe how Satan was cast out of heaven and hurled to the earth. Verses 10 and 11 tell us the historical time frame in which this happened:

> And there was war in heaven. (This happened after Jesus ascended and took His place alongside the Father). Michael and his angels fought against the dragon (referring to Satan) and the dragon and his angels fought back. But he was not strong enough and *they lost their place in heaven* The great dragon was hurled down—that ancient serpent called the devil or Satan, who leads the whole world astray. He was hurled to the earth, and his angels with him. (Revelation 12:7-9. Words in parentheses are the author's.)

> Then I heard a loud voice in heaven say: "Now have come the salvation and the power and the kingdom of our God, and the authority of his Christ. For the accuser of our brothers, who accuses them before our God day and night has been hurled down." (Revelation 12:10,11)

The book of Ephesians specifically tells us when the authority and power of Christ came into being.

I pray also that the eyes of your heart may be enlightened in order that you may know the hope to which he has called you, the riches of his glorious inheritance in the saints, and his incomparably great power to us who believe. *That power* is like the working of his mighty strength, *which he exerted in Christ when He raised him from the dead and seated him at the right hand in the heavenly realms,* far above all rule and authority, power and dominion, and every title that can be given, not only in the present age, but also in the one to come. And God placed all things under his feet and appointed him to be head. (Ephesians 1:18-22.)

Revelation 12:10 and 11 states it was at the time that Christ received His position of authority that Satan was thrown down to earth. The sequence of events, then, that established the life of the church were:

- Jesus was resurrected from the dead and was seated at the right hand of the Father with all authority.
- He received the promised Holy Spirit, and the Holy Spirit was poured out on all who believed.
- There was a great war in heaven and Satan lost his place in heaven. He was hurled to the earth along with his angels.

These events marked the conditions of the spiritual warfare between God's people and His enemy, Satan, which sets the stage for the history of the church. It is a spiritual warfare which involves every believer as a soldier. Again, it is different from the way God dealt with Abraham's first family, the nation of Israel. This is why we find many new spiritual principles taught about Satan in the New Testament that are not found in the Old Testament. The Scriptures warn of the raging spiritual warfare that is going to take place in the life of the church.

John, still speaking about the events of Jesus being given all authority and Satan being cast out, goes on to say:

Therefore, rejoice, you heavens and you who dwell in them!
(because Christ is now on the throne). But woe to the earth

and the sea, because the devil has gone down to you! He is filled with fury, because he knows that his time is short. (Revelation 12:12. Words in parentheses are the author's.)

John is warning those on earth because Satan has been cast down to earth in a different way than before and is filled with fury.

John speaks of two things Satan does when he was hurled to earth as discussed in this chapter.

First:

When the dragon (Satan) saw that he had been hurled to the earth, he pursued the woman (Israel) who had given birth to the male child (Jesus). (Revelation 12:13. Words in parentheses are the author's.)

The next few verses tell of this pursuit and prophetically describe how the people of Israel were protected by being dispersed among the nations of the earth for an unspecified period of time (stated in verse 14 as a "time, times and half time," a phrase used by Jewish scribes to denote an unspecified period of time). This did happen soon after Jesus was resurrected and Satan was hurled down to earth. In 70 A.D., the Israelites were scattered until the twentieth century.

Second:

For nearly 2,000 years the church has been on the spiritual battleground fighting against an enemy who, according to John, is furious. This is why we find many important teachings about Satan in the New Testament that are not found in the Old. For example:

You, dear children, are from God and have overcome them, because the one who is in you is greater than the one who is in the world. (I John 4:4)

Be self-controlled and alert. Your enemy, the devil, prowls around like a roaring lion looking for someone to devour. (I Peter 5:8)

Finally, be strong in the Lord and in His mighty power. Put on the full armor of God so that you can take your stand against the devil's schemes. For our struggle is not against flesh and blood, (people or organizations), but against the rulers, against the authorities, against the powers of this dark world and against the spiritual forces of evil (Satan and his angels) in the heavenly realms. (Ephesians 6:10-12. Words in parentheses are the author's.)

We often criticize people, institutions or organizations rather than standing and fighting against the spiritual force behind them. Satan is the one responsible for making them do what they are doing to wage war against Christians.

The church is a new dispensation—the battle in the spiritual realm. It differs from the Old Testament and the type of battles found in the lives of the Jewish people. This is evident as we proceed through the history of the church, and why a review of history is important if we are to fully understand the battles of the last days.

Warfare Through Persecution

Satan and his angels began their all-out spiritual warfare early in the life of the church through persecution.

Then the high priest and all of his associates, who were members of the party of the Sadducees, were filled with jealousy. They arrested the Apostles and put them in the public jail. They called the Apostles in and had them flogged. Then they ordered them not to speak in the name of Jesus, and let them go. The Apostles left the Sanhedrin rejoicing because they had been counted worthy of suffering disgrace for the name . . . they never stopped teaching and proclaiming the good news that Jesus is the Christ. (Acts 5:17,18,40,41,42)

When they heard this, (the people hearing Stephen preach) they were furious and gnashed their teeth at him. But Stephen, full of the Holy Spirit, looked up to heaven and saw the glory of God, and Jesus standing at the right hand of God. "Look," he said, "I see heaven open and the Son of Man standing at the right hand of God." At this they covered their ears, and yelling at the top of their voices, they all rushed at him, dragged him out of the city and began to stone him. While they were stoning him, Stephen prayed, "Lord Jesus, receive my spirit." Then he fell on his knees and cried out, "Lord, do not hold this sin against them." (This statement tells us Stephen knew it was not the people, but the power of Satan working through these people that was attacking him. They did not know what they were doing.)

On that day a great persecution broke out against the church at Jerusalem, and all except the Apostles were scattered throughout Judea and Samaria. Godly men buried Stephen and mourned deeply for him. But Saul began to destroy the church. Going from house to house, he dragged off men and women and put them in prison. (Acts 7:54-60, 8:1-3. Words in parentheses are the author's.)

That is how Scripture records the spiritual warfare when the church began. Satan has not let up since as we shall see in our brief review of the church's history.

MAJOR HISTORICAL HAPPENINGS

64 A.D. ⟶ to ⟶ 306 A.D.

At first, the enemy worked only through the Jewish religious leaders in his spiritual warfare, but Satan soon got the government officials involved. The first was the Roman Emperor, Nero, in 64 A.D., when he needed a scapegoat for the terrible fire he had started himself in Rome. He began to persecute Christians, blaming them.

Between 64 A.D. and 306 A.D., under the rule of 23 different emperors, history records the Roman government persecuted millions of Christians for their faith.

Satan was loose on earth in a new and different way, and worked through these rulers in a systematic effort, trying to abolish the Christian name. Christians were hunted down like animals, even in caves and forests, and put to death by every cruel torture man could devise. They were torn to pieces, thrown to wild animals, beheaded, burned, crucified and buried alive.

From 64 A.D. to 306 A.D. over three million Christians died because of their faith at the hands of the Roman emperors. Yet most believers endured without flinching—an obvious sign of the power of the Holy Spirit in their lives. I cannot identify with this type of testing, never having experienced it. I am convinced, however, that God would be just as faithful in supplying the power today if similar conditions developed.

Many Christians during this period of time had to live in the catacombs of Rome. They became a place of refuge. The catacombs were tunnels underneath the city, eight to ten feet wide and four to six feet high. Many Christians were born there, lived and died there.

Paul suffered persecution throughout his ministry stating:

> I have worked much harder, been in prison more frequently, been flogged more severely, and been exposed to death again and again. Five times I received from the Jews the forty lashes minus one. Three times I was beaten with rods, once I was stoned, three times I was shipwrecked, I spent a night and a day in the open sea, I have been constantly on the move. I have been in danger from rivers, in danger from bandits, in danger from my own countrymen, in danger from Gentiles, in danger in the city, in danger in the country, in danger at sea, and in danger from false brothers. I have labored and toiled, and have often gone without sleep; I have known hunger and thirst and have often gone without food; I have been cold and naked. Besides everything else, I face daily the pressure of my concern for all the churches. If I must boast, I will boast of the things that show my weakness. The God and Father of the Lord Jesus, who is to be praised forever, knows I am not lying. (II Corinthians 11:23-31)

Paul died a martyr in Rome. All of the apostles died as martyrs. Some of the other early church leaders, too, suffered martyrdom including: Polycarp, 69-156 A.D., burned alive; Ignatius, 67-110 A.D., thrown to the wild beasts in Rome; Papias, 70-155 A.D.; Origen, 185-254 A.D.; John Chrysostom, 345-407 A.D.; Jerome, 340-420 A.D.; and Augustine, 345-430 A.D.

| 306 A.D. ⟶ to ⟶ 476 A.D. |

Despite the enemy's attacks to wipe out Christianity, by 306 A.D., nearly one-half of the Roman Empire's population confessed to being Christians.

In 306 A.D., Constantine became Emperor of Rome and on October 27, 312 A.D., became a Christian. He immediately began to favor Christians. He filled his offices with Christians; exempted ministers from taxes and the military; built churches, made Christianity the religion of his court; ordered handwritten Bibles to be made; made Sunday a rest day; abolished gladiator fights and crucifixions and reformed slavery. Constantine ruled until 337 A.D.

The next two emperors who followed Constantine attempted to restore paganism. This created much turmoil and unrest among a large percentage of the people. They had experienced openness and freedom in expressing their faith during the reign of Constantine and did not want a return of the heavy oppression against Christianity.

When Theodosius became emperor, ruling from 378-395 A.D., he did just the reverse. To gain favor with the people he made Christianity the state religion. He demanded that everyone be a Christian. Church membership became compulsory for believers and heathens alike.

Making church membership compulsory was unfortunate because this move created one of the worst calamities ever to befall the church. Mixing believers and non-believers resulted in internal conflict, bloodshed and many battles over leadership positions and doctrine. It set the stage for the spiritual apostasy that ruled during the Dark Ages. The bishops began to take authority in the church to control the infighting, and it caused the nature of Christianity to move from a spiritual to a political organization.

As the Roman Empire was dissolving amid the storms of Barbarian migration, the bishops of Rome began to claim universal jurisdiction over the church. This became a constant struggle among the people. As the years went by, however, the nature of the church changed into the image of the Roman government.

The first overall bishop of the church was Leo I, 440-461 A.D. Some call him the first pope, and he did claim divine appointment. He advocated the universal papacy and instituted the death penalty for heresy.

476 A.D. ⟶ to ⟶ 590 A.D.

In 476 A.D., the great Roman Empire came to an end. It broke up into many small, new kingdoms of Barbarians. This furnished the church bishop in Rome advantageous alliances as he made an agreement with the leader of each new country, and gradually became the most commanding religious figure. From 476 to 590 there were 17 different bishops in Rome and each attempted to be the spokesman for the entire church. Three prominent changes occurred in this period: all church ministers became priests, the name of priest coming from the Jewish religion; priests were prohibited from marrying; the Barbarians, the Vandals and Huns were accepted into and filled the churches.

The fall of the Roman Empire in 476 A.D. ushered in the Dark Ages, the Medieval Period of history. It was a terrible time of turmoil in the church history.

590 A.D. ⟶ to ⟶ 742 A.D.

In 590 A.D. Gregory I became what most historians regard as the first pope. Gregory was a strong leader and had a great deal of influence over several kings in Europe. They gave him full religious authority and he established control

over the churches in Italy, Spain, Gaul and England. Gregory lived until 604 A.D. After his death in 604 until the year 741, there were 27 different popes.

A major event in religion during these years that affected Satan's spiritual battle against the church was the birth of Mohammedanism. Mohammed was born in 570 A.D. at Mecca. In search of a religious belief, he came in contact with both Christians and Jews in the country of Syria. He was horrified at the idolatry he found in both of these beliefs, and in 610 A.D. declared himself a prophet. He set out to destroy the idolatry he found in the church which had become paganized with the worship of images, relics, martyrs, Mary and the saints. However, his religion was developed around hate, propagated by the sword, which encouraged slavery, polygamy and the degradation of womanhood.

Mohammed died in 632 A.D., but he had accumulated many followers and in the next 100 years the religion of Mohammedanism grew rapidly throughout Western Asia and North Africa, the cradle of Christianity. By the sword, Mohammedanism conquered Syria (634 A.D.), Jerusalem (637 A.D.), Egypt (638 A.D.), Persia-Iran (640 A.D.), North Africa (684 A.D.) and Spain (711 A.D.).

Charles Martel is believed to have saved Christianity from being completely obliterated by the spread of Mohammedanism. At the Battle of Tours, France, in 732 A.D., he defeated the Moslem army and saved Europe from being overcome by this religion.

742 A.D. ⟶ to ⟶ 869 A.D.

Charlemagne, 742-814, became king of the Franks and was one of the world's greatest rulers. He ruled Germany, France, Switzerland, Austria, Hungary, Belgium, part of Spain and Italy. It was Charlemagne who helped the pope bring the papacy to a position of world power. He established the "Holy Roman Empire" in conjunction with Pope Leo III, 795-816 A.D.

In 869 A.D. there was a great split in Christendom. Though there had been many struggles between the popes of Rome and the patriarchs of Constantinople, the church had remained one up until this time. In 869 they were separated into the Roman Church and the Greek Church.

869 A.D. ⟶ to ⟶ 1050 A.D.

These years are considered by historians to have been the "Darkest Period" of the Roman Church. This period is referred to as "The Midnight of the Dark Ages". A portion of this time, 904-963, is known as "The Rule of the Harlots". The corruption, immorality and bloodshed that occurred in the papacy during those years is recorded history, and its reading is almost beyond belief. We can be sure it is a period of time the Roman Church wishes were not a part of its history. Relating any of the sordid details of the immorality that took place during that time would serve no purpose for our study.

1050 A.D. ⟶ to ⟶ 1294 A.D.

This age of the papacy is called "The Golden Age of Papacy Power". A man named Hildebrand led the papacy into this age, bringing reform to the clergy, by purging the immorality and simony (the purchase of church office with money).

It was during this period that the Crusades began. The Crusades were directed by the papacy in an effort to regain the Holy Land of Palestine from Mohammedans. Working through the European kings, the pope persuaded these kings to use their armies to fight the Moslem army for possession of the Holy Land of Palestine.

The first of seven Crusades occurred from 1095 to 1099. The other Holy land wars, as they are sometimes called, were: 1147 to 1149; 1189 to 1191; 1201 to 1204; 1228 to 1229; 1248 to 1254, and 1270 to 1272. Some of the Crusades were successful, but only for a limited period of time. There remain today many historic ruins in Israel from the days of the Crusaders.

During the period between 1198 and 1216, the papacy reached the summit of its power under Pope Innocent III. Historians state he was the most powerful of all popes. He claimed to be "Vicar of Christ." He decreed that all things were subject to him, including salvation. The kings of Germany, France, England and practically all monarchs of Europe obeyed his will. He ordered two crusades. He decreed transubstantiation, established papal infallibility, forbade reading the Bible, ordered extermination of heretics and instituted the inquisition.

The inquisitions have been responsible for hundreds of thousands of deaths. It was the vehicle used by the Roman Church to detect and punish heretics. Under an inquisition, everyone was required to "inform" against heretics (a heretic was anyone who did not believe and/or follow the Roman Church's doctrine) and a suspect was liable to torture. The inquisitions were used for 500 years by the papacy as a means of maintaining power. Two of the most prominent uses of the inquisition were against the Christian movements called the Albigenses and Waldenses.

The Albigenses were located in Southern France, Northern Spain and Northern Italy. They openly preached the Scriptures and denounced the immoralities in the Roman Church. In 1208 a crusade was ordered by Pope Innocent III to extermi-nate them. Town after town was destroyed and hundreds of thousands were killed. In 1229, an inquisition was established and within 100 years the Christian movement known as the Albigenses was extinct. The Waldenses, also a Christian movement in the same area, suffered a similar fate, being repressed by an inquisition.

Our brief account of the papacy is crucial as background information to the Reformation, one of the significant historical events in the history of the church. Obviously, there is a great deal of detailed information on the history of the papacy that prevailed throughout the centuries from the time it arose after the fall of the Roman Empire in 476 A.D. The statements made here can be verified, and are only a few from the many in recorded history. There was much corruption and cruelty in the leadership of the papacy but this does not mean it applies to all of those in the Roman Church. Just as in other times in the history of God's people, the leaders became obsessed with their power. However, there have always been those people who remained true to the Word of God.

It was discontent with the corruption, resistance to the cruelties of the inquisition, and the popes' interference in government matters that led the people to the Reformation.

Some key elements which sparked the Reformation were:

1. The Albigenses Massacre (1208-1300)
2. Repression of another Christian movement, the Waldenses, by an inquisition in the late 1100s
3. The work of John Wycliffe (1324-1384) who translated the Bible into English, advocating that all the people had a right to read the Bible
4. John Huss (1369-1415), a fearless preacher who was a student of Wycliffe, taught the Scriptures about the doctrines of the Roman Church, and condemned the sale of indulgences. In Bohemia (modern Czechoslovakia), 75% of the people became Christians through the influence of Huss' preaching. He was burned at the stake.
5. Savonorola (1452-1498), a Roman Church priest who preached like a prophet, was hanged and burned in the square at Florence, Italy, 19 years before Martin Luther posted his 95 Theses.
6. Discovery of America by Christopher Columbus
7. The Renaissance or "Revival of Learning," which began around 1450—probably the most important event leading to the Reformation

The Renaissance had its beginning with the invention of the printing press, making available dictionaries, commentaries, versions of the Bible and collections of manuscripts. The renewed knowledge of Christian doctrine revealed the vast difference between the simple gospel and church authority. "The Reformation" owed its being to the direct contact of the mind with the Scriptures.

The Reformation

Martin Luther (1483-1546) led the world in its break for Christian freedom and a return to the Scriptures when on October 31, 1517, he posted on a church door in Wittenberg, Germany his 95 theses, which struck at the authority of the pope.

Luther, like the Apostle Paul, had studied law. He was a devout man, loyal to the Roman Church. In 1508, while reading the book of Romans, he was struck by the truth that "the just shall live by faith," and that salvation was to be obtained by trusting in the atoning power of the blood of Jesus Christ, not in rituals, sacraments and penances. It changed his life and God used him to change the whole course of history.

In 1511, Luther went to Rome and was appalled at the corruption and vice of the papal court. It was the selling of indulgences or "the privilege to sin," used as an inducement by the church to go on a crusade to war against heretics and be an inquisitor or informer, that caused Luther to break away from the Roman Church. Then in 1517, he was horrified when a man named John Tetzel went through Germany selling certificates, signed by the pope, offering pardon for all sins. That same year on October 31, Luther posted his 95 Theses on the church door in Wittenberg. Nearly all 95 Theses related to indulgences. It struck at the authority of the pope. Many conditions were already established that preceded this event, but Martin Luther's action was the spark the Lord used to set Europe aflame to reform Christianity.

Within a short period of time, people all over Europe were wanting a copy of the 95 Theses. By 1520 Luther was the most popular man in Germany. And though tried and found guilty by Charles V at the Diet of Worms in 1521, he was released because of his popularity.

Within 50 years the reformation had swept through most of Germany, Switzerland, the Netherlands, the Scandinavian countries, England, Scotland, Bohemia, Austria, Hungary, Poland and France.

The Reformation was a terrific blow to the leadership of the Roman Church. They organized their counter-reformation action at the Council of Trent from 1545 to 1563. With the leadership of the Jesuits, the use of inquisitions, and working through emperors of the various countries, most of whom were loyal to the Roman Church, the Roman Church began the counter-reformation wars. Over the next 100 years, they regained much of the territory lost to the Reformation.

In country after country, Christians were brutally massacred. They were thrown into dungeons, scourged, tortured on the rack, burned at the stake and buried alive.

In the Netherlands, with the help of the Jesuits, Charles V and his successor, Philip II (1566-1598) massacred over 100,000 people. One inquisition condemned an entire population to death.

In France in 1557, Pope Pius called for an extermination of all the Christians, called Huguenots, who were a part of the Reformation. On August 24, 1572, 70,000 were massacred at one time at the order of the king's mother in what has become known in history as the "St. Bartholomew's Massacre."

By 1600 in Bohemia, nearly 80% of the four million population were Christians, following the influence of John Huss' preaching. After the Reformation war, historians report nearly all Christians (about 3,200,000) had been exterminated by a crusade.

In Spain, the effects of the famous Spanish Inquisition left over 100,000 dead and a reported 1,500,000 banished from the country.

In the papacy's attempt to regain England, it influenced the king of Spain to set sail against England. England's historical victory over the Spanish Armada in 1588 was the turning point for Christian freedom over the power of the papacy in the countries of England, Scotland, Holland, Northern Germany, Denmark, Sweden and Norway. The Church of England, which had become an independent church in 1534 and abolished many practices of the Roman Church, now became the official church in England. The Puritans and Methodists came out of the English church.

The last major stand against the political power of the papacy—the French Revolution—occurred in 1789. The elite ruling class and the Roman clergy were oppressing the poor in Europe. The poor revolted and began the French Revolution which was one of the most frightful reigns of terror and bloodshed in history. The poor abolished government, closed churches and confiscated property. When the revolution ended, their leader, Napoleon, restored the churches, but the political power of the popes ended in every country, and this is still true today.

By 1700 the major thrust of restoring Biblical Christianity had moved across the sea to a land called America—a land, it seems, that God kept from being explored until after the Reformation. It became a new and different light in the church's history.

America has held a unique position in the history of God's people as we will discover in the next chapter, "America, America, God Shed His Grace on Thee."

Chapter 3

AMERICA, AMERICA, GOD SHED HIS GRACE ON THEE

Ever since Adam and Eve sinned in the Garden of Eden, there have been *two sides to the history of humankind.* One portion of history deals with the secular aspect of life. All of secular history is reported by men and women about themselves, and should be classified as such. The other side of history focuses on the spiritual realm, which is the guidance and activity of God in the lives of people here on earth.

All the historical information recorded in the Bible is spiritual, and directed toward the involvement of God in the lives of His created beings. For example, we do not find in Old Testament Scripture any account of God's intervention in activities taking place in other parts of the world. Biblical history concentrates on the Israelites and the formation of the nation of Israel. World history as such is not discussed in the Old Testament. The New Testament is an historical account of the life of Christ and the beginning of the church—the spiritual body of Christ.

If we do not recognize the difference between secular and spiritual history, and we try to intermingle one with the other, we run the risk of classifying something as having spiritual significance when it is only secular or political history. To do so can give us a false sense of spiritual victory. In this review of America's church history, then, our aim is to discuss only those areas which have spiritual significance for us.

The discovery of America in 1492 began the Modern Period of world history, and it continues to the present day. I believe the discovery of America, along with the Renaissance (revival of learning) and the Reformation (the church's break for Christian freedom) were God's three major historical events that began to prepare the church for the last days.

For our study the spiritual development of America has been broken down into eight key historical events.

Historical Event #1:
1492—Discovery of America by Columbus

It is common knowledge that Christopher Columbus discovered America. What is *not* common knowledge is his own personal call from God to venture out and discover the new world. Most people recall from school history classes only Columbus' desire to find a new trade route to India.

The following quotation is from some of the explorer's own writings, Columbus's *Book of Prophecies.* These writings were only available in Spanish until recently. They were privately translated by August J. Kling, and quoted in an article in the *Presbyterian Layman* in October, 1971. Columbus said:

> It was the Lord who put into my mind (I could feel his hand upon me) the fact that it would be possible to sail from here to the Indies. All who heard of my project rejected it with laughter, ridiculing me. There is no question that the inspiration was from the Holy Spirit, because He comforted me with the rays of marvelous inspiration from the Holy Scriptures...
>
> I am a most unworthy sinner, but I have cried out to the Lord for grace and mercy, and they have covered me com-

pletely. I have found the sweetest consolation since I made it my whole purpose to enjoy His marvelous presence. For the execution to the Indies, I did not make use of intelligence, mathematics or maps. It is simply the fulfillment of what Isaiah had prophesied . . .

No one should fear to undertake any task in the name of our Savior, if it is just and if the intention is purely for his Holy service. The working out of all things has been assigned to each person by our Lord, but it all happens according to His sovereign will, even though He gives advice. He lacks nothing that it is in the power of men to give Him. Oh, what a gracious Lord, who desires that people should perform for Him those things for which He holds Himself responsible! Day and night, moment by moment, everyone can express their most devoted gratitude to Him.

The next period of 100-plus years after Columbus' discovery offers much recorded history, centering around settlers in Jamestown, Virginia and the Virginia colony. However, all was secular history, and the people of those times made no apparent recognition of being inspired by God, or having a commitment to Him.

After the discovery of America in 1492, the next major move in our country's spiritual history did not develop until the early 1600s. It began in England, with people who had a true desire to worship God freely, without interference and restriction from the Church of England. They experienced many trials because of their faith in Jesus Christ.

Historical Event #2: "The Pilgrims"

After the defeat of the Spanish Armada in 1588, the Church of England became the official church in England, and was headed by the Queen of England. All those with religious convictions were under the authority of the bishops of the Church. These bishops began to create power positions, and rule over the congregations—a dogma of the Roman Church. Several hundred people were having great difficulty in worshipping with freedom, so they began to speak out about their commitment to Jesus and their desire to follow only the writings of the Scriptures. These people became known in England as "Separatists." Since they did not want to obey the rules of the King's Church, which was the law of the land, they began to have secret meetings. However, the king heard they were holding clandestine gatherings, and he began to put some of the men into prison. He caused many problems and trials in an attempt to get these people to bow to the laws of the Church of England.

The church leaders became harsh and cruel, making it more dangerous for these committed Christians to worship according to Scripture. Consequently, they were afraid to stay in England, so they began to contemplate a move to a place where they could worship as they pleased.

In 1608 the Separatists moved to Holland, seeking Christian freedom. They lived in Holland for 12 years, but life there was very difficult. The men had to work extremely hard and they received little to show for their hard labor. The parents also became concerned about their children, fearing that they might forget the cultural customs of their native England. Furthermore, they did not want their children to become sailors and soldiers for Holland, which was customary. It seems the Lord used these concerns and their difficult life to cause them to explore the possibilities of going to the new world, a land called America.

The people began to lay plans for a move to this newly discovered land. Their search for a way to the new world and a means to ship their supplies led these people to some businessmen. They were able to make an agreement for 35 of them to go to the new land if others would work for these businessmen for seven years. They thought this agreement unfair, but it was the only way they could find to get to the new world, so an agreement was made. The departing 35 picked up the name of "Pilgrim," since a pilgrim is someone who goes on a long, long journey.

The Pilgrims returned to England from Holland determined

to set sail for the new world, and boarded a cargo ship acquired by the businessmen, called the "Mayflower." And even though the Mayflower was not designed to carry passengers, this ship did bring 102 people from England to the new world in the year 1620. Out of the 102, 35 of them were Christians from the Separatist group from Holland.

Sailing conditions were extremely poor, and the sailors on the ship became hostile toward the Pilgrims due to their practice of singing spiritual songs and praying. The Pilgrims, in turn, did not like the sailors' use of bad language.

There was little each family could take along on the voyage because there wasn't much room. A mother with a baby could only take along a cradle for the baby to sleep in. The women brought a few cooking utensils, and the men brought a gun or sword and a few tools for building and working in the gardens. Each family could bring one box, which contained the family Bible.

It was dangerous for a small ship like the Mayflower to make such a long voyage—especially by itself. In those days, one ship never sailed alone.

Living conditions on the ship were miserable. The food consisted of salted beef or pork or fish and hard dry biscuits. Sleeping quarters were on the floor below the main deck where hardly any light or air existed. If they wanted to bathe, they had to wash in salty water. Most of the people had to wear the same clothes day after day for the 66-day voyage. Sanitary facilities were non-existent.

During one dangerous storm the main beam cracked. It splintered the main deck, causing water to pour in on the Pilgrims who were living on the lower deck. Their clothes, bedding and food lay in water, making the living conditions intolerable. Many of the people on board became deathly ill. The sickness was so severe even the sailors began to pray with the Pilgrims for an end to the terrible voyage. The Pilgrims knew it was only by God's mercy that they could survive the voyage.

It was the morning of November 9, 1620, 66 days later, when they saw the sandy beaches of Cape Cod in what is today the State of Massachusetts. Many of the people on the ship, led by the Pilgrims, fell on their knees and blessed the God of heaven who had brought them over the vast and furious ocean. And now they were here—in a strange land where there were no homes, no towns, and no friends to greet them. They continued living aboard the Mayflower for another 33 days until a landing site could be found with a place to make their homes.

On December 16, 1620, the Mayflower landed at an area which the Pilgrims called Plymouth because Plymouth, England was their point of departure, and they had received kindness from Christians there. This was the beginning of the first Christian settlement in the new world called America.

In the area surrounding Plymouth, where the Pilgrims decided to stay, they found running brooks, and fields which had already been cleared for planting. Here they would be able to worship God and pray and sing songs with complete freedom.

Trials in building this Christian settlement were many. The Pilgrims had to contend with the cold and snow, lack of food, sickness, death, loneliness, and conflicts with Indians. During February of that first winter, there were times when only six or seven people were well enough to take care of the ones who were sick. By spring, half of the Pilgrims and sailors had died. Three entire families died during the initial days. The rest were alone, except for their God and their commitment.

It was this commitment to Jesus Christ and their faith in Him that gave them the courage and strength to carry on. Their faith had been tested and tried, and built up through the experiences they had endured in England, Holland and aboard the Mayflower. This gave them the strength to persevere, and establish the first light of Jesus in the new land of America. Through these Pilgrims the spiritual history of American Christianity had its beginning.

On April 5, 1621, four months after arriving in America, the Mayflower headed back to England. But not one Pilgrim returned. As summer approached, their faithfulness and commitment to Jesus began to reveal the fruits of this commitment. William Bradford, one of the leaders of the Pilgrims, wrote that they had all things in plenty because the corn had grown well. A friendly Indian named Squanto, who had traveled abroad and knew the English language, taught the people how to plant. It appears he was God-sent. The Pilgrims had plenty to eat and were careful to lay up in store for the next winter.

During the summer they were able to build several homes. Most of the dangers of sickness passed and their friendship with the Indians allowed them to live in peace.

Through the grace of God, they had been able to do what they had set out to do. They found a place where they could live and worship God in their own way with complete freedom.

In autumn of 1621 the Pilgrims decided to set aside a special time to give thanks to the Lord for His faithfulness—a commemoration we now call Thanksgiving. The first Thanksgiving holiday they celebrated lasted for three days. It took place around the middle of October, nearly a year after their arrival in November of 1620.

Historical Event #3: 1628-1644—The Great Migration to America—"The Puritans"

Next in the development of our spiritual heritage is the history of the "Puritans." These people above all others laid America's foundation as a Christian nation.

The Puritans had been given a sense of direction by the Holy Spirit. It was not just a matter of flight from the persecutions they were encountering from the king and bishops in England that caused them to take the drastic action, recorded in history. They were determined to change their society in a way that could make a lasting difference, by giving it a Christianity that worked. They set out to do this, not only by word, but also by example. They felt certain that the place this could be accomplished was 3,000 miles away from their homeland of England, in the new frontier.

While a Christian foundation at Plymouth in the new world was being established by the Pilgrims, the Puritans in England were coming under the mounting pressures of accelerated persecution and advanced moral decay.

The Puritan movement began to gain momentum in the first two decades of the 1600s in England, and since God's will was being made known to them largely through His inspired Word in the Bible, they wanted to get as close to a scriptural order of worship as possible. Their ultimate desire appeared to be to bring the church back to a form of New Testament Christianity.

The Puritans had not really experienced persecution from either King James or the church as long as King James ruled, from 1603 to 1625. However, this situation changed under King Charles I who reigned from 1625 to 1649. In 1628, he made William Laud the Bishop of London and the king received from him a list of English clergy. If a man was Orthodox, he would be in line for a promotion. If the clergyman was a Puritan, he would be marked for suppression.

The Puritans were despised, but not really hated as much as the Separatists were. The Separatists, or Pilgrims, had given up their homes, their jobs, their country—everything, to live as God had called them. The Puritans in England had much more than the Pilgrims—that is, more money, more servants, more friends in high places, more education and more business experience. They attracted people from all social classes and walks of life including some well-trained clergy from Oxford and Cambridge.

Like the Pilgrims before them, the conditions for living a Christ-like life were becoming extremely unbearable for the Puritans. They began to search for the leading of the Lord in how to deal with the problem of whether they should go underground or possibly separate themselves, even though they did not really believe in separation, and did not consider themselves to be revolutionaries. Their objective was to bring reform to the Church. Yet the king and the bishops were making it impossible.

They began to see another alternative—one of establishing and reforming the church. If it could not be done from within, there in England, then it would have to be done from a distant, undeveloped land, in a place that was still untainted by the godless corruption that was now known to the world—a place where people's hearts were not hardened to the truth of the gospel of Jesus Christ. This place, America, was where they would establish a settlement of Puritans who were still loyal to the crown and to the church. Yet they would be far enough away so they could truly have a chance to live committed lives in obedience to Christ.

God began to move among the Puritans, and a massive exodus to America took place—men and women who had found a personal relationship with Jesus Christ. Even though many of them may not have yet discovered the deeper life, and had even been self-righteous, the rebirth was there. The new life in Christ was a reality, and they were being called to a new land to establish a foundation for the dwelling place of God's Spirit. Though all of their actions found in historical accounts are not spiritual as we trace the moving of God in their lives, it is evident that His hand was on these people to develop a strong spiritual base in America.

It was the year of 1628 that marked the beginning of the great migration of the Puritans to the new world. This migration lasted for about 16 years. More than 20,000 Puritans embarked for New England, and 45,000 other Englishmen headed for Virginia, the West Indies, and points south. That number may not seem too significant today, but it could be compared to three million Americans packing up and leaving.

Such a migration was a drastic and major decision for the Puritan people. It seems strange that they felt this was the only solution to their desire to experience a deep relationship with God through the fellowship they had with His Son, Jesus Christ. Obviously, it had to be a most important decision for it would change their lives permanently.

The Puritans were very sincere about their salvation. As the English Puritan theologian, Richard Baxter, put it, "Man's fall was his turning from God to himself; and his regeneration consisted in the turning of him from himself to God . . . hence, self-denial and the love of God are all one . . . The very names of self and own, should sound in the watchful Christian's ear as very terrible, wakening words, that are next to the names of sin and Satan."[1]

Another Puritan minister, Thomas Hooker, spoke for all the New England Puritans when he further identified their commitment to Christ by pointing out that their primary adversary was not only Satan, but self. He referred to it as the "self" in all as their own anti-Christ. "Self" is that old Adam nature in us that seeks ascendancy, and therefore, denies the Lordship of Jesus in our lives.

One of the most dedicated Puritans in England was John Winthrop. He was well educated, and the owner of a sizeable estate. Winthrop was an attorney in the Court of Wards, and a justice of the peace. He wrote these lines in 1612 at the age of 24: "I desire to make it one of my chief petitions to have that grace to be poor in spirit. I will ever walk humbly before my God, and meekly, mildly, and gently toward all men . . . I do resolve first to give myself—my life, my wits, my health, my wealth—to the service of my God and Savior who, by giving Himself for me and to me, desires whatsoever I am or can be, to be at His commandment and for His glory."[2]

The Puritans took sin very seriously—far more seriously than most American Christians today. They knew that sin had to be dealt with swiftly and decisively—first in themselves and also in those who had been called to build this spiritual foundation. They were aware that the secret of success in maintaining a relationship with the Lord revolves around our willingness to submit to Him and have sin dealt with in our lives.

The law book or guide for the Puritans leaders was the Bible, and they were anxious to see a sinner come to repentance. In case after case, we find that mercy, forgiveness, and pastoral concern for the defendant stood out. Our modern writers seem to record only the disciplinary action taken.

The Puritans had submissive spirits, and were willing to face the reality of their own sinful natures. They recognized the harm that sin caused in their relationship with Jesus and their relationships with one another. This willingness to submit to the nature of Jesus produced not only compassion for one another, but a remarkable maturity when it came to meeting the stark realities of life and death.

The Puritans were realists in life as well as in death. They believed that their relationship with God included their children, and because of their love for them, they were no more tolerant of sin in their children's lives than in their own. They followed biblical teachings and subdued the sinful nature in the lives of their children as severely as the situation demanded, regardless of how the child might respond, or the degree of the conflict at the moment.

Here we find one of the greatest differences between the Puritans and modern-day Christian parents. We are not willing to risk losing our relationship with our children by persevering with them in matters of discipline. This has produced one of the biggest single causes for the breakdown of the American family. To withhold discipline, thereby losing control of the life of a maturing child, is not true love. True love is to think of the long-range welfare of the child, not our own personal feelings at the moment. The Bible has much to say about child training.

The Puritans believed it was their God-given responsibility to protect their children, raise them, and teach them—training them up in the way the Lord would have them go. To a

Puritan, parenthood was a sacred responsibility in Christ. If they failed they were directly accountable to God. The Puritans believed in the spiritual value of strong family relationships as taught in Scripture.

Contrary to popular opinion, discipline does not prevent us from loving our children. In fact, just the opposite is true as taught in God's Word. God's love abounds with tenderness, compassion and joy, but it also contains discipline.

> Because the Lord disciplines those He loves, and He punishes everyone He accepts as a son. If you are not disciplined (and everyone undergoes discipline), then you are illegitimate children and not true sons. (Hebrews 12:6,8)

God loves His children too much to permit them to continue in the sin which could harm their development, or to allow them to persist in willfulness. This example of God's love for His children is the example Christian parents should follow in expressing love to their children.

The Puritans saw very clearly that authority, whether spiritual or temporal, had to begin in the home. As one of their outstanding leaders, Cotton Mather, put it, "Well-ordered families naturally produce a good order in society." This statement is still applicable and true today. In Puritan New England, care was taken to preserve discipline and authority in the home. For in the end, an undisciplined home not only threatened the family structure and underminded society, but was a sin against God's plan.

A great deal of emphasis was placed on the matter of parental responsiblity, accountability and authority in the homes of the Puritans. The older men and women taught the younger ones how to establish and develop this proper spiritual atmosphere and teaching in their own homes. These Puritan qualities may seem foreign to our modern American family ways, but since Christian love and caring for the souls of others so characterized the family lives of our forefathers, it might well contain the answer to our own family problems.

The commitment of the Puritans and the way God obviously anointed them and directed them to be His lightbearers in establishing our spiritual direction is historically correct. It appears the main reason many of us are not more aware of the way the Puritans were used of the Lord has to do with our 20th century historians. Relatively few negative comments can be found about the Puritans among the 19th century historians. In fact, almost invariably they give the Puritans credit for setting the course of this nation. Why we find such a prejudice in the hearts of so many American people today against the Puritans and their reported self-righteousness perhaps stems from the fact that in 20th century America the spirit of rebellion has gained such a tight hold on our minds and on our wills.

We rebel against a commitment to God such as the Puritan people had which resulted in submission to biblical authority and teachings. I am sure that our spiritual enemy, Satan, hates the Puritan example of submissiveness more than any other of their qualities. He has tried to eradicate the true picture of their role in the history of our country and their contribution. Rebellion was foreign to the Puritans, and since rebellion is Satan's specialty, it is no wonder the Puritans have received a bad press here in the last 50 years.

Historical Event #4:
The Initial Puritan Light Became a Faint Glow by 1700

As we reflect on the spiritual history of our nation and its development, one might wonder what happened to the spirit of the Puritans. A review of the 1600s reveals the Puritans, after overcoming the frontier wilderness hardships, began to prosper in every way. The hard times were behind them; there was plenty of good land and an abundance of food in the new world. They built spacious houses and were able to live at peace with the Indians. Their obedience of the Word evidenced their deep commitment to Christ. And God blessed them beyond all measure. Then the fire began to slowly die out. Their spiritual life began to dim as the turn of the 18th century approached. What had been a blazing light of the gospel of Christ coming across the ocean had become only a faint glow.

The cause of dimming the light in the lives of the Puritans was the result of the operation of a spiritual principle we all easily forget. This principle is that our faith is not automatically passed on to our children. This pattern was illustrated over and over again in the Old Testament in the lives of the Israelites, and how they could so quickly fall away from their faith. We even see it in the life of the early church. After the first century it too began to fall away from its original call. This seems to be the lot that fell upon the Puritans as the second and third generations who had not personally experienced the original call and commitment became spiritually indifferent.

A dangerous change began to take place in the heart attitude of these Puritans in New England. Several Puritan ministers could see it coming and Sunday after Sunday began to warn their congregations, even though it appears the message usually fell on deaf ears. A favorite Scripture passage of these ministers is found in Deuteronomy:

> Be careful that you do not forget the Lord your God, failing to observe his commands, his laws and his decrees that I am giving you this day. Otherwise, when you eat and are satisfied, when you build fine houses and settle down, and when your herds and flocks grow large and your silver and gold increase and all you have is multiplied, then your heart will become proud and you will forget the Lord your God . . . You may say to yourslef, "My power and the strength of my hands have produced this wealth for me." But remember the Lord your God, for it is he who gives you the ability to produce wealth, and so confirms his covenant, which he swore to your forefathers, as it is today. If you ever forget the Lord your God and follow other gods and worship and bow down to them, I testify against you today that you will surely be destroyed. (Deuteronomy 8:11-14, 17-19)

Apparently, this is what happened to God's new establishment and Satan began to change the hearts of these New England colonists.

The principle of being born into a situation rather than being one of those who had to carve its development prevents succeeding generations from knowing what it means to be persecuted for one's faith or to be mocked and scorned or even imprisoned because they loved God enough to put Him and His will before all else. The sons of the fathers did not know what it was like to have no land, no work and no say in how they were to be governed. Nor would they have memories etched in their minds of several long, wet weeks of misery on the open seas only to disembark in the bitter cold of a New England winter, living in tents or holes in the ground while cold and sickness would take one or two lives at a time. They knew nothing of starvation—of seeing men and women on their hands and knees looking for even a nut or berry to eat to stay alive. The second and third generations of Puritans did not have to forsake all and place their faith only in Him as He had brought them a vision of a new promised land.

How easy it is to be attracted by the power of the world causing us to defect from the path of complete trust in God. This seemed to be what happened to the second and third generations of Puritans.

Consequently the succeeding generations began to develop the spirit of independence. When a man begins to rely on his own achievements and prosperity and forgets the God who is the giver of every good and perfect gift, a spirit of independence develops. He knows how to control his own life, plan his own life and provide for his own life. He begins to conceive of himself as the captain of his own destiny. His need for God diminishes and subsequently his need for other men.

It was this kind of spirit that began to develop in the lives of the Puritans. It was the beginning of one of the strongest and most revered American traits—independence. It's a trait that can be dangerous, for the loner is lauded and the rebel becomes the hero. Today's mass media glamorizes this type of person as a model for our restless youth to emulate. Many of our children believe in them, causing thousands each year to leave home in their attempt to be a king of the road themselves, finding out too late that such a dream is only a frightful nightmare. It is a nightmare because God did not intend for man to live alone. He intended man, and especially His reborn children who are called by the name of His Son, to live and function as a body, providing mutual strength and support.

In the lives of the second and third generation Puritans, a number of them began to forget this spiritual principle of interdependence, and their spiritual health declined. Yes, they still went to church, if the church was within an hour's ride, but their thoughts were often back on their settlement or the house or crops. In other words, their minds were on worldly affairs rather than on their spiritual development. Maybe that principle rings a bell for many of us today.

The grandsons of the Puritan families began to help themselves to more land or drifted into worldly pursuits motivated by self interest. They believed they had to establish their own life on their own land. They were no longer convinced that the first priority was to be the gathering at the church with the corporate body and the development of the spiritual life.

A man was free to go and do as he pleased, or as the Book of Judges puts it, "whatever was right in his own eyes." Many of the early settlers could see it happening and it tore at the very roots of their being.

Cotton Mather, writing many years later, stated: "Religion begat prosperity, and the daughter ignored the mother."[3] And in the same blunt vein, speaking of all New England, Judge Seawall wrote to Daniel Doken, "Prosperity is too wholesome a diet for any man . . . unless seasoned with some grains of adversity."[4]

Was God wrong, then, to honor the obedience of His beloved children with blessings? Of course not, but as John Danforth preached, ".... to turn blessings into idols was a way to have them clapped under a blast. If the Lord loves His people, He will deliver the weapons out of their hands, that they are obstinately resolved to fight with... Better it is that Israel be saved and prosperity lost, than that prosperity be saved and Israel lost."[5]

If God was trying to build a new spiritual base in which to function in the latter days, Satan was doing everything possible to destroy it and tear it down. The spiritual battle that began at the start of the church in the first century was still raging. The people who represented the greatest threat to him, those dedicated to living the daily Christian life in obedience to their Savior, were these Puritans. Satan had waited almost two generations, then as affluence increased, moved in through his worldly systems and began to entice with a heavy influence on the old spiritual scheme of causing these Puritans to look to self, and become independent. Satan had begun to weaken these soldiers of Christ and destruction was his aim. His attack stratagem—deception, rather than persecution—was working well in this new country.

This became more apparent as the 1600s drew to a close and the supernatural manifestations of Satan's power such as cultism, witchcraft and demonology began to surface. Witches hung out their shingles and more and more people, unaware of what was going on, began to turn to this source of power for advice and counsel.

The written accounts of things that happened at the turn of the 17th century are shocking. Demonic possession was nothing new, but whole towns were literally infested with these evil beings and it would appear that God was allowing it as a warning to shake the Christian settlers out of their spiritual apathy.

Cotton Mather wrote a vivid description of what happened

in the home of William Morse.

> In the night he (Morse) was pulled by the hair and pinched and scratched . . . and blows that fetched blood were sometimes given him . . . A little boy belonging to the family was the principle sufferer of these molestations, for he was flung about at such a rate, they feared his brains would have been beaten out . . . all the knives which belonged to the house were one after another stuck into his back, which the spectators pulled out . . . The poor boy was divers times thrown into the fire, and preserved from scorching there, with much ado . . . once the fist beating the man was discernible, but they could not catch hold of it . . . and another time, a drumming on the boards was heard, which was followed by a voice that sang, "Revenge! Revenge! Sweet is revenge!" At this, the people being terrified, called upon God, whereupon there followed a mournful note, "Alas, alas, we knock no more, we knock no more!" And there was an end of all.[6]

Many such cases were reported in those days. The demon possession of a 13-year-old daughter of John Goodwin in Boston was so intense that it actually took two weeks of battling to gain deliverance. In the final struggle, it was won only after several ministers fasted and prayed at length.

Things finally reached a point where the Puritans felt that broad action had to be taken, as the Bible commanded. Cotton Mather in "The Wonders of The Invisible World" comments aptly on the state of affairs: "The New Englanders are a people of God, settled in those which were once the Devil's territories, and it may easily be supposed that the Devil was exceedingly disturbed, when he perceived such a people here accomplishing the promise of old made unto our blessed Jesus—that He should have the utmost parts of the earth for His possession . . . The Devil, thus irritated, immediately tried all sorts of methods to overturn this poor plantation . . .".[7]

Mather and others did their best to get the people of New England to repent, but they refused to listen. As the years passed, the voices of those urging repentance grew fainter until at last they died away. It is apparent that the new generation of ministers coming into the leadership roles of the Puritan churches may have known their theology, but for the most part did not know their Lord, and were content to let this new condition exist.

Historical Event # 5: "The Great Awakening"

When one considers the fact that this land was not discovered until the Reformation period began and the spiritual darkness that had enveloped the whole world during the Dark and Middle Ages was giving way to light, our spiritual history takes on new significance. At various times there was a lull in our country's spiritual development, yet God moved in miraculous ways to bring the people out of these periods of spiritual inactivity. The significance of God's hand in America's spiritual development over and above what is normal becomes more obvious as we continue. For example, as the Puritan era came to an end in the early 1700s, there was nothing spiritually significant in our nation's development for about a half a century. Then, God's hand once again began to move in a supernatural way in the middle 1700s. Historians refer to this period of time as the "Great Awakening."

Possibly the first glimmer of light that began to dawn on this nation's state of spiritual apathy began in 1734 in North Hampton, Massachusetts. It was at a church where Jonathan Edwards, a Puritan minister, was still preaching powerful sermons stating that only God could bring about His own purposes, and the willpower of man leads to spiritual failure.

As this "Great Awakening" began, it became obvious that the Spirit of God began to sweep over a group of preachers, who began to preach the Word with tremendous anointing and great spiritual power. One such man was George Whitefield, one of the greatest evangelists of the 18th century. He was ordained in England on June 20, 1736, at the age of 22.

The first three English cities in which Whitefield preached

were Bath, Bristol and Gloucester, where revival broke out immediately. But Whitefield did not stay in England. He believed his call was to General Oglethorpe's new colony in America, where Charles and John Wesley had already gone and were urging him to join them. He traveled to this new land with the thought of evangelizing the Indians. But soon after his arrival the whole state of Georgia responded in spiritual revival to the young man's preaching. He was able to capture the hearts and minds of those who heard him.

In New Jersey, Theodore Freilinghuysen was proclaiming the gospel with power throughout the Dutch Reformed Church. In Virginia, the Presbyterian minister and hymn writer, Samuel Davis, was preaching the message with spiritual anointing. In the woods of Pennsylvania, Connecticut and also in New Jersey, a missionary named David Brainerd was proclaiming the gospel to the Indians, as he rode horseback throughout the area under the auspices of the Presbyterian Church. Brainerd admitted awe at the power of God that fell on one village after another as he preached. Indians would change so dramatically that skeptical whites would come to the meetings to mock, only to be converted themselves.

Brainerd drove himself unmercifully. He preached three times a day often for hours at a time. He died at the age of 29 of tuberculosis. Other preachers, influenced by his commitment, considered his sermons to be irresistible. As he proclaimed the message of Christ thousands came to the knowledge of Jesus as their Savior. Wesley said of him, "Find preachers of David Brainerd's spirit and nothing can stand before them. Let us be followers of him, as he was of Christ, in absolute self-devotion and total deadness to the world, and in fervent love to God and man."[8]

These early evangelists of the "Great Awakening" performed a magnificent service within their denominations and transformed the geographical areas to which the Lord had called them, but it was George Whitefield who was used by God to tie it all together. Wherever he went, revival accompanied him in a dramatic way. The other evangelists who were also preaching the gospel of renewal welcomed him and his anointed message as an answer to prayer.

In North Hampton, for example, Jonathan Edwards lit the fires of the new awakening but was having difficulty in keeping them alive. He offered Mr. Whitefield his pulpit and was moved to tears by his preaching. Concerning this event, Edwards' wife, Sarah, wrote to her brother stating, "It is wonderful to see what a spell he cast over an audience by proclaiming the simplest truth of the Bible . . . Our mechanics shut up their shops, and the day laborers threw down their tools to go and hear him preach, and few returned unaffected."[9]

In Philadelphia, an aged minister by the name of William Tennent saw George Whitefield as the prophet who would bring the people to repentance. His first night in Philadelphia, Whitefield preached from the courthouse steps with Mr. Tennent standing by his side. The streets were jammed, yet the people stood perfectly hushed and still. Mr. Whitefield's message eliminated denominational barriers as he called out for God to help them forget about divisions, and to become Christians in deed and in truth.

The name of George Whitefield was well known all along the New England coast. Even if he came to a town unexpectedly, there would be an astonishing turnout. On one occasion he felt that God wanted him to change his itinerary at the last minute and preach at Middletown, Connecticut. The moment they heard of his coming, riders galloped down all the nearby roads spreading the word that the man who had preached in Philadelphia "like one of the old apostles" would soon be preaching in front of the meeting house. Farmers dropped their hoes and left their plows, corraled their wives and mounted their horses. It was described as the sound of distant thunder by one of their group as he saw a great cloud rising along the road—everyone was riding as fast as he could down the dirt road to Middletown. When Whitefield arrived, several thousand tied horses could be seen behind the vast crowd of dust-covered farmers. It looked as if an entire cavalry division had dismounted and was awaiting him.

It was apparent that God was using George Whitefield to set America ablaze for Him. Year after year, up and down the East Coast, as far as known civilization extended, Mr. Whitefield traveled and preached the gospel of Jesus Christ. He seemed happiest in the saddle, covering new territory and meeting new people along the way. In the summer of 1754, he wrote to Charles Wesley, "My wonted vomitings have left me, and though I ride whole nights and have frequently been exposed to great thunders, violent lightning, and heavy rains, yet I am rather better than usual, and as far as I can judge am not yet to die. Oh, that I might at length begin to live! I am ashamed of my sloth and lukewarmness, and long to be on the stretch for God."[10]

The true spirit of his tireless devotion to the Lord is revealed in his shame of his personal sloth and lukewarmness even though he preached 100 times in six weeks that year, riding the main roads and the back woods of New England and covering nearly 2,000 miles in five months. It was a miracle that he felt as well as he did and his health sustained such a grueling schedule.

Whitefield had elected to go the way of the cross, and counted it nothing but gain to have the privilege of picking up his cross daily. It took a fearful toll on his health, as he stretched his endurance to the limit. But no matter how sick he was, as long as he had the strength to stand and the breath to speak, he would preach and trust God to sustain him through the sermon and to provide the power and the anointing.

The power of the Holy Spirit of God fell practically every time he preached, and one has to think that it was bestowed in response to his obedience and willingness to lay down his life for God. If he had not driven himself and had taken an easier path, as most of us do, would God's tremendous purpose for him have been accomplished? Wherever Whitefield went, he preached the same gospel. The same Holy Spirit quickened his message in people's hearts regardless of their denomination. They all accepted the same Jesus Christ as Lord in the same way.

By the sovereign act of God and the obedience of a few dedicated men, revival broke out in the colonies and the body of Christ was forming in America. This "Great Awakening" made believers aware of their identity as a people chosen by God for a specific purpose—to be a true light in a darkened world.

Both the Pilgrims and the Puritans as evidenced by their commitment to the Lord had seen the challenge for the church. When they had all died there was a short period in the early 1700s when it appeared as though their vision had died with them. However, through the shared experience of coming together in large groups to hear the gospel of Jesus Christ, Americans rediscovered God's plan to unite them by His Spirit in the common cause of advancing His kingdom.

The rekindling of faith in the lives of His people in the mid-1700s was miraculous. One can only attribute it to a mighty movement of the Spirit of the Lord in our land. The message these early settlers were hearing and committing themselves to during this "Great Awakening" was more than just lip service. The emphasis was on action. Their preachers did not merely discuss theology, but challenged people to make life-changing decisions, and to act upon them as an expression of their faith in Jesus Christ. One part of the message they heard defined a true Christian as one who spends his life in active service for the common good of others, and desires to live according to the Word of God, not according to the world.

To illustrate this principle of action, Whitefield and the other evangelists would travel hundreds of miles on horseback and preach until their lungs practically collapsed. Whitefield preached more than 18,000 sermons between 1736 and 1770.

God called George Whitefied to help awaken the people in this new country. But many others also had a part. Charles Wesley, for example, traveled 4,500 to 8,000 miles per year on horseback, preaching more than 40,000 sermons. He started his day at 4:00 A.M. and began preaching at 5:00 A.M. He lived during Whitefield's time, and died March 2, 1791. The biographies of many others could be included, and would be supporting evidence of the same special anointing of God on this land.

America was becoming a new nation with her principles of foundation established through the preaching of the Word, and her spiritual history being formulated for the purpose God had planned—to be that geographical nerve center in the last days from which God would take the gospel of Jesus throughout the world. Our spiritual history now confirms this fact.

Historical Event #6: 1776—"The American Revolution"

A new nation was born with a governing Constitution that allowed freedom of worship. Historians agree it was the powerful preaching during the "Great Awakening" that set the tone of our Constitution. America was a "new event" in the history of man.

By the time the colonies broke away from their mother country, England, the spiritual strength of the new nation had been so established that she could now stand firm, regardless of the adverse conditions which might come upon her in later years from the secular world and world systems. The quality of believers was being emphasized more than ever in American churches. It was only natural that they would therefore have an impact on the civil government. This was to become one of the seeds of democracy that would be embodied in the Constitution of the United States as the political segment of our country was being founded, with all men equal and entitled to vote. In the eyes of God, one man is equal to another, for He is no respecter of persons. This principle has allowed the message of Jesus to be preached to this day, even though the enemy has obviously introduced many elements to water down the message, to attack it and try to defeat it.

Because the foundation of Jesus Christ had been set so firmly, believers in America knew the importance of their freedom in Christ, and recognized that they could never again submit to the yoke of slavery. That was what the new Americans would have been guilty of if they had allowed themselves to go back under the rule of England. Having the freedom to worship, to serve the Lord, and to spread the gospel of Jesus became the standard by which God had moved in this nation so it could become the light-bearer for Jesus in the last days.

Today there are thousands of churches across this land, and the gospel is preached every day through a number of various ways. We can see how God has used Christians in this country to take the gospel throughout the world during these last days.

Unfortunately, it appears that many today in the body of Christ are not taking the time to distinguish our unique spiritual history from our country's secular history. Yet this is crucial, for ever since Adam, Satan has raised up secular world systems alongside spiritual developments by God, to counter-attack, undermine and try to wipe out God's purpose. This was true in the spiritual history of the early church by the way Satan used the Roman government in his attempt to destroy the church. We can expect it to happen today, and it is.

Historical Event #7: 1800-1900—Christian Churches are Established Throughout the Land

The period of time between 1800 and 1900 saw hundreds of churches established throughout America. The revivals that started during the "Great Awakening" period in the 1700s continued in the 1800s under men such as Dwight L. Moody,

Charles Finney and A. B. Earle—men whose testimony of labor for the Lord and their anointing resembles that of George Whitefield and Charles Wesley. The effect of Moody's work in Christian education continues today. Charles Finney saw 100,000 give their lives to the Lord in one two-year period, 1857-58, and it is stated that 85% of those converted under his preaching stayed faithful to the Lord.

The 1800s saw positive church growth as church membership rose from 10% to 40%. Some called it the "second awakening," and it has continued to this day.

With the introduction of the industrial revolution and the development of great economic resources in this country, the opportunity was presented to establish many missionary organizations and take the gospel to other parts of the world.

But the spiritual battle raging between the power of the Holy Spirit and the forces of Satan did not cease. It seemed to continue in intensity but not in method. The use of persecution was not apparent. Satan was using a different mode of attack in this country. Rather than using the horrible persecution of thousands upon thousands, which was prevalent in the early church and throughout the Dark Ages, (as was prophesied in God's Word and will be examined in later chapters of the book), his attack method in this country would be by deception.

Some of the key issues the church began to deal with in the 1800s included:

1. The industrial revolution, which often brought oppression of the masses.
2. The development of Socialism, which proclaims that man's problems are caused by environment, not through spiritual laxity; that unequal distribution of property and goods is the main source of all evil, not the spiritual forces of Satan. The strongest advocate of Socialism during this period was Karl Marx, 1818-1883, who was a militant atheist.
3. The theory of evolution first became a factor of conten-

tion in the 1800s when Charles Darwin introduced this concept through his writing, "The Origin of the Species", published in 1859. This helped create a school of biblical criticism.

4. "Secularism". This is no doubt the most dangerous of all Satan's deceptive attacks against Christianity. Secularism is the substitution of worldly values and standards for Christian standards set forth in the Word of God. Very often this type of attack is most difficult to recognize and requires thorough study and spiritual commitment to avoid.

5. Another issue which began to plague the church was the many splits that began to occur in local congregations over doctrinal differences. In the 1800s slavery was a key issue, which caused splits in three of the most prominent denominations: Presbyterian, Baptist and Methodist.

6. Another factor which challenged the church was the change in immigrant origin that took place in the late 1800s. Up until this time, most immigrants were Protestant, if they had a religious belief. Now, more immigrants were coming from Southern Europe and other parts of the world and had different beliefs.

7. There also began a rise in new religious groups in the 1800s such as: Adventists, Mormons, Christian Scientists, Jehovah's Witnesses, plus several new denominations.

Historical Event #8: 1900 to Present Day

Satan's battle in America is intensified through his use of deception. The most persistent challenge to the church has become "Secularism." Secularism is characterized by replacing biblical Christian standards with worldly standards. The substitution is not necessarily evidenced by words, but by our lifestyle.

Biblical Standards

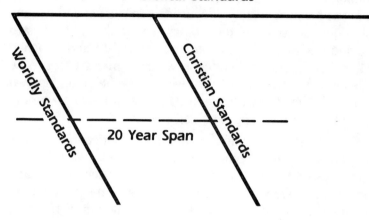

20 Year Span

To better illustrate this, examine the chart. Biblical standards always remain the same. But if we, as Christians, accept and rub elbows with the world's standards and activities, then Satan will slowly and constantly lower the world's standards. So if we continue only to maintain the same distance between the world's standards and Christian standards, then our Christian standards will also drift downward. The net result is that what was a world standard 20 years ago, is today an accepted Christian standard. Many such happenings in the church today are causing a great deal of hurt and defeat for God's people. One example is divorce, which was seldom found in the church 30 years ago, yet today is as common as in world circles. Most people who have been divorced will admit to the terrible pain involved.

When Satan attacks through deception using secularism, the society around God's people is not likely to persecute as the Roman society did in the days of the early church. The prevailing environmental spirit of secularism is characterized by attitude control. Tolerance and eventually indifference to sin is the product of secularism. It develops in us a lack of commitment to biblical standards, and the concept that man controls his own destiny. It causes us to trust in and depend on education, science, technology, and political systems to provide our needs. We become committed to and attached to the "Great Society" concept, which is man's effort to be independent and self-sufficient with everyone doing his own thing. It is the characteristic of the spirit of Babel, a worldly system which the Scriptures call Babylon.

Other factors affecting the church in America in the 1900s include: The rise of Communism, which began with the Bolshevik Revolution in 1917; the growing influence of cults and the occult; the rapid changes in the fundamental living nature of American society such as urbanization and our high degree of mobility, which has caused us to lose our family roots. We avoid commitments to our neighbors, and often project a lack of concern for others.

Theological liberalism is another major concern in our churches. We handle too lightly God's view of sin. I do not say this critically, but by examining the Scriptures, I see the devastating effects and personal defeat this concept causes for God's people in their everyday lives. It has caused us to adulterate the Word and develop what is called "the Social Gospel."

To eliminate the breakdown of moral values we see taking place in our country through our liberalism, we must be careful of how we attempt to rectify proper moral values. We have the perfect example which *worked* in the middle 1700s during the "Great Awakening." Men and women became personally committed, through the power of the Holy Spirit, to bring national revival. It was demonstrated through their living out the moral values taught in the Word. We must be careful not to attempt to replace the power of the Holy Spirit at work in each person's life by using political action or legislative change as the only means to bring about national revival of biblical moral values.

God's Geographic Base

America truly became God's geographical base for spreading the gospel throughout the world. Our spiritual history reveals the discovery of America was delayed until just the right time. America has had the funds and resources to spread the Word of God throughout the world in these, the last days. America has a special calling by God.

But the enemy is not idle. As we grow in the Lord, we learn from the Word and our experience that anything of God involves great spiritual battles. Briefly, seeing, as we have reviewed in this chapter, the way God has developed our spiritual history, one would think our nation would be in for fierce spiritual battles. In fact, prophetic Scripture brings to light the method and means that Satan will use here in America to try and defeat the spiritual base which God has established in our land in these last days. The enemy's methods will be thoroughly examined as we advance through the teaching of this book and you will then be able to acknowledge and know *God's next move in America based on the prophetic word of God.*

Our country was a new beginning in the life of the church, something the enemy had not before encountered. Satan's attack has been different in America than what we see throughout the church's history. But, it is just as severe. The difference is that in our country he is using the attack method of deception rather than persecution. This was prophesied in the New Testament Scriptures.

Throughout the balance of the book, we will focus on showing this teaching from the Word so we can know our spiritual enemy's deceptive schemes, and how the Word of God says he will deploy them against Christians in THE LAST DAYS IN AMERICA.

Chapter 4

KNOWING OUR ENEMY

America is God's chosen land for the center of Christianity in the last days. There is a church located every few blocks in most towns across this nation. Teaching from the Bible can be heard day and night on radio and television. The Bible is the number one best seller. Millions of books with a Christian message are sold each year; religious publishing has become a major business. Christian missionary organizations are spending millions of dollars to take the gospel of Jesus Christ throughout the world.

"But wait a minute!", you say. "Though all of that may be true, and it's evident God has established our land as His geographical center in these last days, where are the persecutions? Why don't we have the kind of spiritual warfare we saw throughout the history of the church? What about the great battle when the Holy Spirit was poured out, and Satan, with his angels, was cast down to earth? Why don't we hear much about this conflict these days? Has it subsided?"

Let me tell you, dear friend—the spiritual battle is just as fierce today, if not more so. However, it is decidedly different! You see, the Bible teaches us that Satan attacks God's people in two different ways in the combat of spiritual warfare: persecution and deception.

We saw through our review of the church's history how fierce this battle has been throughout the ages by the persecutions Christians have had to endure. In the last days, the Bible warns us the battle is just as severe; however, Satan will attack the core of Christianity through deception, not persecution.

Deception centers on motivating Christians to step out independent of God's Word, primarily for the purpose of satisfying, serving or pleasing our "self life."

The following are some of the Scriptures which warn us of the deceptive conditions in the end times:

> At that time if anyone says to you, "Look, here is the Christ!", or, "There he is!", do not believe it. For false Christs and false prophets (prophets are teachers) will appear and perform great signs and miracles *to deceive* even the elect (Christians)—if that were possible. See, I have told you ahead of time. (Matthew 24:23-25. Words in parentheses are the author's.)

In Matthew 7:15-23, Jesus teaches we are to examine the fruits of a teacher—not signs, miracles or works. While I do not want to belittle the miracles of our God, miracles and works *can* be counterfeit and deceptive. Only fruits reveal the heart of an individual. Miracles and works can be for self-satisfying purposes.

> No one knows about the day or hour, not even the angels in heaven, nor the Son, but only the Father. As it was in the days of Noah, so it will be at the coming of the Son of Man. For in the days before the flood, people were eating and drinking, marrying and giving in marriage, up to the day Noah entered the ark; and they knew nothing about what would

happen until the flood came and took them all away. That is
how it will be at the coming of the Son of Man. (Matthew
24:36-39)

In the last days people will be overly concerned about
what they have to eat. Their lives will be caught up in partying
and drinking. Marrying and giving in marriage will be the spirit
of the day concerning matrimony. In other words, there will
be an attitude of freedom to marry, marry again and again, if
one so desires.

Did you know that in our country there is nearly a 50%
divorce rate in the church? Even prominent church leaders
have gone through divorce. This is indicative of the deceptive
force coming to attack Christians.

Be careful or your hearts will be weighed down with dissipa-
tion (excessive indulgence in pleasure seeking), drunkenness
and the anxieties of life, and that day (Jesus' second coming)
will close on you unexpectedly like a trap. (Luke 21:34. Words
in parentheses are the author's.)

The pressures from our society to seek pleasure and be
weighed down with the anxieties of life are very strong and
powerful today. I think most of us would honestly admit that
there is some effect on nearly everyone.

So, because you are lukewarm—neither hot nor cold—I am
about to spit you out of my mouth. You say, "I am rich; I
have acquired wealth and do not need a thing," but you do
not realize that you are wretched, pitiful, poor, blind and
naked. (Revelation 3:16,17)

The pressure to obtain material things can become spiritually devastating. Our commitment to the attainment of
"things" becomes greater than it is for our need to be obedient to the Word of God. The pressure to believe that things
and wealth give us our security rather than our faith in the
Lord Jesus has become extremely strong in America.

But mark this: There will be terrible times in the last days. People will be lovers of themselves, lovers of money, boastful, proud, abusive, disobedient to their parents, ungrateful, unholy, without love, unforgiving, slanderous, without self-control, brutal, not lovers of good, treacherous, rash, conceited, lovers of pleasure rather than lovers of God – having a form of godliness, but denying its power. Have nothing to do with them. (II Timothy 3:1-5)

Paul is prophesying of the self-serving lifestyle that will prevail, the spirit of everyone wanting to do his own thing, as a sign of the conditions used to deceive the major Christian society in the last days.

Paul says people will go to church, have a form of godliness, but he refers to the spirit of their character as "terrible times" (II Timothy 3:1) — people loving money, disobedient to parents, ungrateful, unholy, immoral, conceited, proud, loving pleasure rather than God will be characteristic. The spirit of this society here described by Paul will be to satisfy one's own personal desire, to please ourselves.

All of these Scriptures relating to the conditions of the last days confirm one another. They speak of a self-serving spirit that will prevail — excessive pleasure, commitment to possessing material things, marrying and remarrying, over-concern with food, partying, a proud spirit and disobedience to authorities.

In the history of the church, all of these conditions which describe the last days have not occurred prior to the present generation here in America. Nowhere else have these prophecies been fulfilled in the past, and nowhere but in this country do all these conditions exist.

Throughout the church's history, the spiritual warfare between the Holy Spirit and Satan has usually been expressed through Satan causing hard times or persecutions of Christians, with the Holy Spirit providing the strength for God's people to endure.

In these latter times, however, Satan has changed his

scheme just as Scripture has predicted. He has developed a means by which Christians are deceived, causing us to change our inner character and nature in our commitment to the ways of the world. Our way of life often demonstrates the self-serving lifestyle we read about in II Timothy 3:1-5: We have become lovers of money, proud, seeking pleasure more than God, disobedient to authorities and coveting what is not ours.

This type of attack by the enemy is causing much spiritual defeat. Families are suffering and many are falling apart because of poor marriage relationships and problems with children. Emotional stress and depression are at record levels.

No one knowingly chooses the pressures of life which are coming our way today. However, Scripture warns that if we are not extremely careful and alert during this period of time in which we are now living, God's enemy, Satan, will cause even Christians to be overcome by these pressures.

To think we cannot succumb to the temptation of today's deceptive pressures because we are Christians is misleading. Recall what happened in the beginning with Adam and Eve. Even Israel, God's chosen people, was overtaken by the pressures of its time and fell away.

Remember—God's enemy is Satan. Therefore, Satan's most enticing attacks are reserved for God's children. This is how he gets at God. Satan is no dummy; he attacks where it will hurt God the most—in the geographical areas where God's people are the strongest. We learn this from Adam and Eve, Israel, Jesus and throughout the history of the church.

We need to understand the tactics of Satan—especially those which are used to attack Christians.

In international relations, government leaders realize the importance of knowing their enemies thoroughly—politically, militarily, economically and in any other way vital to survival. In business, sports or any other endeavor, it is essential to *know* the competition. The same is true in the spiritual realm.

As Satan observes the strength of God's people in any area, he is going to strike out and attack. Scripture never implies that it will be any other way. This attack may be direct and obvious through persecution, as we saw throughout most of the church's history, and still see today in some countries, or, Satan may attack through the use of deception. God's prophetic Word warns that in the last days, Satan will attack through deception rather than persecution. We have established that America is the center of Christianity in these end times. Therefore, it is critical that we understand the nature of Satan's deceptive attacks.

Many people today acknowledge that something has gone wrong with the attitude and spirit of our country, and that it appears the power of evil is being openly released as never before. An examination of many of the fruits of our society reveals this truth:

- The practice of Satan worship, sorcery, witchcraft, the occult and astrology has increased beyond belief. Over ten million witches are reported to live in America.

- Use of drugs and narcotics are at epidemic levels.

- Sexual freedom is the cry of our day—"Do whatever satisfies you." Over 20 million sex magazines are sold each week. Each day television and movies further tear down biblical sex standards.

- *Parents* magazine recently stated that adultery in the United States seems to be as widely practiced as it must have been in the days before the flood. One result is that divorce was up 160% from 1961 to 1976. Fifty percent of all marriages are ending in divorce. This fulfills a prophecy made by Jesus about the end times, stating people will be "marrying, and giving in marriage." (Matthew 24:38)

- Another result in America has been the murder of 13

million human beings over the past ten years through abortion.

- Another is the current plague of venereal and so-called "social" diseases, including AIDS and herpes.

- Crime and violence increased 59% between 1970 and 1980 to a total of 13.3 million crimes in America, by far the worst in the world. A major crime is now committed every three seconds in our country, and in one out of every six homes, someone has been raped, robbed or assaulted.

- Organized crime is the largest business organization in the United States generating ten times the profits of Exxon, the nation's largest corporation.

- Over 50 billion dollars is spent each year by Americans on gambling.

- Over 50 billion dollars is spent each year on alcoholic beverages—a cause of many family conflicts. There are 3½ million alcoholics under the age of 17.

- Statisticians report God's name is now used over one billion times each day in our country as a curse word.

These are but a few examples of what is taking place in today's society. The important thing is to recognize that we are under a tremendous attack by evil forces. Whether we like to accept this fact or not, Jesus says in Matthew 7:15-20 that fruits reveal false spiritual influence and teaching.

It is important to realize that Satan is relentless in his attacks against Christians. And that is why so many Christians are plagued with problems today—all brought about by the enemy's use of deception. He is causing Christians to lose their sense of dependency on God, primarily for the purpose of satisfying or pleasing their own "self" desires. And that is causing many to suffer spiritual defeat. It may be reflected in a number of ways such as troubled family relationships, pressures, and emotional stress.

The same independent character we see developing in our country is the nature that caused Satan's own downfall.

> Now you have fallen from heaven, O Lucifer, son of the morning! How you are cut to the ground—mighty though you were against the nations of the world. For you said to yourself, "I will ascend to heaven and rule the angels. I will take the highest throne. I will preside on the Mount of Assembly far away in the north. I will climb to the highest heavens and be like the Most High." (Isaiah 14:12-14, Living Bible)

We see the independent attitude. "*I* will do this. *I* will do that. *I* will do what *I* want to do." Everybody doing their own thing has become a strong spirit in our land. That is the nature of Satan, and it is bringing pain and destruction to the lives of many.

Though we may have had great favor with God in this country, the attitude of "serving self" will cause us to fall, just as it happened to Satan. At one time he had great favor with God. Speaking of Satan, the Bible says:

> I appointed you to be the anointed guardian cherub. You had access to the holy mountain of God. You walked among the stones of fire. (Ezekiel 28:14, LB)

Satan was God's right hand man, so to speak. But he became independent, wanting to do what *he* wanted to do, as we read in Isaiah 14. The cause of his rebellion and self-seeking attitude was because his beauty and position of power and wealth filled him with pride.

The following passage refers to Satan:

> Your great wealth filled you with internal turmoil and you sinned. Therefore, I cast you out of the mountain of God like a common sinner. I destroyed you, O overshadowing cherub, from the midst of the stones of fire. Your heart was filled with pride because of your beauty; you corrupted your wisdom

for the sake of spendor ... you defiled your holiness with lust for gain. (Ezekiel 28:16-18,LB)

We find that the same conditions have developed in our country. Our great beauty, wealth and position of power has caused us to corrupt our wisdom and allowed a spirit of independence to develop among the people.

Paul refers to this type of character in candid language:

But mark this: There will be terrible times in the last days. People will be lovers of themselves, lovers of money, boastful, proud, abusive, disobedient to their parents, ungrateful, unholy, without love, unforgiving, slanderous, without self-control ... conceited, lovers of pleasure rather than lovers of God. (II Timothy 3:1-4)

UNDERSTANDING SATAN'S USE OF DECEPTION

The fall of Adam and Eve gives us understanding of the attack methods Satan uses against God's people through deception.

As the story of humankind begins to unfold in the book of Genesis, we notice that at first everything was good. We see no sign or hint of rebellion.

God saw all that He had made, and it was very good. And there was evening, and there was morning—the sixth day. (Genesis 1:31)

There was no opposition present. We see only a lovely picture of fellowship between God and His creatures, with God providing the perfect setting for man. God and man walked together in happy communion. The Bible presents this scene as a blessed picture of peace. We see here a God of love providing for and having fellowship with His loved ones, and in turn, seeking the love of those He created. God's word to Adam and Eve at that time to obey and express their love was short and simple.

The Lord God took the man and put him in the Garden of Eden to work it, and take care of it. And the Lord God commanded the man, "You are free to eat from any tree in the garden; but you must not eat from the tree of the knowledge of good and evil, for when you eat of it you will surely die". (Genesis 2:15-17)

The method Satan used to cause Adam and Eve to fall from the will of God in the very beginning was deception. The temptations and choices we meet every day are displayed for us in this tragic story. Satan has not changed his method of attack for the child of God.

There was a sweet fellowship existing in the Garden of Eden. Satan knew if he could only break the bonds of that fellowship and cause those two in the garden to step out and be independent of the command of God (not to eat from the tree of the knowledge of good and evil), then God would lose something which was most precious to Him. Satan cared nothing for the suffering that would follow. He wanted to accomplish a breakdown in the holy communion and relationship between God and His children. This was his objective throughout the history of Israel and the church, and it is still his basic objective today.

Satan employed several tactics and temptations to accomplish his goal in the Garden of Eden. He would love to remove the third chapter of Genesis from the Bible, for here we see the plan of Satan's attack in the garden—and, most important—the unique pattern of assault he employs against God's children. He has used the same basic pattern throughout history. I believe that is why he has caused so much confusion over the acceptance of the early Genesis chapters. By promoting the concept that no educated person can believe this really happened, he clouds our understanding of how he brings about deception.

Now the serpent (the animal Satan spoke through) was more crafty than any of the wild animals the Lord God had made.

He said to the woman, "Did God really say, 'You must not eat from any tree in the Garden'?"

The woman said to the serpent, "We may eat fruit from the trees in the garden, but God did say, 'You must not eat from the tree that is in the middle of the garden, and you must not touch it, or you will die.' "

"You will not surely die," the serpent said to the woman. "For God knows that when you eat of it, your eyes will be opened, and you will be like God, knowing good and evil."

When the woman saw that the fruit of the tree was good for food and pleasing to the eye, and was also desirable for gaining wisdom, she took some and ate it. She also gave some to her husband, who was with her, and he ate it. (Genesis 3:1-6. Words in parentheses are the author's.)

There are four techniques displayed in Satan's attack on Adam and Eve.

Satan's First Attack Technique:

He implants thoughts of doubt and then, if not dealt with, outright denial of the meaning of God's word.

Daily, hourly, as we are confronted with issues in our everyday lives, we can count on the enemy to raise doubts in our mind concerning the meaning of God's Word. He can implant doubts through our subconscious, through the many teaching avenues of the world such as television, movies, books and magazines, through friends and in many other ways. And if we are not alert and careful, we will begin to reason these thoughts in our own mind. If we do, next there will be a strong temptation to question, "Does it really make any difference to God?", or "God's Word doesn't really mean that, does it?" The next step then is that Satan will cause the doubt to become an outright denial. "No, God doesn't really mean what He has said." If we accept that position, we move out, ignore God's Word as Adam and Eve did, break communion with God, and suffer a spiritual defeat.

Jesus called Satan the father of lies:

He was a murderer from the beginning, not holding to the truth, for there is no truth in him. When he lies, he speaks his native language, for he is a liar and the father of lies. (John 8:44)

Satan's Second Attack Technique:

He deceives people to elevate themselves, "to be like God," so that people will make their own decisions about right and wrong.

"For God knows that when you eat of it, your eyes will be opened, and *you will be like God,* knowing good and evil." (Genesis 3:5.)

Satan deceived Eve to rebel against God's spoken Word by tempting her to be independent and use human wisdom and reasoning to decide right and wrong, "knowing good and evil." The one thing God did not equip humans with was the knowledge of good and evil. And when we become independent and attempt to reason and decide "right and wrong" on our own apart from God's Word, we can be sure Satan will be right there. He will lure us into rebelling against the standard found in God's Word, in favor of our own "self" interest to serve our desires, just as he did Eve.

This characteristic of people wanting the freedom "to be their own God" was prophesied by Paul to be a deceptive attack method Satan would use against the central stronghold of Christianity in the last days.

"Concerning the coming our Lord Jesus Christ and our being gathered to him (this introductory statement lets us know Paul is talking about the last days), we ask you brothers, not to become easily unsettled or alarmed by some prophecy, report or letter, supposed to have come from us, saying that the day of the Lord has already come. Don't let anyone deceive you in any way, for that day will not come until the rebellion occurs and the man of lawlessness is revealed, the man doomed to destruction. He opposes and exalts himself over everything that is called God or is worshipped and even sets himself up in God's temple, proclaiming himself to be God." (II Thessalonians 2:1-4. Words in parentheses are the author's.)

In II Thessalonians, Paul makes several comments about the second coming of Jesus, and he didn't want to confuse the people into thinking it had already happened.

As we recall our review of church history, we discover that the prophetic points made by Paul in these verses have not happened until now.

An understanding of these verses in II Thessalonians requires a study of some of the key words.

In speaking of the second coming of Jesus in the last days Paul says, "For that day will not come, until the rebellion occurs and the man of lawlessness is revealed". (II Thessalonians 2:3)

The Greek word Paul uses here for rebellion is "apostasia." It means to defect or fall away. Paul calls those involved in this falling away "a man of lawlessness." It has become common teaching over the last few years to apply the word "man" to mean one individual who sets himself up to rule —called the Anti-christ.

However, I found the Greek word used for man in this verse is "anthropes". It is used most often in Scripture with reference to everyone or many people, not just one man. To illustrate, II Timothy 3:17 says, ". . . so that the man (anthropes) of God may be thoroughly equipped." This refers to all people of God.

Hebrews 2:6 states "What is man (anthropes) that you are mindful of him?" Hebrews 2:9 talking about Jesus says, ". . . so that by the grace of God, he might taste death for everyone (anthropes)." In this verse, "anthropes" is translated "everyone." In Hebrews 13:6, we find ". . . the Lord is my helper; I will not be afraid. What can man (anthropes) do to me?", and again in James 1:19, "anthropes" is translated "everyone." "My dear brothers, take note of this: Everyone (anthropes) should be quick to listen, slow to speak and slow to become angry." "Anthropes" is the Greek word Paul used for man in the phrase, "man of lawlessness," and carries the meaning of "many men."

Paul is describing a condition that will occur in the key Christian society in the last days. He didn't know where that would be, but listen to the warning of his prophecy.

Rebellion, a falling away, will take place before Jesus comes. Many (anthropes) will defect and fall out of the will of God due to the spirit of lawlessness. Paul calls them "The man of lawlessness." The spirit of lawlessness means having no real conscience against sin. Some translations refer to those in this rebellion as "a man (anthropes) of sin." A general apathy toward sin will be the spirit of the day.

It is the same type of deception the enemy used to deceive Eve and cause her to fall. Recall that Satan tempted Eve saying, "You will be like God, knowing good and evil." When we decide what is good or evil, Satan knows he can get us out of the will of God because we have a "self interest" nature. This is what Paul describes as the cause of this rebellion—the falling away from God's will in the last days.

> "He (referring to the man of lawlessness, those in rebellion) opposes and exalts himself over everything that is called God or is worshipped, and even sets himself up in God's temple, proclaiming himself to be God." (II Thessalonians 2:4. Words in parentheses are the author's.)

Notice that Paul, in speaking of the state of man in this society, uses the word *himself* three times. That is the sin of the rebellion that takes place. He doesn't say this man will quit going to church. His sin will be that of putting his own self-serving interests ahead of God, and he will believe that he has the right to decide right and wrong as though he is God. That is exactly how Satan got Eve to fall. She reasoned in her heart as though she were God, and determined she could decide "right and wrong" rather than follow God's Word.

In this verse, Paul has explained how the characteristic of rebellion will be expressed in the geographical center of Christianity in the last days. The rebellion must take place in a society of strong Christian teaching. Otherwise, how could there be a "rebellion" or "falling away" from Christian standards if it were not the prominent religious teaching of that society? How can you fall from something if you were not there first? And we know he is talking about the last days— the second coming of Jesus—because he states that clearly in II Thessalonians 2:1.

To understand what Paul is talking about in verse 4, I found the key to be the word *temple*. And again, this required a word study because of the common teaching which states this word refers to the temple in Jerusalem and how some man (usually referred to as the Anti-christ) "sets himself up in God's temple, proclaiming himself to be God."

That teaching makes sense and sounds correct, but it doesn't fit the Greek word used for man (anthropes). And it doesn't really fit the Greek word used for rebellion (apostasia), the falling away. I am sure Paul was speaking of more than one man falling away. Then, through a study of the Greek words used for temple, I found there are two. "Hieron" is the Greek word usually used when referring to the temple in Jerusalem. However, Paul uses a completely different Greek word, "naos," in this verse 4 of II Thessalonians.

I discovered "naos" is the Greek word used for temple in the Scriptures which refers to man as the temple of God. For example, "Don't you know that you yourselves are God's temple (naos) and that God's Spirit lives in you?" (I Corinthians 6:16) "Do you not know that your body is a temple (naos) of the Holy Spirit, who is in you, whom you have received from God?" (I Corinthians 6:19) "For we are the temple (naos) of the Living God . . ." (II Corinthians 6:16)

With that discovery, Paul's prophecy began to make sense and fit perfectly with other prophecies about the last days. If Paul is talking to Christians about Christianity (which he is), his terminology would refer to meanings as used in Christianity. In Christianity, the word "temple" refers to the body of man. And that is the word temple (naos) Paul uses in this verse, not temple (Hieron) which is usually used when referring to the temple in Jerusalem.

Paul was not speaking of the temple in Jerusalem in II Thessalonians 2:4, but was referring to man who is the temple of God's Spirit in Christianity. And the way Satan deceives man and gets him to fall away fits the pattern of what caused the fall of Satan, Adam and Eve and others. He deceives man to set himself up as his own god, to "exalt himself," to place his own desires first and ignore God's Word.

To summarize Satan's second technique, I believe Paul's prophecy is mainly addressing Christians in America, because he is talking about the primary Christian society in the last days and its falling away. The laws of our society were founded on Christian principles which were followed until recent years. But now man wants to be like a god. He wants to decide right and wrong. He has become the living definition of humanism.

Paul described the signs and characteristics of this prophecy, "man exalting himself and setting himself up in God's temple", when he said:

> But mark this: There will be terrible times in the last days. People will be lovers of themselves, lovers of money, boastful, proud, abusive, disobedient to their parents, ungrateful, unholy, without love, unforgiving, slanderous, without self-control, brutal, not lovers of good, treacherous, rash, conceited, lovers of pleasure rather than lovers of God — having a form of godliness (Christianity), but denying its power (having victory over sin through the indwelling power of the Holy Spirit). (II Timothy 3:1-5. Words in parentheses are the author's.)

What Christian society in these last days fits these two

descriptions of Paul's prophecy in II Thessalonians 2:1-4 and
in II Timothy 3:1-5? There is only one.

Satan's Third Attack Technique:

*When attacking Christians through persecution, Satan
causes them physical harm. When attacking through deception, however, Satan causes them spiritual harm. He, Satan,
attacks his victims through the desires of the flesh—those
things that serve the self-life such as beauty, material possessions, knowledge, wisdom, immoral thoughts, pride, position,
power, and others.*

When the woman (Eve) saw that the fruit of the tree was
good for food (lust of the flesh) and pleasing to the eye (lust
of the eyes), and also desirable for gaining wisdom (pride of
life) she took some and ate it. (Genesis 3:6. Words in parentheses are the author's.)

It was these three types of temptations (to serve the self-
life) that caused Eve to be deceived and go against God's
Word.

Then the Lord God said to the woman, "What is this you
have done?" The woman said, "The serpent deceived me,
and I ate." (Genesis 3:13)

Satan's Fourth Attack Technique:

*When attacking through deception: Satan tempts us to use
the name of God, since we are the sons of God, for self-serving
interests.*

Satan was very free to use the name of God in his discussion with Eve. He didn't ask her to deny God or to quit walking
with God. He knew it was important for her to follow God so
he just encouraged her to step out and disregard God's Word.
He caused her to wonder if God really meant what He had
said. He said to the woman, "Did God really say, 'You must
not eat from any tree in the Garden?'" (Genesis 3:1)

This fourth method is graphically illustrated when Satan

tried to trap and deceive Jesus. Satan did not tempt Jesus with the obvious vices of the world. He didn't tempt Him to deny God or to quit being religious. He tempted Jesus with self-serving attractions, just as he had tempted Eve. He wanted Jesus to step out on His own — to become independent and make His own decisions, rather than following the principles of God's Word as to how He should serve God and be godly.

Notice that each of the ways Satan tempted Jesus had to do with serving the self-life.

The first temptation was the lust of the flesh.

Then Jesus was led by the Spirit into the desert to be tempted by the devil. After fasting forty days and forty nights, he was hungry. The tempter came to him and said, "If you are the Son of God, tell these stones to become bread." Jesus answered, "It is written: 'Man does not live on bread alone, but on every word that comes from the mouth of God.' " (Matthew 4:1-4)

I am sure God was not going to deprive Jesus of food, but it was to be provided according to God's timing and will, not Satan's. Jesus knew He was not to perform a miracle to serve His own self desires, even if it would help prove who He was.

The second temptation was the pride of life.

Then the devil took him to the holy city and had him stand on the highest point of the temple. "If you are the Son of God," he said, "throw yourself down. For it is written: 'He will command his angels concerning you, and they will lift you up in their hands, so that you will not strike your foot against a stone.' "

Jesus answered him, "It is also written: 'Do not put the Lord your God to the test.' " (Matthew 4:5-7)

This time Satan tempted Jesus with pride by trying to get Him to perform a miracle to serve His own self-interest. He tried to get Him to be proud of the fact He was a child of

God, causing Him to do a foolish thing to prove God would save Him. Jesus again responded to the temptation by quoting Scripture.

The third temptation was the lust of the eyes.

> The devil led him up to a high place and showed him in an instant all the kingdoms of the world. And he said to him, "I will give you all their authority and splendor, for it has been given to me, and I can give it to anyone I want to. So, if you worship me, it will all be yours."

> Jesus answered, "It is written: worship the Lord your God and serve Him only." (Luke 4:5-8)

What a heavy temptation — to be offered all the authority and splendor of the things of the world! We have difficulty in not bowing to this temptation when offered far less than what was shown to Jesus. Again, notice that Satan tempted Jesus' self-life — something that would serve His personal being.

When attacking through deception, all of Satan's temptations are directed toward serving or doing something for our "self." He will even use what appears to be a godly cause. But, if the inner motivation is to serve, promote or do something only for ourselves, be on guard.

One other confirming example is found in Matthew 16. Jesus had asked His disciples the question, "Who do you say I am?" Peter answered, "You are the Christ, the Son of the living God." Jesus then told Peter, "This was not revealed to you by man, but by my Father in heaven." (Matthew 16:17) Peter had received a revelation from God. Now notice what happened immediately following this revelation.

> From that time on Jesus began to explain to His disciples that He must go to Jerusalem and suffer many things at the hands of the elders, chief priests and teachers of the law, and that he must be killed, and on the third day be raised to life.

> Peter took him aside and began to rebuke him, "Never, Lord!" he said. "This shall never happen to you!"

> Jesus turned and said to Peter, "Out of my sight, Satan! You are a stumbling block to me; you do not have in mind the things of God, but the things of men." (Matthew 16:21-23)

Peter receives a revelation from God, then in the very next scene states the desire of Satan. Why? The motivating force was self-preservation for Jesus over and above the will of God. Again, Satan tempted Jesus—this time through one whom He loved to seek for self-interest—to think of self first. Jesus knew the will of God and, therefore, let Peter know that his thoughts of self-preservation were the ways of man, and were from the enemy.

Knowing the ways in which our enemy attacks us through deception is critical for us to understand in these last days. The Scriptures warn us that this is to be his method of attack in our country. The facts prove this to be true. Here again are the four major ways Satan attacks God's children through deception:

1. He implants thoughts of doubt, then outright denial of the meaning of God's Word when it conflicts with our desire or will. These thoughts can come from many outside sources or from our own inner being.
2. He tempts us to elevate ourselves "to be like God"—to think that we have the capacity to decide and make our own decisions about right and wrong.
3. Satan attacks us through the desires of the flesh, the eyes and pride of life. He uses those things that will serve the desires of the self-life. He will use a variety of things such as beauty, material possessions, knowledge, immoral attractions or position.
4. Satan even uses the name of God and tempts us to serve God according to his (Satan's) direction, rather than God's.

We have all fallen victim to deception in one way or another, and at various times in our Christian walk. When this occurs victory in our spiritual walk is lost. This can result in a multitude of personal problems, pressures and conflicts, and requires that we understand another important biblical teaching—that of repentance and confession—if we want to regain our position of living in victory.

Deception by Satan is difficult to discern in these days because the enemy has so many weapons at his disposal. That is why we need all the insight we can gain on this subject. If it were not important, God's Word would not contain such stern warnings about Satan using this method of attack in the last days.

I found the following story to be both helpful and meaningful in my understanding of deception. Perhaps it will be of benefit to you, also. It is the story of an eagle.

A LESSON IN DECEPTION

The eagle is an amazing specimen of God's creation. This bird is mentioned over 30 times in Scripture. Eagles are swift, clocked at 120 to 150 miles per hour in flight. Their powerful seven-foot wing span allows them to soar and glide effortlessly at heights up to one-half mile, and the aerodynamics of their wing construction permits flight in winds of hurricane force.

The eagle's eye has two fovea (areas of acute vision) which gives them the ability to spot a rabbit two miles away. Their great depth perception allows them to dive at speeds up to 200 miles per hour. They have 270-degree peripheral vision. Their two sets of eyelids permits closing one, which is clear, and protects the eyes from dust and wind during flight.

The eagle's decisive appearance is different from other birds, due to a bony protrusion which extends outward over the eyelid, and is not found in most other fowl. A stern and decisive appearance, along with its other unique characteristics, gives the eagle a "royal" pose. Its grandeur and grace have been revered and esteemed for centuries. The eagle has been chosen as the official symbol of some of the greatest countries and leaders including the Romans, Charlemagne, Napoleon and the United States.

Picture this monarch of the sky perched high on a mountain ledge overlooking a valley below with a beautiful stream, trees and mountains in the background. This majestic eagle you have envisioned has a clear view of the entire area below him as he sits basking in the morning sun.

After bathing in the sun for awhile, enjoying his domain on this particular morning, the eagle launched himself into the air. He sailed over the green valley and swooped down toward the stream, heading for his favorite fishing spot to catch his breakfast.

When he arrived at the stream's bank his keen eyes noticed there was a slight change near the area where he normally fished. There, near the shore, close to his fishing spot, was a large rock, about two or three feet in diameter and two feet high. It was something new. The eagle knew this rock had never been there before. Therefore, to him it appeared dangerous.

The eagle flew right on by his fishing spot without stopping, sailed to a nearby tree, and perched on a limb so he could observe the area. He wanted to determine if this new and strange object might be harmful. He sat there for better than an hour, his keen eyes looking up and down the stream. In time he could tell there was no activity around; he saw no danger, so he sailed down and landed on the rock.

Next to the rock—not by the stream, but in the nearby grass—was a large, beautiful fish. Fish are one of an eagle's favorite foods. He was quickly drawn to the fish, but he was puzzled. If the fish had been on the shore near the stream, he thought, that would have been normal. But there it was on the grass, several feet from the shore—that was puzzling.

The eagle sat for awhile. He was suspicious. Things didn't seem right to him. His sharp eyes scanned every grassy area around, all the nearby bushes, and the shore of the mountain stream. There seemed to be no danger.

He jumped off the rock, clutched the fish in his claws and was about to fly away when he noticed another fish lying nearby in the grass. Then he saw another! There were three or four beautiful, plump fish. The wilderness was caring for his needs this morning in a most amazing way!

On the other side of the stream, however, a wise trapper hiding in a thick clump of bushes watched every move the eagle made. This trapper had been promised a large sum of money to capture an eagle alive. And he knew the wise eagle would require him to use his best and most crafty skills.

The eagle ate well that day. The next day, after his morning sunbath, he returned to his favorite fishing spot. The rock was still there. He sailed to the nearby tree to observe the area — this time for only a few minutes. He was more quickly satisfied there was no danger. The eagle flew to the rock and after landing, found the supply of fish had been miraculously renewed. This was unbelieveable! Mother nature was surely providing for him in a beautiful way. And it would give him more time to sit on his perch and soar through the heavens, viewing his lovely mountain and valley domain.

After several days had passed, the eagle was becoming conditioned. Now each morning he would fly directly to the rock. He had found that each day the supply of fish was being replenished. After landing, he would jump down, grab a fish, jump back on the rock and sit there to eat and enjoy his breakfast. When finished, he would again jump down, clutch another fish in his claws and fly off, taking the second fish to his nest high on a cliff for a meal later in the day. The eagle loved it! This was saving him better than half of every day which could be used for soaring through the sky and perching high in the cliffs, his two favorite pastimes.

Several days passed and the eagle had developed a frame of mind of acceptance. The trapper was now ready for his next move. He made a strong hoop like a fish net about four feet in diameter. He attached to the hoop a long handle with a curved bow. The next night he went to the mountain stream where he had placed the rock and carefully dug the long handle into the ground, positioning it at an angle. The hoop hovered about three feet above the rock, yet the bow in the handle kept the net fairly level over the rock. Then, as he had been doing every night, he spread fish out in the nearby grass.

The next morning, the eagle sat perched on his high cliff lookout as usual, enjoying the beauty of the mountains, forest and stream below. In about an hour, he lifted off his perch and began what was becoming a leisurely flight to his favorite spot. The eagle's acceptance that mother nature was providing his food without any effort on his part was beginning to develop in him a dull and sluggish nature.

As the eagle drew near to the rock, he was suddenly puzzled and annoyed. There was an odd structure erected above the rock. He checked his flight and began to soar in circles. He flew fairly high, around and around, trying to make out the strange object. He could see the fish were there as usual. After 20 to 30 minutes of flight, there wasn't any evidence of danger in the bushes near the rock, so he descended to a nearby tree top where he landed. There he spent over an hour in complete silence, observing. His keen eyes kept watch for any strange movement and he listened for any unusual sound. There was nothing!

Far off, however, a good 200 yards away, hidden in the thick bushes, was the motionless trapper, patiently watching every move the eagle made.

After sitting in the tree top for over an hour, the eagle could sense no danger, so he believed it was safe to investigate. He flew down to the shore, landing away from the net. He found a fish in the grass, ate it, grabbed another in his claws, and flew back to his nest. He had not determined that the strange object over the rock was harmless, but it appeared so.

That afternoon as the eagle was soaring through the sky, he couldn't erase from his mind that new object over the rock. He had to know if it was going to interfere with the beautiful way his food had been provided the last couple of weeks. He flew back to the rock and after circling several times, landed on the handle of the net. Nothing happened! The structure appeared to be harmless.

There were still a couple of fish near the rock under the net. He hopped down to test this strange structure. He reached out with his beak and claw clutching one of the fish under the net, then quickly hopped back. The object didn't move.

The next few days the eagle proceeded with caution. With each visit he surveyed the area closely, making sure there was nothing else new. He would move quickly, devouring one fish and carrying a second off to his nest, all the time staying away from the rock.

As the days passed, he regained his confidence that all was well. He was overjoyed that his food was still miraculously being provided. Once again he began to get a fish and perch on the rock, which was directly under the net, to eat his banquet.

The trapper was now ready. Before dawn the next morning, he made some important changes in the arrangement of the net. He tied a strong cord to the rim of the hoop. He ran the cord down to the ground in front of the rock, under a small root, and then ran the cord into the nearby thick bushes. To test the cord, he pulled on it, bending the rim of the net down until it covered the rock.

The trapper satisfied himself all was ready. He baited the trap with the usual fish. Then he moved into the nearby thicket where he had run the cord to wait in silent anticipation.

Right on time, the eagle came the next morning. The trapper watched. The eagle, now full of confidence, had no hesitation. Though wise, he had been deceived into accepting this strange structure and free fish every day as a part of the established order.

He landed on the sand near the rock, grabbed a large fish and perched on the stone under the net to enjoy his meal.

At that very moment, the eagle sensed there was a slight movement in the nearby thicket. His muscles tightened! He was ready to spring into the safety of the air, but before he could move, the four-foot hoop with the net attached came down over him with a vicious swish.

There was an intense battle—the eagle against the net. Beating his wings, tearing at the net with his beak and claws, he fought for his freedom. He strained with every ounce of energy, but soon the eagle became helpless. He was entangled in the mesh of the trap. The mighty and glorious monarch of the sky had fallen to defeat through deceit.

Deception—the tool Satan is using to undermine biblical standards in the last days! It is this tool of Satan which is causing Christians to suffer spiritual defeat. Our fruits confirm this is true when we examine family relationships, pressures and anxieties in the lives of Christians in America.

The story of the eagle demonstrates several principles of deception. We can learn from this story some of the aspects of danger that draw us into being deceived. Most deceptive traps are usually hidden, but there will usually be visible evidence of their presence. Spiritually, we are warned not to believe every spirit, but to try the spirits. (I John 4:1) This is accomplished through using the Word of God as our guide, just as Jesus did when Satan tempted him. (Matthew 4:1-11)

- The eagle trusted what he saw with his eyes. He ignored his instinct. Adam and Eve were first lured into deception by what they saw with their eyes (the lust of the eyes) rather than listening to the word they had from God.
- The eagle was drawn to the trap through an appeal to one of his basic needs—food. The deadly temptations of Satan always include an appeal (lust of the flesh) to one of our basic needs such as food, clothing, security, acceptance or sexual drive. He offers these as bait.
- The eagle had inner warnings of the hidden dangers,

but his desires caused him to go against his wisdom. God provides us with warnings and insights of spiritual danger. Like Jesus, we must follow His Word instead of our wants or wishes.

- The eagle fell victim to not realizing the hidden cost of getting something for nothing. He gained his provision of food every day without labor, but it cost him his natural instinct to be alert. He became dull and sluggish, and it eventually cost him his freedom.

Satan is a master in tempting us with the pleasure and advantages of sin without revealing the spiritual defeats in our life that we will suffer.

The last principle we notice is the eagle's dullness which caused him to develop a false sense of pride in thinking he had all things under control, regardless of the new surroundings. How easy it is for us to let our guard down and accept a watered down biblical standard. It is our spiritual pride and false confidence that tells us we can enjoy the pleasures and sins of the world, and not get caught in its consequences.

The eagle became conditioned to his surroundings through the lust of the flesh, lust of the eyes and pride because he was more interested in satisfying his "self" desire for food. Though contrary to the laws of nature, he soon accepted new standards because they pleased him. He accepted new standards because they were "self" serving, allowing more time for pleasure. In like manner, God's Word warns us that our spiritual enemy, Satan, will attempt to deceive us into accepting or changing biblical standards through "self-serving" traps, just as he deceived Eve.

To know our enemy and his methods of deception is of critical importance in these last days. This is especially so here in America, the center of Christianity, where the Word tells us this is the area where Satan will set many deceptive traps. We are told they will follow a pattern similar to what we found in the story of the eagle. We are warned that Satan's method of attack will be to get us to set aside sound biblical standards and accept the standards of our society—the world—in order that we may serve our own desires. We are tempted at every turn today "to be like God" and determine right and wrong through our own reasoning power.

> Be self-controlled and alert. Your enemy, the devil, prowls around like a roaring lion looking for someone to devour. (I Peter 5:8)

In our next chapter, we learn of the vehicle Satan uses to bait his deceptive traps.

Chapter 5

SATAN'S ATTACK VEHICLE

In the previous chapter we saw how the wise old trapper outsmarted the eagle. Did you know that Satan has his rock, his fish and a net, always planting traps for you and me, hoping to cause us to fall from God's will? It is Satan's way of doing battle in the spiritual realm. Every Christian is a part of this battle, though many do not realize the warfare that is now taking place.

As we explore areas that apply to the Christian community today and discover what the enemy's strategy is concerning this warfare in the last days, the teaching gets tougher. I am quick to acknowledge that I am not attempting to avoid unpopular issues. And simply because the Lord has burned some strong truths into my heart over the past 12 years about what the enemy is doing in these last days, I don't presume to have it all put together, and feel that I can claim spiritual victory in everything. I don't want you to sense that kind of spirit in my writing.

I am writing this study to share some things about what is happening here in America in the last days—how the enemy has conceived a masterful weapon to keep us from walking in the power of God's Spirit. The evidence reveals Satan is experiencing far too much victory in the personal lives of Christians. There is an obvious lack of peace, patience, serenity, caring for others, and all-around victory over sin. I am interested in sharing as much as I know about the reason for this, believing it will benefit you.

Our enemy is Satan and he is out to trap everyone he can, to cause many of us to fall victim to his deceptive snares.

> Be self-controlled and alert. Your enemy, the devil, prowls around like a roaring lion looking for someone to devour. (I Peter 5:8)

We Have a Need

Christians need to understand the method Satan uses to bring about his attacks. The vehicle through which he sets his traps is what Scripture calls "the world." "Oh, come on!", you may say. "The world? That's a worn-out term in Christianity." But before you draw any conclusions, follow through with me on a few points I found to be helpful.

Did you know the subject of "the world" is one of the most widely discussed topics in the New Testament? In the Old Testament, the word "world" is seldom used. It is not a common word at all. Yet in the New Testament, it is used over 200 times.

It is the vehicle Satan uses to wage his spiritual warfare against Christians. Therefore, we want to have a proper understanding of its biblical meaning for these last days. Many Christians, however, don't have a solid understanding of this tool of Satan and its application. That is not to say I am an expert. But let me be open and honest. If God allows the subject of "the world" to occupy as much space in the Bible as He does, then it must be important. When something is mentioned more often than "the Holy Spirit" or "love" or many other subjects, then I personally believe the Lord meant for us to spend some time on what it means.

God's warning is clear. Note the number of times the word "world" is used:

> Do not conform any longer to the pattern of this *world*, but be transformed by the renewing of your mind. (Romans 12:2)

Notice what Paul says next:

> Then you will be able to test and approve what God's will is. (Romans 12:2)

God teaches us to keep unspotted from the world.

> Religion that God, our Father, accepts as pure and faultless is this: to look after orphans and widows in their distress and to keep oneself from being polluted (spotted) by the *world*. (James 1:27)

God wants us to avoid friendship with the world.

> You adulterous people, don't you know that friendship with the *world* is hatred toward God? Anyone who chooses to be a friend of the *world* becomes an enemy of God. (James 4:4)

God's people are to be "in," but not "of" the world.

> Jesus said, "My prayer is not that you take them out of the *world*, but that you protect them from the evil one (Satan). They are not of the *world*, even as I am not of it." (John 17:15,16)

According to Scripture, we are warned not to love the world.

> Do not love the *world* or anything in the *world*. If anyone loves the *world*, the love of the Father is not in him. For everything in the *world* ... comes not from the Father but from the *world*. (I John 2:15,16)

Why is there such a strong warning against what is called the world? Because Scripture says Satan is the god of this world.

The god of this age *(world)* has blinded the minds of unbelievers." (II Corinthians 4:4)

He is the ruler of the kingdom of the air.

As for you, you were dead in your transgressions and sins, in
which you used to live when you followed the ways of this
world, and the ruler of the kingdom of the air, the spirit who
is now at work in those who are disobedient. (Ephesians 2:1,2)

To follow the ways of this world — the ruler of the kingdom
of the air, the spirit who is at work in those who are
disobedient — is to follow Satan. And the world is under his
control!

We know that we are children of God, and that the whole
world is under the control of the evil one (that is Satan). (I
John 5:19. Words in parentheses are the author's.)

To win the battle with Satan, we are told how we must
prepare:

Finally, be strong in the Lord and in his mighty power. Put on
the full armor of God so that you can take your stand against
the devil's schemes. For our struggle is not against flesh and
blood, but against rulers, against the authorities, against the
powers of this dark *world.* (Ephesians 6:10-12)

All of these passages warn against what the Bible calls
"the world." "The *world*" is Satan's attack vehicle in spiritual
warfare. He is called the god of this world. The Bible states
that the world is under his control, and he is its ruler. He is
constantly at work, setting his traps to entice and deceive
Christians.

Some Christians seem to have extreme difficulty in understanding who runs "the world" order. They acknowledge
Satan has an *influence* in the world, and like to think that
this is a more proper term to describe his position. But that
is not what God has said in His Word. The Bible says Satan
controls the world.

I believe Satan fights this biblical truth. There seems to be a constant temptation in our minds to reason against such a possibility that he controls the world, regardless of what Scripture says.

"World" In Greek

The Greek word used for "world" in the Scripture is "kosmos." We find this word has three primary meanings.

First, it is used with reference to the material universe, this earth, as noted in Matthew 13:35, Acts 17:14, John 1:10 and Mark 16:15.

I will open my mouth in parables, I will utter things hidden since the creation of the *world.* (Matthew 13:35)

The **second** use of the Greek word "kosmos", or world, refers to the inhabitants or men of the world, as in John 3:16, 12:19, 17:21, and in many Scriptures which focus on the whole race of mankind.

For God so loved the *world* that He gave His one and only Son, that whoever believes in Him shall not perish, but have eternal life. (John 3:16)

In this verse, the word *world* refers to all human beings.

The **third** use of "kosmos" means the moral and spiritual systems we call "human society." A society is that realm of the world which has been developed through the efforts of man. It consists of man-made religious systems, political and governmental systems, economic systems, educational systems, business and financial systems, pleasures, medicine and the arts, legal systems, science and technology, endowments, riches, advantages, and so forth. Eliminate these things, and you eliminate a society.

Do not love the *world* or anything in the *world.* If anyone loves the *world,* the love of the Father is not in him. (I John 2:15)

> We know that we are children of God, and that the whole
> *world* is under the control of the evil one. (1 John 5:19)

It is this third use of the word "world" that Satan controls. He is the ruler in charge of societies according to Scripture.

As just stated, society consists of those elements that are developed by man. Unless converted, man is in an unregenerate or lost state spiritually. Therefore, spiritually he is not in God's family and under God's control, but under Satan's control. Therefore, all things which man develops in this spiritual condition fall under the control of Satan. These are the "things" that make up a society or what Scripture calls "the world." In a sense, it is that part of the world developed by man, rather than created by God.

This is not to say that these things developed by man cannot be converted out of the world system and used for the glory of God, just as man himself can. But on the whole, God warns that the systems and things developed by man that make up a society are controlled by our spiritual enemy, and he uses them as his attack vehicle to wage warfare against Christians.

Key Points About Societies

There are several key points to emphasize concerning the society systems of the world. **First,** since the day Adam opened the door for evil to enter God's creation, the whole world order (which includes all societies) has shown itself to be hostile to God.

> Jesus said, "If the *world* hates you, keep in mind that it hated me first. If you belonged to the *world,* it would love you as its own. As it is, you do not belong to the *world,* but I have chosen you out of the *world.* That is why the *world* hates you." (John 15:18,19)

> The *world* cannot accept Him, because it neither sees Him nor knows Him. (John 14:17)

Jesus said, "In this *world* you will have trouble. But take heart!
I have overcome the *world* (the pressures and influence of
society)." (John 16:33. Words in parentheses are the author's.)

Other related passages include John 18:36 and I Corinthians
1:21.

The **second** point to emphasize is that there is a mind
behind societies—a controlling spiritual influence—referred
to in the Bible as the "prince of this world," and "he that is
in the world." This, of course, is Satan. There is an order to
all of the societies, biblically called "the world," which is
governed from behind the scenes by the spiritual ruler, Satan.

As for you, you were dead in your transgressions and sins, in
which you used to live when you followed the ways of this
world, and the ruler of the kingdom of the air, the spirit
(Satan) who is now at work in those who are disobedient. All
of us also lived among them at one time, gratifying the
cravings of our sinful nature, and following its desires and
thoughts. (Ephesians 2:1-3)

Finally, be strong in the Lord and in his mighty power. Put on
the full armor of God so that you can take your stand against
the devil's schemes. For our struggle is not against flesh and
blood, but against rulers, against the authorities, against the
powers of this dark *world* and against the spiritual forces of
evil in the heavenly realms. (Ephesians 6:10-12)

To stand against the devil's schemes and his deceitful traps,
we need the full armor of God.

Our struggle is not against flesh and blood, against people,
organizations or institutions. That is why Jesus, Stephen and
others down through the ages have said, "Forgive them
(talking about people who did them harm) for they know
not what they do." Jesus and others who felt this way knew
their conflict was not with people or the establishment—it
was against Satan and his angels who were working through
various individuals and the world (society) system.

When we see people or organizations against Christians or Christian teaching, we cannot stand in our wisdom or power. We are no match for Satan; we are dependent on God. Our struggle is not against them, but against the spiritual mind behind them. We saw this in our review of church history.

The **third** key point to emphasize about societies—the world—is that Satan has authority and control over them.

> The devil led him (Jesus) up to a high place and showed him in an instant all the kingdoms of the *world.* And he said to him, "I will give you all their authority and splendor, for it has been given to me, and I can give it to anyone I want to. So if you worship me, it will all be yours."
>
> Jesus answered, "It is written: worship the Lord, your God, and serve him only." (Luke 4:5-8)

Jesus did not deny what Satan said about his authority over the world systems.

> We know that we are children of God, and that the whole *world* is under the control of the evil one. (I John 5:19)

Several times the Bible refers to Satan as being the ruler of this world. Satan is called the "ruler of the world" eight times. Some translations use, "prince of the world", but it is the same Greek word and it means the one who is in control, the one in charge.

The **fourth** key point about society is that the apostle Paul considered "this world" dead to him and himself "dead to the world," as did Jesus.

> May I never boast except in the cross of our Lord Jesus Christ, through which the *world* has been crucified to me, and I to the *world.* (Galatians 6:14)
>
> Jesus said, "You (talking to the Pharisees) are from below; I am from above. You are of this *world;* I am not of this *world.*" (John 8:23. Words in parentheses are the author's.)

Jesus was not of this world spiritually because He was conceived by the Holy Spirit. Likewise, if we receive Jesus into our heart, we experience a spiritual rebirth (called being born again) by the power of the Holy Spirit, and are no longer a part of this world's family. For it is Satan's family. Colossians 1:13 states, "For He has rescued us out of the darkness and gloom of Satan's kingdom and brought us into the kingdom of His dear Son." (Living Bible) Our function here on this earth changes to represent God's family, which is to be a light of good in a darkened world, and a preservative salt of good in an evil world.

Though Satan may have authority over and control of the world society, all Christians are equipped with a greater power, as was Jesus, to carry out the functions of God's family to do good.

> You, dear children, are from God and have overcome them, because the one who is in you (the Holy Spirit) is greater than the one who is in the *world* (Satan). (I John 4:4. Words in parentheses are the author's.)

To prevent Christians from carrying out the function of being light and salt, we saw in our review of Church history how Satan uses his vehicle, the world, to attack Christians. Persecution is still taking place is some countries today. Satan uses this same vehicle (things of society) when attacking through deception. He deceives Christians and causes us to disobey God's Word. Our society system attempts to prevent us from carrying out the purpose of God's family to be the light of the world and the salt of the earth.

The spiritual objective of Satan's society systems, then, according to biblical teaching, is to bring about the downfall of God's will and purpose for our life. This may be in a direct way, through persecution, or it may be indirect through deception—tempting us to adopt the world's standards and thus cause us to sin.

Deceptive Temptations

Scripture teaches us that the temptations of deception fall into three major categories.

1. The lust of the flesh
2. The lust of the eyes
3. The pride of life

These three areas of "man's being" incorporate what Scripture terms man's "sinful nature." In other words, there is a part of our natural makeup that enjoys certain sinful things—those contrary to God's standards. We didn't ask to have this as a part of our inner nature, but the Bible says none of us had a choice in the matter. We all inherit this nature from the first man, Adam, because of his fall. (In all of the Scripture passages that follow, words in parentheses are the author's.)

> Therefore, just as sin entered the world through one man, and death through sin, and in this way death came to all men, because all sinned. (Romans 5:12)

Speaking to Christians, Paul said:

> As for you, you were dead in your transgressions and sins, in which you used to live when you followed the ways of this world, and of the ruler (Satan) of the kingdom of the air, the spirit who is now at work in those who are disobedient. All of us also lived among them at one time, gratifying the cravings of our *sinful nature* and following its desires (lust) and thoughts. Like the rest, we were by *nature* objects of wrath." (Ephesians 2:1-3)

John breaks down this sinful nature of man into three different parts of his inner being.

> "For everything in the world—the cravings of sinful man *(lust of flesh)*, the *lust of* his *eyes* and the boasting of what he has and does *(the pride of life)*—comes not from the Father, but from the world." (I John 2:16)

Satan is aware of man's three areas of weakness; *the lust of the flesh, the lust of the eyes* and *the pride of life.* Therefore, when attacking through deception, he will tempt us in one or all of these three ways.

We saw this application of Satan's temptation when he tempted and deceived Eve.

When the woman saw that the fruit of the tree was good for food (lust of the flesh) and pleasing to the eye, (lust of the eye) and also desirable for gaining wisdom (pride of life) she took some and ate it. (Genesis 3:6)

Then the Lord God said to the woman, "What is this you have done?" The woman said, "The serpent (Satan) deceived me, and I ate." (Genesis 6:13)

Satan caused Eve to disobey the Word of God.

In his temptation of Jesus, Satan appealed to the same three areas of Jesus' nature, trying to cause Him to disobey.

The devil said to him, "If you are the Son of God, tell this stone to become bread." (lust of the flesh, Luke 4:3)

The devil led him up to a high place and showed Him in an instant all the kingdoms of the world. And he said to him, "I will give you all their authority and splendor ..." (Luke 4:5,6, lust of the eyes and pride of life)

If we yield to the cravings of our sinful nature, its lust and desires, then we are following the ways of the world and will seek for "self" interest, "self" satisfaction and "self" glorification.

Do not love the world or anything in the world. If anyone loves the world, the love of the Father is not in him. (I John 2:15)

Understanding Worldliness

Worldliness is closely associated with "lust," which means "desires" or "passions" exalted or pursued to the point that they cause us to sin. What has been translated "lust," "desires" or "passions" in Scripture is all the same Greek word.

For the grace of God that brings salvation has appeared to all men. It teaches us to say "No" to ungodliness and *worldly passions* (desires, lust) and to live self-controlled, upright and godly lives in this present age. (Titus 2:11,12)

Threrefore, do not let sin reign in your mortal body so that you obey its *evil desires* (lust). (Romans 6:12)

All of us also lived among them at one time, gratifying the cravings of our sinful nature and *following its desires* (lust) and thoughts. Like the rest, we were by nature objects of wrath. (Ephesians 2:3)

When tempted, no one should say, "God is tempting me." For God cannot be tempted by evil, nor does he tempt anyone; but each is tempted when, by his own *evil desire* (lust), he is dragged away and enticed. Then, after *desire* (lust or passion) has conceived, it gives birth to sin; and sin, when it is full-grown, gives birth to death. (James 1:13-15)

So I say, live by the Spirit (power of the Holy Spirit within) and you will not gratify the *desires* (lust) of the sinful nature (lust of the flesh, lust of the eyes and pride of life). For the sinful nature desires what is contrary to the Spirit, and the Spirit, what is contrary to the sinful nature. They are in conflict with each other, so that you do not do what you want. But if you are led by the Spirit, you are *not under law*. (Galatians 5:16-20)

Do you know *what law* Paul is referring to here? It is the law of sin. It is the law of our sinful nature which enjoys sin. In Scripture it is called the law of sin. Did you know we are born with an inner force in our being which causes us to do things we know we shouldn't, and keeps us from doing things we know we should?

After becoming a Christian, Paul discovered this law of sin in his inner being. See if you can identify with what he says.

So I find this law at work: when I want to do good, evil is right there with me. For in my inner being I delight in God's law; but I see another law at work in the members of my body, waging war against the law of my mind and making me a prisoner of the *law of sin* at work within my members. So then, I myself, in my mind am a slave to God's law, but in the sinful nature a slave to the law of sin. (Romans 7:21-25)

Paul goes on to say in Romans chapter eight that it is only as we are led by the Holy Spirit that we have the power to overcome this natural law of sin in our being.

Everyone is born with a sinful nature. It explains why young children are *naturally* going to learn to lie or cheat or fight as they look after and seek their "self" interests. Parents do not purposely teach them to be that way.

Satan knows we have a nature within us that is a slave to the law of sin. He knows that when a person becomes a Christian, spiritual rebirth includes the power of the Holy Spirit coming to live within—a power greater than the power of this universal law of sin in our sinful nature.

Therefore, Satan's objective is to keep Christians from walking in the power of the Holy Spirit, that supernatural power to overcome the law of sin in our sinful nature. If he is successful, Satan will cause Christians to do many things they shouldn't do, and act like people in the world. And he will cause us *not* to do things we know we should that please the Lord.

He accomplishes this by tempting the desires of our sinful nature—the lust of the flesh, the lust of the eyes and the pride of life—through his attack vehicle, the world (society) system. Observe how often you can identify these three desires of our sinful nature being tempted through TV and movie productions, books and magazines, advertisements and many other elements of our society.

That is the nature of the deceptive spiritual warfare we encounter. It is all around us. We must constantly be alert and self-controlled, because the devil is like a roaring lion, seeking someone to devour. (I Peter 5:8) A perfect example is the way the Christian community has followed a recent standard of society and now records a 50% divorce rate.

Understanding Our Sinful Nature

To comprehend the strategy behind Satan's deceptive warfare, we need to understand the makeup of our weaknesses in our sinful nature.

We will first examine the lust of the flesh and the lust of the eyes. It includes things that will be pleasing to our "self-life" regardless of the act. It is a primary desire to satisfy "good 'ol me!"

The lust of the flesh and the eyes might include things such as sexual drive, food, sleep, luxuries, cars, our household, paintings, clothes and jewelry. There is nothing wrong with any of these things within themselves. When our lust or desires for these things is so powerful it causes us to sin, then we can be certain they are not of God.

The sinful nature of the flesh and of the eyes will normally be tempted in one of two ways.

The **first** is materialism. This is accomplished when the desire for material things of our society tempts us to ignore sound spiritual teachings and biblical standards. The result is that we seek to obtain material things by the use of white lies (manipulation), deceitful tactics, not paying bills when due, being otherwise dishonest, greedy, not tithing properly, and so on. We are tempted by the standards of society to use these practices, if the opportunity arises, as our rule of conduct for the purpose of obtaining materialistic benefits. It has probably happened to all of us. I am not discounting God's blessings and all the provisions He may supply for anyone. However, Satan uses his world attack vehicle to tempt our natural desires. That is a strong biblical teaching.

The way to know whether a material thing is a blessing from God or a part of Satan's trap—something worldly—is to examine its effects. Will it cause me to sin in any way to obtain it, or could it cause me to neglect God's will for my life after I obtain it?

Remember, the fish offered to the eagle was his normal

diet. However, the fall came later, due to his becoming dull and lazy. Examine again the temptations of Jesus. (Matthew 4:1-11) At first they appeared harmless, not causing Jesus to break any of God's Word, but He knew the after-effects would bring sinful results.

Keep in mind that it is Satan's objective to tempt us with material things to cause us to sin. Sin is what quenches the power of the Holy Spirit in our lives. And when we are not walking in that power, the Bible teaches that the law of our sin nature, our own selfish desires, controls our actions. And that is what causes us to do some things we know we shouldn't, and not do others we know in our mind we should. It is our sinful nature that causes us to become irritated, angry, boastful, conceited, haughty, proud, disrespectful to others, selfish, self-centered, wanting our own way, speaking unkind words about others and having immoral thoughts. I'm sure we could all list many characteristics that describe the nature of our inner being at times. The list is virtually inexhaustible.

The Bible teaches there is only one way to overcome any of these natural sinful characteristics. It takes a greater power than we have within ourselves. Our nature needs to be changed from within. That requires the power of God, which is given to us as a gift at the time we accept Jesus into our hearts. (Acts 2:38) It becomes Satan's scheme then to keep us from walking in this power because he knows that when we do, the light of God will flow through our lives and draw others to Him. But if we don't, we as Christians, God's people, will not act or live our daily lives much different than many people in the world.

In the same way the trapper caught the eagle, Satan uses material things to lure us into his trap. The world system, or society, is his vehicle through which he offers this type of deceitful temptation.

The **second** way Satan uses his world system to tempt our sin nature is to create a desire in us for *excessive pleasure.*

It will cause either an over-commitment of our time to do pleasurable things, or to be entertained by pleasurable things, that are sinful. The many resources at Satan's disposal in America today create a tremendous temptation for most of us in this area. I am not speaking against good and wholesome things like enjoying God's creation and its beauty, the company of friends, playing wholesome games and so forth. But the enemy is attacking us fiercely in the area of the "lust of the flesh and eyes" to enjoy the pleasures developed and produced by his society system—the many sinful things that have been developed by man.

For example, Satan's demons are capitalizing on man's sinful and natural tendency to immorality through the eyes by every available means. It is evidenced by immodest dress, impure magazines, pornographic books and pictures, and many TV and movie productions. A discerning person who glances at the newsstands, reads the advertisements on the theater page of the newspaper or watches the programs and commercials presented on television knows full well that the "lust of the eyes and flesh" is being exploited by the power of the devil. One cringes when walking into a store and seeing the covers of pornographic or suggestive magazines openly displayed, or when thinking about immoral TV and movie productions, all available to anyone who will pay the price or give them the time.

It hurts even worse when I think about the devastating effect it is having on our society. Crime and terrorism are at an all time high. Sex and violence explode through almost every medium of entertainment, becoming a steady diet for many.

We have developed an apathetic and receptive attitude toward the standards of nudity, sexual perversion, incest, group sex and wife swapping. Venereal and other "social diseases" have reached epidemic proportions in our society occurring more often than any other infectious disease except the common cold. Illegitimate children by the millions, (adultery so common *Parents* magazine stated it must be as widely practiced in America as it must have been in the days before the flood), disregard for marriage vows, over 13 million abortions in the past 10 years, homosexuality proclaimed out in the open, immoral dress, and countless other things which have become part of our lifestyle.

As a result, families are suffering and many are falling apart because of poor marriage relationships and problems with children. Emotional stress and depression are at record levels. One out of every five Americans suffers from emotional or mental problems.

As the prophetic Scriptures warn, there will be tremendous pressures for excessive pleasure and materialism in the last days to cause us to become overanxious about the cares of this life.

The temptations that arouse our desires for material things and to accept most forms of pleasure come through every available communication medium. We are bombarded daily to accept the world's standards over God's standards. We have a need to develop the heart of David when he said:

> I will sing of your love and justice; to you, O Lord, I will sing praise. I will be careful to lead a blameless life—when will you come for me? I will walk in my house with a blameless heart. I will set before my eyes no vile thing. The deeds of faithless men I hate; they will not cling to me. Men of perverse heart shall be far from me. I will have nothing to do with evil. (Psalm 101:1-4)

Pride Of Life

Society tempts the natural sinful characteristic of the lust of the flesh, the lust of the eyes and the pride of life.

The "pride of life"—being somebody—is the **third** characteristic developed by a world society. It is expressed through our desire to be "noticed," be "seen," be "exalted," be "important," be "popular," be "right," and be "esteemed." We are taught to exert maximum effort for money, applause, recognition, and position to help build "self" ego. The struggle for power, prestige and honor is now at the heart of almost every human endeavor including many of the good things that are done.

It was the nature of Jesus to have no personal ambition of His own.

> Jesus gave them this answer, "I tell you the truth, the Son can do nothing by himself; he can do only what he sees the Father doing, because whatever the Father does the Son also does." (John 5:19)

> By myself I can do nothing; I judge only as I hear, and my judgment is just, for I seek not to please myself, but him who sent me. (John 5:30)

Ultimate Development

According to the Bible, the whole social structure of this world is controlled by a prevailing principle of life that is foreign to God, and leads men away from Him. This principle penetrates education, literature, science, business, religion, economics, politics, government, medicine and the many other segments of society which together constitute the "world."

Satan is utilizing the material world, the people of the world and the value systems of the world. He has raised up one society that is exalted far above all the other societies of the world—one in which all of the characteristics of his world system are being perfected, giving it great power in all worldly areas to tempt and deceive Christians to step outside of God's Word. Remember how Paul described the character of this society:

> There will be terrible times in the last days. People will be lovers of themselves, lovers of money, boastful, proud, abusive, disobedient to their parents, ungrateful, unholy, without love, unforgiving, slanderous, without self-control, brutal, not lovers of the good, treacherous, rash, conceited, lovers of

pleasure rather than lovers of God—having a form of godliness, but denying its power. Have nothing to do with them. (II Timothy 3:1-5)

There are many who believe that Satan's end-time society will result from a tremendous increase in the occult, to the extent that society as a whole will embrace these practices. However, an examination of Scripture does not suggest this teaching. Satan is too wise and much more deceitful than that. You see, he can get us to worship him if we worship "self" by stepping out and being independent. "Self" is against Christ—therefore, the main characteristic of the anti-Christ society of Satan will be a preoccupation with self: my possessions, my pleasures, my desires, my ambitions, my welfare and the "things of my world." It will be a society Satan can use to deceive and influence Christians to become overly concerned about serving "self." We must remember that the Christian community is Satan's only enemy.

Consider Our Society

No longer is it necessary to go out into the world in order to make contact with it. The influences of our society come and search us out. Its forces are so strong that it captivates people daily. As never before the Christian family today feels the power and the pull of a worldly society and its ways. Our apathy toward crime and world problems has revealed that we are willing to let Satan and the world do anything, as long as it doesn't affect our bank accounts. Wherever you go, even among Christians, the things of the world are usually the topic of conversation. Most of our conversations are centered around food, clothing, housing, pleasure, buying, the deals we've made or the items we've purchased, or the pleasures in which we have been involved.

Through the powerful influence of the value standards set by our society, many of us place a greater emphasis on supplying the physical needs and wants of our families than in supplying their spiritual needs. We commit our time and

money to obtaining things from our society, yet fail to dedi-
cate ourselves to spiritual growth in nearly the same propor-
tion. This attitude has been overly developed in Christians
through the influence of the deceiving worldly power behind
our society.

The demonic power that now prevails in our society can
be noticed everywhere. Observe the way we rush here and
there, feverishly making business deals. People in our society
are caught up in a whirlwind of buying that is unprecedented.
Our present state of affairs is not natural to man, as history
bears out. There is a super, hidden satanic power which now
captivates people every day, causing them to lose sight of
their priorities concerning material goods.

All of us have been in the bondage of sin and readily agree
that sinful things are from Satan, but we do not believe
equally that many things in our society are of Satan. Many of
us are still of two minds about this. Yet the Scriptures clearly
affirm that "the whole world (societies) is under the control
of the evil one." (I John 5:19) Satan well knows that to
influence and deceive Christians through activities that are
clearly sinful is vain and futile. The Bible does not teach that
this will be his method. Satan is too smart for that. He knows
the Christian community will usually sense these dangers
and flee. Instead, he has developed an enticing worldly
society, the mesh of which is so skillfully woven so as to
entrap the most innocent of men.

Should We Run?

The answer is not to flee from a society because that too
would reflect Satan's will. If we run, we would not be the
light and salt this world needs, or the soldiers God wants us
to be. To run may bring about physical separation, but it
does not bring about the spiritual separation which is the
key to our victory and that which inwardly sets us free from
the pressures and influences of a world society.

We live in the world and are to convert the things out of the world, but only to bring glory to God. We are not to strive to build a future in this world, for the cross of Christ has shattered all our hope in the things this world has to offer. The cross of Christ has put to death our hopes for gain from any of its societies. Satan does not want us to have this attitude so he uses every trick possible to deceive and destroy this kind of thinking.

> Paul said, "May I never boast except in the cross of our Lord Jesus Christ, through which the world has been crucified to me, and I to the world." (Galatians 6:14)

The key to our victory is always our faith relationship with the victorious Son. "Be of good cheer," He said. "I have overcome the world." (John 16:33) "As He is, so are we in this world." (I John 4:17) Jesus is the only one who ever overcame the pressures and influences from the world. The depth of our victory is completely dependent upon Christ Jesus and the faith we have in Him living His life in and through us. There is no room for any victory through "self." We now live in a society which trains us to look to "self" for power and fulfillment, and to become independent. This is purposely planned by Satan in his attempt to destroy the only key to our source of delivery from the law of our sinful nature.

A Warning From Jesus

> Watch out! Don't let my second coming catch you unawares; don't let me find you living in careless ease, carousing and drinking, and occupied with the problems of this life, like all the rest of the world. Keep a constant watch. And pray that if possible you may arrive in my presence without having to experience these horrors. (Luke 21:34-36, Living Bible)

The Lord is warning all of us, especially those living close to the time of His second coming, to beware or we will be unduly pressed and overly concerned with this life's cares.

From these words of Jesus, it is obvious that He foresaw

the methods of Satan's attack which we in America are now experiencing. There is a growing tendency among Christians to become occupied with the problems of this life. We even feel anxiety over such ordinary matters as food and dress — allowing ourselves to be deceived and ensnared into one of Satan's worldly traps.

We need to emphasize that the Christian's attachment to the things of the world is abnormal Christian behavior. It's no longer just a question of food and drink. We are meeting the work of demons. Satan, in his control of world societies, is using demonic power through the things of the world to lure us into the traps of the world. The present state of affairs cannot be accounted for in any other way. Christians must wake up to this point!

> Be self-controlled and alert. Your enemy, the devil, prowls around like a roaring lion looking for someone to devour. (I Peter 5:8)

The problem that confronts us is not how to refrain from buying, selling and eating, but how to avoid this satanic power in our society, which has been able to change the course of man's response and commitment to these things. Satan has prompted us to step out independently like Eve, and accept the temptations of our society which have caused us to embrace many of its standards. It is through these methods that Satan has been able to attack Christians, preventing many in the church from experiencing spiritual victory over sin.

In Summary

Everyone is born with a sinful nature. We should not try to hide from this fact, but be open and honest about it. It is a spiritual law. We are sinners by nature. Spiritually, we all are born on the wrong side of the tracks. We are by nature self-centered. We want to satisfy ourselves. We sin because of our heritage.

At the time of being born again and becoming Christians, Jesus sets us free from the power of the law of our sin nature through the power of the indwelling Holy Spirit.

> Jesus said, "If you hold to my teaching, you are really my disciples. Then you will know the truth, and the truth will set you free." They answered Him, "We are Abraham's descendants and have never been slaves of anyone. How can you say that we shall be set free?" Jesus replied, "I tell you the truth, everyone who sins is a slave to sin. So if the Son sets you free, you will be free indeed." (John 8:31-36)

However, as Paul discovered, even though Jesus forgives the sins in our lives, the power of our sinful nature is still present in our inner being after we become Christians.

> Now if I do what I do not want to do, it is no longer I who do it, but it is sin living in me that does it. So I find this law at work...the law of sin at work within my members...I myself in my mind am a slave to God's law, but in my sinful nature, a slave to the law of sin. (Romans 7:20,21,23,25)

God does not do away with our sinful nature. He gives us the Holy Spirit as a gift, which is a power greater than the power of our sinful nature. The battle is the Lord's. So as we learn to walk in His power we have victory over the law of sin in our nature.

Recall the important biblical concept we discussed which began at the formation of the church. The Holy Spirit was poured out on all believers and Satan was cast down to earth. This set up the battle of the Holy Spirit (God) and the evil spirit (Satan). It is a spiritual warfare of good and evil, light versus darkness, kingdom versus kingdom, as it is expressed through the lives of individuals.

Satan knows the character of our sinful nature. We are the center of this spiritual warfare. The power of the Holy Spirit empowers us so we might walk upright, blameless and righteous. But Satan still tempts our old sinful nature to yield to its power and the law of sin, so we might walk according to our desires and the ways of the world. The decision is ours. However, most Christians do not seem aware of this warfare and how Satan goes about tempting our old nature, causing us to yield to its desires. Thus, we experience spiritual defeat.

When Satan succeeds, then our actions, our decisions and many of the standards by which we live will not be much different than those of the society in which we live. We will probably be considered good citizens. He doesn't usually tempt us with gross sin. We won't be as bad as the world in many things; Satan doesn't use that tactic. But as long as he can persuade us to drift from the standards of God's Word, then he is winning the spiritual battle within and quenching the power of the Holy Spirit. He knows that will dim our Christian light in this dark world.

Remember—the key vehicle Satan uses in this spiritual warfare to tempt our old sinful nature is what the Bible calls "the world." We call it "society." That is why God's Word gives so much warning about the subject of "the world."

The factors which make up our sinful nature are "the lust of the flesh," "the lust of the eyes," and "the pride of life." These three elements are concerned with the "self" life. These are opposite to the nature and character of God. The lust of the flesh and eyes will normally be tempted through material things and pleasure, and the pride of life through the development of an independent attitude and desire to be somebody.

Satan's worldly traps lure us in these three areas to serve "self," and according to Scripture, will be extremely powerful in these last days.

It is prophesied that the influence of Satan's world vehicle will be extremely powerful in the center of Christianity in the times which we now live to deceive and overcome many Christians in the battle of spiritual warfare. This will cause a casual acceptance of many worldly standards in the name of Christianity.

Chapter 6

HOW IT ALL BEGAN

Let me share with you the events that inspired me to spend these many years seeking the Lord concerning THE LAST DAYS IN AMERICA.

On Saturday, October 4, 1969 my wife, Barbara and I spent the day with friends in Detroit, Michigan, and it was late that evening when we returned home to Youngstown, Ohio. We had left our oldest son, Perry, at our minister's home for the day and stopped there to pick him up. It was then we learned of the tragedy that had happened earlier in the day. One of the elders from our church, along with his wife and three of their six children, had been in an automobile accident, near New Castle, Pennsylvania. Both parents had been killed.

I was compelled to go immediately to the hospital. I arrived to find that Andrea, their ten-year-old daughter had been pronounced hopeless and the normal patient clean up procedure was being left for the mortuary. Alice, fours year old, was on the critical list. Sixteen year old, Larry, had escaped with only minor cuts and bruises.

As I drove home from the hospital in the early hours of that Sunday morning, I experienced something new and different in my Christian walk with the Lord. For the first time, the Lord spoke directly to me through His indwelling Holy Spirit. He said, "Build a new house on the land you recently bought and take these six orphan children to raise." A few months earlier Barbara and I had purchased 15 acres of land near the edge of the community where we were living, thinking that we might someday build a new house on it.

I later discovered the Lord had revealed this same message to my wife. At first such a task appeared insurmountable to Barbara and me. We were already busy people, involved in many Christian activities. That coupled with my responsibilities as Vice-President and General Manager of an aluminum company consumed our time. Now the Lord wanted us to be responsible for six more children—four of whom were teenagers. We began to pray, asking the Lord how we were to handle His directive. It soon became clear that He would have to supply both the power and the wisdom. We could only be vessels.

In an act of obedience to this command from the Lord, we stepped out in faith and volunteered our availability to the children's relatives and to the State Probate Department. Most of our friends, including many Christians, spoke up and said, "You're the last people we ever thought would consider such a responsibility in your lives. Everything is so perfect in your home. You have so much going for you."

As we became involved with these six children, we saw what was perhaps the Lord's greatest work in the entire situation. Ten-year-old Andrea had been left to die at the hospital because of the severity of her injuries in the accident. Unexpectedly, she lived through the first night so they transferred her to a hospital in Youngstown, Ohio, which was closer to home. There they began administering special treatment to keep her alive. Surgery was scheduled but doctors warned that even if the operations were successful, Andrea could not expect to be back in school until the next fall—eleven months away. The prognosis was that she would never completely recover, and would remain an invalid both physically and mentally.

Not only did Andrea live, but the Lord completely and miraculously healed her fractured skull and reversed the severe brain damage received in the crash. She returned to school three weeks after the accident. The doctors never had a chance to perform their operations.

Our obedience to that command from the Lord to take these children and raise them as our own was the dawn of many miracles the Lord has since worked in our family. One has been His unmistakable leading in directing me to write on the subject covered in this book.

The Motivating Force

For more than a decade, an intense interest in Bible prophecy has caused me to spend hundreds of hours studying the Word of God, doing research on the subject and praying for spiritual insight and direction. I'm convinced that the Lord has been the motivating force in making the study of end-time prophecy one of the top priorities in my life. Some background information will help explain my desire to share with others what God has revealed to me.

There were 13 children in our family, and I was the youngest. We were raised on a farm near Greenville, Ohio, in the southwestern part of the state. I was nine years old when I accepted Jesus as my personal Savior and Lord. It happened during an evangelistic meeting at our church. My brother Charles, who is two years older than I, also accepted the Lord at the same evangelistic service. In a very real sense, his experiences as a Christian had a decided impact on my life, and are an important part of my story.

Our parents were godly people, sincerely dedicated to serving the Lord Jesus. As we grew up we were trained by precept and example. Many who knew our mother testified that she lived an exemplary life—much like those of the outstanding godly women described in the Bible.

My brother Charles lived in obedience to the Lord, and throughout his school years sought to walk righteously. I always had a high regard for his spiritual dedication.

After graduating from high school he entered the navy. Charles then developed a compulsive desire to know God better, and soon realized this could only be accomplished through knowledge of the Bible. He spent many months studying God's Word during most of his spare time, often rising two hours before reveille to study and pray.

After four years in the navy, Charles felt led to attend Nyack Missionary College in New York. By that time he was literally living in God's Word. He had memorized 850 Scripture verses letter-perfect, and reviewed 150 verses each day.

Whether or not you believe God's people still have visions, please stay with me through the following account before drawing your conclusions. Perhaps what you are about to read will be difficult for you to accept, as it was for me. But God's Word is true, and I challenge you to examine the things I share by the evidence of the fruits produced.

A Sign from God

During that first year at Nyack, while waiting for the Lord to give him further direction in his life, Charles experienced the first of what would be several visions in the years to come. In this vision, the Lord directed Charles to become a doctor and go to Africa as a medical missionary. The thought of being a physician had never entered his mind, but the leading of the Lord was so strong he simply stepped out in faith, knowing little of all that would be involved. But my brother was obedient to God's call and entered pre-med school at Taylor University in Upland, Indiana.

Preparing for a Career

The Lord honored Charles' obedience, and he graduated from Taylor cum laude. He earned an A in every course of his pre-med studies with two exceptions—a B in literature and another for a semester of physical education during his junior year. My brother was a good basketball player, and the coach wanted him on the team that year. Charles decided against it because he didn't want to spend the required time away from his studies.

Charles continued his studies in medicine at Ohio State University. Ours was a relatively poor family, and though funds were in short supply, God always provided for my brother's financial needs during college and medical school. When he had completed his work at Ohio State, he took one year of internship and four years of surgical residency at St. Elizabeth Hospital in Youngstown, Ohio. For 13 years he prepared for the task to which the Lord had called him.

Though Dr. Charles Fraley, Surgeon, chosen and prepared by God, was ready for the mission field in Africa, he had gradually slipped in his relationship with God during the latter years of training. He had lost sight of the commitment he had made to become a missionary. It seemed to him he could serve the Lord just as well in America, and simultaneously enjoy all the material advantages he had learned went along with being a successful physician. Christian Collegues, friends and others were in agreement. He listened to these voices and followed his persuasive personal desires, though they were not the original leading of the Lord. Charles chose to begin a private practice in New Madison, Ohio, near the area where we had been raised.

A Life-Changing Experience

Charles' medical practice flourished. He and his wife, Marlene, were now the parents of two children. They had an expensive home in a beautiful residential area of Greenville. Charles enjoyed flying, and was soon the owner of a four passenger plane. He purchased the old homestead, the farm where we grew up. There were fine cars and furniture — seemingly everything the family desired.

Materially, things appeared to be going extremely well. But as his material welfare increased, my brother's interest in God's Word became less important to him, and his spiritual commitment continued to diminish. His plans for the mission field were put on the back burner. Though he did not know it, he had left his first love. It wasn't noticeable to others, but Charles would tell you today that this was the condition of his heart. Deception had taken him out of the Lord's will for his life.

Spiritually, my brother grew weaker. More and more the natural desires of the flesh dominated his life. Then the unthinkable happened. He began to develop an interest in the nurse who assisted him in his office. As is so frequently the case when a believer is out of the Lord's will, the spiritual power to wage successful warfare with temptation is weakened.

Charles' relationship with his nurse grew, despite the fact that both of them were married. The nurse was not a Christian, and somehow Charles got the idea that the Lord was permitting this fondness for one another to grow, so my brother could teach her the Bible. He began to do this, but only when the two of them were alone together.

Then in natural thought progression Charles began to feel that perhaps something was going to happen to his wife, and that the Lord had brought this person into his life to replace Marlene when that "something" happened. How insidiously our spiritual enemy plants thoughts in our minds to get us to accept something contrary to God's Word. This is why it's so essential to test such thoughts by the truth of God's Word, and through prayer. Otherwise, when we're tempted, the old sin nature of our flesh will override the truth of God's Word.

Nothing immoral happened between Charles and his nurse, and their marriages did not break up. But both have confessed that they became inordinately fond of each other.

My brother had now been practicing medicine for about five years. It was then the Lord opened his spiritual eyes and revealed to him how he had been walking in disobedience as far back as five years, when he had finished his surgical training. Charles had given in to his own deceptive desires and had been lured to the attractions of the world, rather than following God's direction for his life.

When I asked Charles what had brought him to his senses and lifted the deception in his heart, he answered, "Ironically, it was the nurse, herself, along with Marlene. After I had shared God's Word with my nurse, she accepted Christ as her Savior, and began to feel convicted about the way we were thinking. She would go home and cry under conviction. This happened for several weeks. Then she would come to the office and show me Scripture revealing that our thinking had to be wrong. She soon decided to quit working with me and concentrate on becoming the kind of wife to her husband that the Lord was teaching her to be.

"At the same time," Charles continued, "my wife kept telling me something was wrong with my relationship with my nurse. I, of course, would not admit it at first, but when I finally had to face up to it, I was literally crushed to think I had gotten so far from the Lord that such a thing could even happen. It did have such an impact on me, however, that it compelled me to seek the Lord with every ounce of strength I had."

My brother went into a place of repentance and began to seek the Lord for the fullness of the Holy Spirit and direction for his life. He desired to renew the relationship with the Lord he once had many years earlier. He longed to have again that inner motivation to know God's Word, to seek Him and spend time with Him, and to experience the peace and joy of the Lord's presence. He wanted to walk righteously and be pure in heart.

Seeking After Righteousness

Charles' intense search for this renewed relationship with the Lord went on for seven months. It came to a climax when at the end of that time, my brother and his family took

a two-week vacation. It was Charles' purpose to totally seek
the Lord during this time away. Though Marlene and the
children were with him, he spent practically the entire two
weeks alone, seeking God in fasting and prayer and meditation
in the Word.

During the second week, Charles awoke one night and
sensed the presence of the Lord in the room with him in an
unusual way. Then he began to have visions. The first vision
was that of a beast with a huge head and big mouth, gulping
down Christians through pleasure and materialism. The Spirit
of the Lord showed Charles that this represented the wordly
attractions of society, and how Christians were being deceived
by this. Charles saw himself as a prime example, and realized
how he has grieved the Holy Spirit.

Several other visions of Jesus appeared next, confirming
the presence of the Holy Spirit. He saw Jesus as One who led
a life of discipline, with His face as a flint. *Nothing* could
deter the Lord from His purpose and calling. Charles also
saw Jesus enduring the suffering of His crucifixion, and saw
in a new and different way the tremendous price Jesus paid
for the salvation of the world. He saw the great and persevering love Jesus has for us, and that He was standing at the
heart's door, knocking. Yet, incredibly, here were the children
of God's family—selling themselves out to the beast and its
world system, oblivious to what was really happening in their
lives.

This series of visions troubled my brother greatly in his
spirit. The following morning he felt strongly led to look
through the book of Revelation, recalling that it had something to say about a beast. When he came to the thirteenth
chapter he began to read: "And I saw a beast coming out of
the sea. He had ten horns and seven heads, with ten crowns
on his horns, and on each head a blasphemous name. The
beast I saw resembled a leopard, but had feet like those of a
bear and a mouth like that of a lion. The dragon gave the
beast his power and his throne and great authority. One of

the heads of the beast seemed to have had a fatal wound, but the fatal wound had been 'healed'." (Revelation 13:1-3)

As Charles finished reading the third verse of the chapter about the wound, the Spirit of the Lord seemed to lift this verse off the page and sear it into his mind.

The meaning of this verse was suddenly crystal clear. It was revealed to him that this verse had been fulfilled at Pearl Harbor. Charles had never heard of or thought of such an interpretation. He can only say that he knows the meaning of this verse about the wound of the beast came in a super-natural way from the Spirit of the Lord. He knew without a doubt the wound of the beast was the bombing of Pearl Harbor.

It was a miraculous happening. My brother was over-whelmed with this meaning and it would not cease. This revelation was branded deep within by the Spirit of the Lord.

He also realized that if this was its fulfillment, then the beast was referring to the United States government and not to some man who was to receive a head wound, as he had always been taught. This was very hard for Charles to believe, but he could get no peace from the Lord about the matter until he accepted it.

Then as he began to think back to World War II and Pearl Harbor, it seemed to fit. Though we had been kids at the time, we were old enough then to have had some appreciation of the impact of that death blow to our country's military strength and the seemingly miraculous way in which we recovered. The whole world was awestruck by the way the war ended. Truly everyone thought there was no way to fight against such a power, which was demonstrated at that time with the atom bomb. The apostle John states this fact: "Who is like the beast? Who can make war against him?" (Revelation 13:4)

A day or two later, scales seemed to drop from my broth-er's eyes. He recognized that we were in a great spiritual warfare here in this country. The enemy forces seemed to be going all out to overcome the saints of God in their battle against the sinful forces of the world. John also prophesied of this: "It (the beast) was given power to make war on the saints and to conquer (overcome) them." (Revelation 13:7) This war still rages, with greater and greater force!

Anointed by God's Power

The visions just described came to my brother in May of 1971. During the days that followed he spent a great deal of time studying the book of Revelation. He sensed that many of the things recounted there were in the process of being fulfilled, and many of the ingredients for their fulfillment were already present. He sensed that the second beast (Revelation 13:11) had something to do with electronics and computers. We share that possibility in chapters 8 and 9 of this book.

Back home a few days later, my brother was lying in bed just worshipping the Lord before going to sleep when an unusual immersion in the power of God took place. He was filled with an overwhelming desire to serve the Lord and worship Him. The anointing from that experience remained for many weeks, and miraculous things happened. It seemed that anyone with whom he came in contact—anyone who talked to him—would come under total conviction from the anointing of the Holy Spirit. For example, Charles was asked to share his message at the Church of the Brethren in Eaton, Ohio. It was not the custom of this church to invite people to come to the altar after a service. However, the week after he spoke, practically the entire congregation came forward in repentance, due to the power of God evident in what he had told them.

During this period of about six weeks, while my brother was under a special anointing of the power of God, my wife and I decided to take a trip back to the area where we had both grown up. Our weekend visit at home was routine. We spent some time with Barbara's parents and with my mother. (My dad had died five years earlier.) On Sunday afternoon we went to visit Charles and his family. I knew nothing about his unusual experiences of the past several months, or his involvement with his nurse and all that had followed.

As my brother and I sat down in the living room to relax and talk he asked, "Have you ever studied the book of Revelation?" "No," I answered. "Whenever I've tried, I always become confused because of all the symbolic language. To me," I continued, "the Lord shows us in this book just how dependent we are on Him, because any true understanding of its meaning could only come from Him." He then asked a more specific question: "Have you ever studied or thought about the thirteenth chapter of Revelation which deals with the beast of the end times—the antichrist?" Again I replied, "No." Charles then began to share his thoughts on this subject just as the Lord had given it to him during his recent times of fasting and prayer.

As my brother talked to me about the identity of the beast in Revelation—the antichrist—the Spirit of the Lord suddenly fell on me in a way that I had never before experienced. I even began to tremble. The Lord filled me with His presence and His love. He confirmed to me with an overpowering conviction the truth of what my brother was saying.

Then, so I would know without a doubt it was the power of the Spirit of God, He filled me with an inner awareness of Jesus and His Lordship that far surpassed anything I could imagine. Words can't begin to express the tremendous anointing of love and joy that came from the Lord at that moment. And the beauty of it all has been its lasting effects. Since that day, any time of the day or night, there has been an assurance of faith from the Spirit of God to help me know the Lord Jesus is with me. He has created in my heart a desire to continually pray to the Father, and praise the Lord Jesus and serve Him with my being.

The Lord had a purpose in filling me with His Holy Spirit at that particular time, and in the overpowering way He did it. I didn't know it then, but realize now it was to cause me to commit my whole being and all my thoughts to the prophetic truth my brother was sharing on the identity of the beast — often called the antichrist. The Lord knew, as I would later discover, that I would be chosen by Him to present this message to the Christian community. He also knew then this would not be an easy task, because the enemy, Satan, would fight this truth and fight it hard. The Lord knew I would need His peace and the presence of a strong indwelling faith in Him.

I truly believe I can relate to the experience Paul had on the road to Damascus — not to the same degree, but in principle. If you get hit hard enough, regardless of how contrary it may be to your present thinking, you are going to listen. I knew what my brother had said was true.

The truth and the anointing that came to me then has caused me to commit my life to sharing this prophetic revelation to this day. I know it is just one message of many needed by Christians in these times. But it is one particular part of the message for which I have a responsibility.

The Year That Followed

My brother's discussion on the identity of the beast, the infilling of the Holy Spirit and the Lord's undeniable confirmation of the truth of what my brother had said came to me as a complete surprise. Until this time I had not studied the Scriptures relating to prophecy and I was not intending to do so. I really didn't know exactly which passages dealt with the subject of the beast.

Because the Spirit of the Lord's leading was so unshakable, research and study of those prophetic Scriptures became a daily habit. At that point I was doing it strictly for my personal edification and confirmation. I discovered there are many different views on the exact meaning of the symbolic words which describe the characteristics of the beast, but not once did I find someone who stated the Lord had revealed to that individual the exact meaning of these Scriptures. They had simply offered their own personal views. As I studied the Word of God on this subject I could not gain any peaceful understanding from the Lord on the precise meaning of other prophetic Scriptures that describe the characteristics of the beast even though I now knew its identity and the exact meaning of Revelation 13:3. So, I concluded, "When and if the Lord wants me to know the exact meaning of other prophetic Scriptures, He will show me."

Next, the Lord led me to study other books such as *Love Not the World* and *The Normal Christian Life,* both written by Watchman Nee. As I studied this material I recognized my need to understand and have as a part of my spiritual life a greater fullness of the spiritual principles shared by Brother Nee in *The Normal Christian Life.* I read and studied this book three times, completely outlined it, and taught a Bible class using it as my discussion guide. The Lord used that book along with other Bible studies to increase my faith to walk in the power of the indwelling Holy Spirit and to become sensitive to His leading.

The Lord also led me to research and accumulate a mass of statistical facts and historical information to help confirm what He had revealed to be the identity of the beast. He directed me to search and study the Bible on Satan's ways and means of attacking not the unsaved people in the world, but God's very own family—we who make up the Body of Christ. This was necessary because John prophesies in Revelation it is the "beast" that Satan will use as his end time means to attack the saints.

Later I again looked to the Lord for an understanding of those specific prophetic scriptures in Daniel, II Thessalonians, I John and Revelation that relate to and give descriptive characteristics of the beast. In time the symbolical prophetic words in these Scriptures started to come alive—not because of human wisdom, but because the Lord began periodically to reveal their exact meaning.

Such a statement will probably raise some eyebrows, but I

knew the Lord's revelations on these prophetic Scriptures were true, and were from Him. They came just as the previous directives had come from the Lord—directives that had proven to be true. Each of them had been according to God's Word, and had produced fruit for the Lord.

Over the years the Lord has given Barbara and me the opportunity to be involved in a number of things that have blessed our lives and borne spiritual fruit. Yet there has remained a constant compelling command and motivation from the Spirit of the Lord to seek God's direction in understanding and sharing this message about the deception of the beast.

There is much I do not know about prophecy. At times I become weary with this message. But over and over, the Lord has faithfully confirmed my understanding of the identity of the beast—the means used by Satan to attack and overpower the saints in these last days.

The historical facts and biblical teachings on the last days which I share with you in this book have been given by the Lord as strong evidence to support the revelation my brother had on the identity of the beast.

You will be interested to know that Charles has now served several years as a missionary doctor in East Africa under the auspices of Africa Inland Mission. He is currently the missionary Medical Coordinator for the country of Kenya, working for Africa Inland Church, which operates two major hospitals, four smaller hospitals and about 15 clinics and dispensaries throughout the country. His field address is:

> Dr. Charles Fraley
> A.I.C. Medical Co-
> ordinator
> Box 21010 Nairobi
> Kenya, East Africa

I am convinced it was so my brother Charles could be obedient to his call to the mission field that I was touched by the Lord in 1971 to search His Word and share this vital message to America. Also, Jesus stated that a thing is established by the testimony of two witnesses. To this day, my brother and I have the assurance that the Lord chose us to bear witness of these truths revealed to us in such a miraculous way.

In the next chapter I'll share with you the exact meaning of several verses from Revelation 13 which biblically identify the surprising and prominent role of the American government in end-time events.

Chapter 7

SATAN'S WORLD
VEHICLE—THE BEAST

Revelation chapter 13:1-10 is the text where John specifically describes "the beast." We will examine these distinct identifying characteristics of Satan's ultimate world vehicle for these last days.

The United States government's identity as that world power to which John is referring in Revelation 13 is the biblical truth that was revealed to my brother. This is not to be construed as political disagreement or dissatisfaction with our country as a nation, just as Paul did not speak out against Rome and its ruling authority. However, Rome was called a beast in relation to its world position of power. Similarly, we are a world power—in fact, the greatest world power in history when we consider all facets, such as economics, military strength, industrial power, agricultural output and political influence. It is interesting to note John uses some of the same prophetic phrases to describe our government as Scripture uses elsewhere to describe the Roman government. Scholars agree the two are very similar in their organizational structure.

Spiritual Warfare

Christians have been involved in spiritual warfare through-out the history of the church. The record begins in the book of Acts. This truth and the way our spiritual enemy attacks through world political powers helps identify why he is work-ing through our governmental system and society to under-mine and sabotage the biblical standards on which our country was founded and developed.

Because Satan had never encountered a nation whose beginning laws were built on Christian principles, he had to devise a different plan of spiritual attack. Persecution at the hands of the governing officials wouldn't work in this new land, so deception through worldliness became his plan. It would be carried out through a world system. John prophet-ically describes this world system in Revelation 13 as a "beast," because all great world powers that have affected God's people have been referred to in prophecy as "beast." We today refer to them as "superpowers." Both the United States and Russia are powerful enough to scripturally be called "beast." Either could destroy the world.

I realize that you may have difficulty in accepting that our governmental world power could be the one John is talking about. All I ask is that you stay with me through the rest of this study. I have no interest in trying to force this teaching on anyone. My responsibility is to share what the Lord has burned in my heart concerning the type of spiritual warfare our spiritual enemy has developed for this period that closes out the church age.

The meanings of descriptive words and phrases used by John in Revelation 13, coupled with other passages about the beast in the book of Daniel, should give sufficient scrip-tural evidence to support the identity that was revealed. *Please keep in mind as we discuss these verses that they are referring to our secular history. Likewise, some of the histor-ical accounts I share deal with secular history. In no way do*

I wish to take away from the spiritual history of our country. We must be careful not to confuse the two. In fact, I believe it is because of the strong spiritual history in our country that Satan has raised up such a strong worldly society to wage spiritual warfare against us. John describes it as a beast because he saw its dominant world position.

The Identity of the Beast

The Scripture passages from Revelation 13 which follow are from the Revised Standard Version Bible.

> Then the dragon (Satan) was enraged at the woman (Israel) and went off to make war against the rest of her offspring— those who obey God's commandments and hold to the testimony of Jesus. And the dragon stood on the shore of the sea. (Revelation 12:17. Words in parentheses are the author's.)

The spiritual church of Jesus Christ is the offspring of Israel, (the woman) brought about through the child she bore who was Jesus Christ. They that "hold to the testimony of Jesus" refers to Christians.

In the last verse of Revelation 12, John changes the scene of his prophetic discussion as he begins to prophesy of the future methods of attack Satan will use against Israel's offspring—those who bear testimony to Jesus, His church. In verse 6 of this chapter, John saw the early church going into a general state of obscurity for 1260 years (the Dark Ages), a time when the truth was protected by God. Then after this period, the people in the church once again began to speak out openly of Jesus Christ, and of their spiritual commitment to Him. We know this began to take place in Europe. However, after this period of obscurity was over, John implies in Revelation 12:17 that the central area of those who testify of Jesus would move across the seas and the center of Christianity would be in another land. This occurred after the Reformation when thousands of Christians, known as the Puritans, crossed to America.

Beast Out of the Sea

> And I saw a beast rising out of the sea with ten horns and
> seven heads, with ten diadems upon its horns and a blas-
> phemous name upon its heads. (Revelation 13:1)

John begins to explain in Revelation 13:1 the method Satan
will use to make war with the saints in the last days. He
states that Satan will bring about this attack by raising up
(developing) a beast or a world governmental superpower
in this new land which has become the new center of Christianity. Then John describes this worldly tool of spiritual
warfare developed by Satan to make war on the saints. Just
as Satan had used the world empire of Rome to attack Jesus,
he again develops a beast (a government with awesome
world power) near the end time to attack the Body of Christ
in the hub of Christianity. But as Scripture warns it will be
through *deception, not persecution.*

To understand how John has used the word "beast" in
Revelation 13:1, we need to see if the word is used elsewhere
in the Scriptures in a similar manner and under similar cir-
cumstances. In Daniel 7:3 we find the statement, "And four
great beasts came up out of the sea, different from one
another." From Daniel's own words in his book, and as confirmed by history, we know that the four beasts Daniel mentions are the four great world powers who have had a distinct
influence upon Israel.

The first of these four beasts was Babylon, which became
a world power in 606 B.C. when she conquered Egypt. Daniel
calls her a beast like a lion. The second beast or world power,
described as being like a bear, was the Media-Persian empire.
(Daniel 8:20) The Media-Persian empire conquered the Babylonian empire in about 539 B.C. and ruled until 331 B.C. The
third beast in Daniel's prophecy was Alexander the Great's
Greek empire when, in 331 B.C., he conquered the Persians.
As prophesied in the eighth chapter of Daniel, Alexander's
empire disintegrated when four of Alexander's power hungry

generals took over the empire and divided it into four kingdoms. They lasted until about 31 B.C. when the Romans
conquered the last of these four powers. It was then that
Rome became the fourth beast and the greatest world power
to that date.

History shows that the prophetic phrase, "coming up out
of the sea," has reference to world powers made up of people,
geographical areas, laws and customs of many different
countries. And since John introduces the "beast" in Revelation
13:1 as "rising out of the sea," we know his use of the word
"beast" also has reference to a world power, and that this
governmental power will be made up of many different
nationalities and cultures of people. The people and their
customs that develop this new world power will come primarily from Europe or the geographical area which was the
Roman empire, according to Daniel 7:20 and 24.

Many current Bible students apply the word "beast" in
Daniel as meaning a world empire, yet in Revelation 13 want
to change it to mean a man. We will examine the reason for
this.

John's Use of the Pronoun "it" or "He"

Bible versions differ in their translation of the Greek word
"avrov," a pronoun which makes reference to the beast
throughout Revelation 13. It is found in verses 2 through 8
and 11 through 18. Some Bible translations, such as the
Revised Standard Version, Phillips translation and the early
Greek papyrus manuscripts, translate this pronoun as "it,"
meaning the beast is a government with awesome power as
used in Daniel. However, other Bibles (King James and New
International Version) translate this pronoun as "he," "his"
and "him," which leaves the impression the beast could be a
person or a man.

The true meaning is significant in view of the revelation
given to my brother. I needed to establish which Bible translation was correct. I knew a pronoun should always carry

the same gender as that word to which it refers. The same should hold true in this case. Therefore, the pronoun throughout this chapter which refers to "the beast" should carry the same gender—neuter or masculine—as the Greek word for "beast."

Please note: The Greek word for "beast," *onpiov,* is neuter gender, not masculine.* Therefore, this pronoun which makes reference to the beast in Revelation 13 should be translated "it," which is neuter gender, not "he," "his" or "him," which is masculine. Translating the gender incorrectly by using the words "he," "his" or "him," has caused many to assume the word "beast" refers to some man. The Revised Standard Version Bible gives the correct Greek translation. Therefore, I am using the Revised Standard Version for the verses quoted from Revelation 13 in this teaching.

The Beast with Ten Horns

John states that the "beast" or this new world empire will have "ten" horns. All numbers in Scripture have a symbolic meaning. Ten, for example, has the meaning of *order* such as the Ten Commandments, the ten plagues, the ten virgins or the numbering system which is based on the numeral ten. There are many examples of *order* through the symbolic use of the number ten in Scripture.

The word "horn" is symbolic of a country with world power and influence, but not an empire like a "beast." For example, several countries in the United Nations would be classified as horns, but they are not world governmental empires.

To have "ten horns" would mean then that the beast or this world government will maintain order over several other countries of prominent world influence and power.

John points out, however, that this beast or new world power does not rule politically or have direct governmental control of these countries. This point is made where John

---

*The Interlinear Greek-English New Testament using the Nestle Greek Text, Zondervan Publishing House, Grand Rapids, Michigan.

states, "the diadem is upon each horn." Therefore, it is upon each country. The word "diadem" or "crown" prophetically means governing authority. It's a word that was used among the Greeks and Romans to represent a distinctive badge of royalty and symbolizes ruling governmental power and authority. John states that each of these countries will have its own governing political body even though the beast (U.S. government) would be stronger.

It is noteworthy to see the slight difference in John's description of the Roman government in Revelation 12:3 and how he describes the government of our world empire in Revelation 13:1. In Revelation 12:3 he states that the "diadem" (governing authority) is upon the *heads* or the leadership of the Roman government. This refers to the regions or areas of the world over which Rome had direct control. In other words, it was the government of Rome that controlled politically all of the countries in which she had a great influence. In Revelation 13:1, John states that the "diadem" is upon the *horns,* or that each country the U.S. government strongly influences will have its own government under which its people are ruled.

This truth had great significance to me in that it shows how accurately the Word of God describes all things. The Roman Empire did have political control over the people under her influence, whereas the many people under the influence of the U.S. are not under our political control. For example, the people in the countries of western Europe have been greatly influenced by our industry, economic power and military power, but each country has its own government (the diadem is upon each horn).

I am aware of the common explanation of this phrase "ten horns," which says it refers to the ten countries in the European Common Market. That explanation concerned me, however, because it appears to have a major flaw. Scripture uses the same phrase to describe the Roman rule, yet they controlled many more than ten countries, so limiting the meaning to just those ten in the common market holds some inconsistency. The discovery that numerical words are often used with their symbolic meaning in prophecy rather than their literal meaning eliminated this major hurdle. If at some future date there are more or less than ten countries in the European Common Market, it will not contradict God's prophetic Word.

The Beast with Seven Heads

The number "seven" throughout God's Word has a symbolic meaning of "complete" or "full." This symbolic meaning definitely describes our world power in these end times. In this first verse of Revelation 13, seven is associated with the word "heads" which means leadership ability. Therefore, John is stating that this beast (world power) will have seven heads, or in terms of its world position, will be complete and full in its leadership authority. This would include world leadership position in all areas, such as politics, economics, military strength, industrial output and agriculture.

I have heard people state they believe Russia might be the beast, the world empire, John is speaking about. However, Russia does not fit several of the identifying phrases given in Scripture. "Seven heads" is one of these. Russia is a leader in military strength and political rule, but is not a world leader in economics and agriculture. John qualifies the identity of the beast he saw. He says it has "seven heads" or is complete in all areas of world leadership. No world power fits that description except our own government.

Blasphemous Name Upon its Heads

The world power which rises up in the end times will have a blasphemous name upon its heads. In this prophetic statement John is warning us how the leadership of this empire will use the association of the name of God in leading the people. (This characteristic also eliminates Russia.) The political head will present itself or its government as being under the name of God. The economic head or spiritual influence of its economic position in the world will claim that its number one position in material things of the world came from God. Its leaders in military power will claim to be representing God and protecting its godly position in the world, even though it performs many selfish and unrighteous acts. John says that each head of our empire will be blasphemous because all use the name of God in association with justification and promotion of a worldly cause and a number one position in Satan's kingdom, "the world." (See chapter 5 concerning who the Bible teaches is the god of this world.) Analyzing the many unrighteous laws and standards now accepted by our government system confirms the truth of this statement made by John. Again, we are the only world governmental power that fits this descriptive phrase.

More Characteristics Revealed

And the beast that I saw was like a leopard, its feet were like a bear's, and its mouth was like a lion's mouth. And to it the dragon gave his power and his throne and great authority. (Revelation 13:2)

First: In this verse John reveals to us some of the true characteristics of our empire. He does this by referring to three wild animals as a symbol of our empire. Daniel used similar prophetic language in describing world empires. However, Daniel used only one animal for each empire, stating that the Babylonian Empire was like a lion, the Media-Persian Empire like a bear and the Greek Empire like a leopard. John uses all three of these animals to characterize this beast empire in Revelation 13, indicating the tremendous world authority and power it develops. The leopard characterizes the quickness of our power and military genius. The bear characterizes our superior strength. The lion characterizes not only our strength, but also the pride we develop in our elegance, beauty and splendor, along with the pride in our world leadership. John without doubt affirms that our empire will boast and promote the idea of how great and powerful a nation she has become.

Second: The dragon (Satan) gives this empire his power, his throne and great authority. Satan is the "god of this world" (II Corinthians 4:4), or as we studied in chapter 5, he is the "god of the societies of this world." All societies are in his power. (I John 5:19) He is the spiritual mind working through people and governments to control the various worldly societies. (Ephesians 6:12)

Only when we comprehend Satan's position of power and authority in the societies of this world can we begin to understand John's statement in this verse. This evidence of Satan giving the U.S. empire his power is noticeable when we observe the position the U.S. has in military, political, industrial and economic strength. Satan is the "god of the world;" therefore, the power he has to offer an empire would be a position of power to gain for itself the number one status in the "things of the world." We have been in the number one position in the world in every category since World War II— economics, military strength, politics, agriculture and industry.

In this verse, John says that Satan gives our empire his throne. This means we will be the number one government in the world (his throne) and that our society will be number one in goods and services of the world. Keep in mind that the world is Satan's kingdom; therefore, his throne would be the top position in the world.

John also states that our empire will have great authority. This applies not only to our position in the world, but also to our ability to promote and advance "the things of the world" and thus keep people, including Christians, living under its influence.

Satan's power, throne and authority are given to the U.S. governmental power. We should apply the characteristics of Satan that he uses to attack God's people to our understanding of this beast (empire)—a beast used to attack the testimony of the saints. (Revelation 12:17) When we do, we can see that this power of Satan's, his throne and his authority, will appear beautiful to those with a worldly sense of thinking.

They will offer much human wisdom and will be presented in the name of God. However, the spirit of our government's influence will be most deceitful because it will develop in us an attitude of "self" sufficiency, independence and pride, attacking the fiber of our spiritual commitment and loyalty. It will promote the "great society" concept which is man's attempt to control his own destiny. It is the spirit of "Babel" —humanism.

> One of its heads seemed to have a mortal wound, but its mortal wound was healed, and the whole earth followed the beast with wonder. (Revelation 13:3)

First: In this verse John prophesies that one of our government's heads will seem to receive a mortal wound. John does not tell us here the type of wound it would be — only that it seemed to be mortal, or would appear impossible to overcome. However, if we look at verse 14 of this chapter, we find that John describes the wound in more detail as "the beast which was wounded by the sword and yet lived." This tells us that the wound received by our empire was through military attack. It is in verse 3, then, that John is prophesying of a military attack which will at first appear to have fatally wounded our nation in its military leadership.

Second: However, John then states that the wounded empire will be healed. The U.S. will overcome this military attack which appears to be fatal. Then, John states, the whole world will follow our empire with wonder. People will be amazed at the strength which our empire displays as it sets out and overcomes the wound.

The mortal wound our nation received which John foretold in this verse was the bombing of Pearl Harbor on December 7, 1941. The light given by the Lord on this verse was revealed with such clarity to my brother, then to me, through the Spirit of God that I cannot question its validity. Our historical study of this event then confirmed exactly what the Spirit had revealed. When the U.S. received this great military wound at the bombing of Pearl Harbor, facts indicate that the world concluded our military strength had been shattered beyond recovery.

The Japanese did not pursue their first attack, however, and we recovered quickly. We went into war on two different military fronts, Asia and Europe. In a period of about 42 months we actually won two wars at the same time, demonstrating a power the world had never seen. We ended World War II with a show of awesome power that man had never before witnessed or experienced—the release of the atomic bomb. According to John's prophecy, after this wound healed "the whole earth followed the beast with wonder." The world stood amazed at the magnificent power of our country at the end of Word War II, and consequently many nations aligned themselves with us. After the war was over, our country emerged as the greatest military and economic power that has ever existed on the face of the earth.

> Men worshipped the dragon, for he had given his authority to the beast, and they worshipped the beast saying, "Who is like the beast, and who can fight against it?" (Revelation 13:4)

To worship means to serve or to venerate. It can be direct or indirect. In this verse John deals with an attitude that generally prevailed after World War II, which he prophetically called an attitude of worship. He describes the attitude of worship which the people had toward our country's might and power, noting that it was one of awe. This is expressed in the statement of the people, "Who is like the beast and who can fight against it?" If anyone doubts that this was the prevailing attitude of people throughout the world after we defeated Japan and Germany, I recommend that they study this point John makes and review the attitudes of the people at the end of World War II.

> And the beast was given a mouth uttering haughty and blasphemous words, and it was allowed to exercise authority for forty-two months. (Revelation 13:5)

First: In this verse John names two identifying characteristics of our empire. The first is haughtiness—the feeling and promotion of self as being better than others. It is the displaying of pride in self and personal accomplishments. John is saying our empire will promote the idea that the United States is better than other countries, and that as a people we will show pride in our accomplishments, and great satisfaction in our conquests. This characteristic of haughtiness is one that God hates. (Proverbs 6:16)

Second: The second characteristic John mentions is the uttering of blasphemous words. He is prophesying that our empire will be blasphemous in character while having this haughty attitude. It will openly promote and advance its position, its superiority, acclaim its accomplishments in the world, and reflect its pride. Regardless of how evil some of its ways may be, they are done in the name of God, implying that they are godly teachings. John calls this "uttering blasphemous words," because no government can possess this attitude and truly serve God.

John's next point begins in Revelation 13:5 and continues into verse 6. He states:

> It (the beast) was allowed to exercise authority for forty-two months; it opened its mouth to utter blasphemies against God, blaspheming His name and His dwelling, that is, those who dwell in heaven.

In the context of the beast's exercise of great authority for 42 months, we relate this activity to verse 2 where John states we were given this authority, and verse 3 where he declares that one of our heads seemed to have received a mortal wound which was healed. Please recall that what seemed to be a mortal wound was military in nature—the bombing of Pearl Harbor. This wound, however, aroused our wild beast fighting instinct. Following this event we exercised our military authority for 42 months during World War II. We demonstrated this great authority of power by winning wars on two widely separated fronts while our own homeland remained untouched. After the war, we emerged on the throne of Satan's kingdom, "the world." The mortal wound was healed.

John also says in verse 6 that we uttered blasphemies against God. We were claiming that this authority and power came from God and that we were serving a godly purpose as we exercised it.

Historians reveal our government's purpose for entering World War II was self-interest — to receive economic and military gain. It brought about conditions which allowed our government to become the strongest and most influential power in the history of man. We have been exposed to many influences which identifies that war with moralistic purposes. We were led by Franklin Roosevelt, Winston Churchill and other political leaders to believe we entered the war to defend ourselves and our allies from unprovoked aggression. But many facts, including some from our own State Department files, such as the official Army's Pearl Harbor Report, reveal that our main purpose in entering the war was to establish a stronger military and economic position in the world.

America as a World Power

Historical records prove it was primarily the outcome of World War II that allowed our country to become the leading world power. Whereas other leading powers had both their military and economic strength destroyed, ours was actually enhanced. Other powerful countries lost a large number of their fighting forces. This alone seriously affected the structure and strength of those countries. So when we consider that all the fighting was done on the soil of the other leading powers, destroying many of their industrial complexes, cities, farms and homes, we can begin to realize why we emerged as the world's leader.

We like to think that one of the major reasons we fared so well in World War II was because of our national righteousness and our claim to trust in God. But the teachings of

Jesus Christ and His examples are quite contrary to such a concept.

We even try to justify this thinking by relating Scripture passages from the Old Testament concerning God's direction and formation of Israel. It's true that Israel fought many wars in its development as a country. But remember, this was the nation descended from Abraham, through which God had chosen to come to earth. After God came in the flesh in His Son, Jesus Christ, a new nation or kingdom was established. It was a "spiritual kingdom." It is a kingdom that reigns and works through the hearts of men. God's Word never teaches the principle that the protection or advancement of this new "spiritual kingdom"—Christianity—will be accomplished through war.

As we think about what has taken place in our society since World War II, we can see our nation rising above all others in its world position and possession of "things" of the world (Satan's kingdom). We can see the United States government rising up in power in the area of the center of Christianity. Then parts of prophecy and their meanings will begin to form and be confirmed by historical review, just as Moses stated, in Deuteronomy 18:21,22.

Our country made a leap in its "world position" after World War I. After World War II, when similar conditions existed, the United States emerged as the most prosperous and mighty of all nations. It became a world superpower which no other country was in a position to challenge. As John prophesied, we received the throne of Satan, "the world."

For many years the American people did not know that the primary objective of our State Department in entering World War II was to increase our economic and military position in the world. But an abundance of information, even some from our own State Department reports, has revealed this truth. This can be substantiated from numerous sources.[1]

After World War II, Secretary of War Henry L. Stimson revealed the decision that had been made by President

Roosevelt and his cabinet prior to Japan's attack on Pearl Harbor—that they were going to try to get Japan to attack us. In an entry in his personal diary for November 25, 1941, approximately two weeks before the bombing of Pearl Harbor, Stimson wrote: "The question was how we should maneuver them into the position of firing the first shot without allowing too much danger to ourselves. It was a difficult proposition." (Stimson refers here to Japan).

When the attack came it was not a surprise to our State Department. Washington had cracked the Japanese code more than one year prior to Japan's attack on Pearl Harbor. Our State Department was fully informed of the timing and the preparation by Japan for this attack. The headlines on the front page of the *Honolulu Sunday Advisor* dated November 30, 1941, warned, "Japanese May Strike Over Weekend."

As a nation, we were surprised by Japan's bombing of Pearl Harbor. However, it is now known that Washington expected this attack. Government officials withheld this information from the American people so they could shock us and gain our unquestioning support for declaring war.

The administration knew that the great majority of American people (records show 85%) did not want to enter into this war. Therefore, for the administration to implement their objectives of world military supremacy and economic control, events had to be well planned, so we the people, would follow their leadership in entering this war. The tool of deceit was their means. As we observe and gain a better understanding of how world government employs deceit and exploits its people to accomplish objectives, we can see the strength of satanic forces at work behind the scenes. These forces fulfill a basic principle that the Word of God warned us about hundreds of years ago.

For our struggle is not against flesh and blood, but against the rulers, against the authorities, against the powers of this dark world and against the spiritual forces of evil in the heavenly realms. (Ephesians 6:12)

One reason for President Franklin Roosevelt's strategy in using Japan was that he and his cabinet knew the treaty between Germany, Italy and Japan would require the United States to fight all three countries. It was in reference to this treaty that Rear Admiral Robert A. Theobald wrote, "The fact that war with Japan meant war with Germany and Italy played an important part in President Roosevelt's diplomatic strategy. Throughout the approach to the war and during the fighting, the primary U.S. objective was the defeat of Germany." This statement is from Theobald's report, "The Final Secret of Pearl Harbor," page 51. Prime Minister Winston Churchill, in a statement made to Great Britain's House of Commons on January 27, 1942, confirmed the suggestion that Roosevelt's strategy in using Japan was to get us involved in the war in Europe.

History shows that any country which is a conqueror, as we were in World War II, accomplishes victory through acts of brutality, greed and power politics. We are the youngest and yet the mightiest of all the great powers of our day. We have looked back in our history and on the basis of our spiritual Pilgrim heritage justified many unrighteous secular acts that have taken place in our country's growth.

A biblical analysis directly contradicts the idea that the teachings of Christianity allow the fighting of wars to promote its values or its interests. This concept has caused us to rationalize and justify our government's actions, and allowed us and others to be deceived into thinking we have been virtuous. Satan has been able to deceive us into identifying evil with good, often rationalizing our government's actions as being of God, when the Bible says that all the world is controlled by the evil one.

The real cause of World War II was not made known until after the war ended and was never made public knowledge by the press. Our involvement in this war was due to man's age-old sins of self-centeredness, selfishness, greed and covetousness.

Many people do not realize the tremendous gains we made from World War II which allowed us to become the leading world power. Satan had destroyed the power of the other nations in this war, thereby setting up one nation to become his world empire (on his throne) as his time draws short—a world empire he could use to attack the spiritual commitment of the saints. He gave over his authority to our nation, which exercised it for about 42 months during World War II, establishing a power above all other powers ever developed.

If you are a Bible scholar, you may find significance in the period of 42 months. This prophecy was written by John, a Jew. Therefore, he wrote consistent with Hebrew custom for measurement of time. Remember—in those days they did not have clocks and watches, so time was not measured in the exact fashion we are accustomed to. For example, a day was from sundown to sundown. Jesus died on Friday and was resurrected early Sunday morning. Yet the measurement of time as recorded in Scripture by the Jewish writers was three days, even though in total hours it was less than 48. Friday was counted as the first day and Sunday was the third day, regardless of what time of day Jesus was buried and rose again.

World War II began on December 7, 1941, and it ended during the forty-second month, according to the Jewish calendar. Germany surrendered on May 7, 1945. The exact dates are not as important as the fact that the war ended during the forty-second month when using a Jewish calendar.

It was also significant to me to discover that the measurement of recorded time, 42 months, is based on the war in Europe and the Middle East area—the area associated with the Jewish people and their history—and not the date our conflict ended with Japan in the Pacific. The Jewish people were not involved in our war with Japan.

America's Post-War Position

A study of the post-war era reveals the tremendous strength of the United States, both economically and militarily. We occupied many of the countries in Western Europe and Asia that were once invaded by Germany and Japan. We brought a number of former British and French colonies into our governmental control. The real objectives of our State Department were accomplished as the war developed our economic and military position of world control. Solidification of our world position was the total gain of World War II. At the end of this war the world looked at the beast and said, "Who can fight against it?" We were able to set up our industrialized strength throughout much of the world — especially the Christian world — along with military bases to protect this industry.

We maintain a military presence in more than 50 foreign countries and hundreds of major overseas military installations. Our navy patrols every ocean and we have military missions on every continent. When we combine this with the strength of our business community, which has been the decisive economic factor in country after country around the world since World War II, we should begin to comprehend that we indeed have been the strongest governmental superpower in all the history of mankind. The Apostle John has appropriately used the names of all three animals in Revelation 13:2 to characterize our awesome power.

To illustrate this concept of our industry being supported by the power of our military, notice how Major General Smedly T. Butler expressed his experiences even though they were in the early 1900's: "I spent 33 years and four months in active service as a member of our country's most agile military force — the Marine Corps. I served in all commissioned ranks from Second Lieutenant to Major General. And during that period I spent most of my time being a high-class muscle man for big business for Wall Street, and for the bankers. In short, I was a racketeer for capitalism. During those years I had, as the boys in the back room would say, a swell racket. I was rewarded with honors, medals, promotions. Looking back on it, I feel I might have given Al Capone a few hints. The best he could do was to operate his racket in three city districts. We Marines operated on three continents."

Most American Christians, influenced by our communications media which is generally under Satan's control, believe that the foreign policy of the United States in recent years has been mainly concerned with the extension of freedom to other peoples. Because of this teaching we have become somewhat blinded to the biblical teaching that governmental systems are of the world. Therefore, they generally serve a worldly purpose. This is not to say that they overrule God's providence, but they are often the vehicles used by Satan to attack and influence God's standards and God's people. Our society has been used to develop a stronger attachment to the things of the world as we approach the end time. It is promoting policies for "self" interest as Satan has set out to attack the testimony of the saints in the central area of Christianity.

This is one of the reasons Christ did not become involved with the political problems of His day. He said He came to save mankind from the influence of these Satan-controlled systems. He came to truly set people free—spiritually free, detached from the things of the world and its worldly systems. Man's way to set people free is at the expense and death of others, and their freedom is not really established —only a change from one worldly system to another. I do not speak out against serving in the military forces or being involved in politics, for God can use His people in many areas. We must let the Spirit of God direct us in these areas. I'm referring to the general spiritual attitude which prevails today in the Christian community that has implied more loyalty by our actions to the teachings and ways of our world society than to the teachings of Jesus Christ.

Also, it (the beast) was allowed to make war on the saints and to conquer them. (Revelation 13:7)

To "conquer" in this verse means to overcome, defeat, subdue, or prevail against, as when a country is conquered. The country still exists, but in a defeated state. John saw this happening to the spiritual state of those saints living under the "beast" system in the last days. To make war with and conquer the saints would be to attack and overcome them in their spiritual battle against yielding to the power of their old nature's characteristics and desires.

Christians in Spiritual Conflict

Because John could look into the future he saw that the spiritual victory over sin we can have with our Lord would be a rarity in the Body of Christ during the time the beast was on the throne of the world. He saw that the power of the beast would be so great that most believers in our society would not fully commit themselves to Jesus Christ. Our "self willpower" would not become spiritually detached from the ways of the world. He saw that the Christian community would be a "self" seeking people.

Notice that Daniel also makes note of this prophecy. "As I looked, this horn (the one which became the end time beast) made war with the saints, and prevailed over them." (Daniel 7:21. Words in parentheses are the author's.)

The fruits often displayed among Christians reflect the truth of this prophecy of the "beast system" conquering the saints in their spiritual walk. Many Christians in our country are experiencing severe defeats in their spiritual battles against the present worldly standards and the influence of our society. We are being conquered in our family relationships, business ethics, moral issues, acceptance and involvement with world entertainment standards, etc. Our apathy toward sin is a true barometer of this condition.

Because most of us have been deceived on this point, we do not acknowledge that we have been overthrown in the spiritual battle by the influences and pressures of the world. This is what Scripture warns is the overall attack plan in Satan's use of the beast system—to deceive those Christians living under this system to accept the standards of the world rather than persecuting them.

There are two influencing spirits in the world. **First** is the spirit of Satan who causes service to self. The **second** is the Holy Spirit of God who dwells in a reborn Christian and who gives motivation and power for righteousness and obedience to God's will. Both want to capture our inner spiritual being. God has made us free moral agents and we can yield to whichever master we choose. John says that in a certain period of time (the Lord has revealed that we are now living in that time), Satan, through the power and authority he gives over to the beast, will make a severe attack on the saints as he sees his time drawing to a close. He will be able to overcome many, keeping them from yielding to the power of the Spirit of God in directing their lives and, therefore, from walking in the Spirit. To walk in the power of God's Spirit is to walk victoriously over the power of our sinful nature. (Romans 8:4-8 and Galatians 5:16-18)

It is only by God's spiritual strength that we can bring true glory and honor to Jesus and the power of God as He reigns in our life. It is the victorious position over sin in the world that God intends for us to have that John saw the beast overcome in many of the saints.

> And authority was given it (the beast) over every tribe and people and tongue and nation. And all who dwell on earth will worship it, every one whose name has not been written before the foundation of the world in the book of life of the Lamb that was slain. (Revelation 13:7,8)

We do not know if John refers in the first part of this sentence to the authority of our economic, military and industrial power. We have controlled many countries through our economic and industrial might. We do know that the Scriptures often speak in this manner in prophecy—that is, making reference to an empire having conquered or having authority over the world—not because this empire physically takes control of all of the world, but because it has the power to do so. An example of this is recorded in Daniel where he speaks of empires conquering the world, when in actuality they only conquered a small portion of the world physically, though they had the power to conquer it all. We also find that words of prophecy in the Scriptures center around those areas affecting God's people. John may be using the words spoken here in a prophetic sense, referring to our world economic, military and industrial authority over the Christian world.

> If anyone has an ear, let him hear: If anyone is to be taken captive, to captivity he goes; if anyone slays with the sword, with the sword must he be slain. Here is a call for the endurance and faith of the saints. (Revelation 13:9,10)

Let me emphasize again that I am sharing the light which our Lord has given me. I have not received any definite leading which I know to be revelation from the Spirit of God on verses 9 and 10, as the other verses I have discussed. Perhaps someone else has. It appears that John is talking about a period of time in which there is going to be a direct attack by society and government on the saints in our country, rather than an indirect attack such as we have been experiencing through the influence of society in recent years. A direct attack would be by means of worldly trials and tribulations. Regardless of what kind of tribulations the world may throw at us, however, we can be assured that God will give us the power to endure with peace and joy just as He did the early Christians. Of course, this power to endure will be relative to our desire to yield our "self willpower" to the "power of His Spirit."

As for the balance of the verses in Revelation 13 (11 through 18), I will share in the next two chapters what light has been given on these.

More Biblical Teachings on the "Beast"

To develop an even better background and understanding of the identity of the "beast" in Revelation 13, we can also review a few verses from chapter 7 of Daniel. Daniel gives us some additional insight into the origin of this beast, or last great governmental superpower, that John does not give in the book of Revelation.

After this I saw in the night, visions, and behold, a fourth beast, terrible and dreadful and exceedingly strong; and it had great iron teeth; it devoured and broke in pieces, and stamped the residue with its feet. It was different from all the beasts that were before it; and it had ten horns. I considered the horns, and behold, there came up among them another horn, a little one, before which three of the first horns were plucked up by the roots; and behold, in this horn were eyes like the eyes of a man, and a mouth speaking great things. (Daniel 7:7,8, RSV)

Then I desired to know the truth concerning the fourth beast, which was different from all the rest, exceedingly terrible, with its teeth of iron and claws of bronze; and which devoured and broke in pieces, and stamped the residue with its feet; and concerning the ten horns that were on its head, and the other horn which came up and before which three of them fell, the horn which had eyes and a mouth that spoke great things, and which seemed greater than its fellows. As I looked, this horn made war with the saints, and prevailed over them, until the Ancient of Days came, and judgment was given for the saints of the Most High, and the time came when the saints received the kingdom. Thus he said: "As for the fourth beast, there shall be a fourth kingdom on earth, which shall be different from all the kingdoms, and it shall devour the whole earth, and trample it down, and break it to pieces. As for the ten horns, out of this kingdom ten kings shall arise, and another shall arise after them; he shall be different from the former ones, and shall put down three kings. He shall speak words against the Most High, and shall wear out the saints of the Most High, and shall think to change the times and the law; and they shall be given into his hand for a time, two times, and half a time." (Daniel 7:19-25, RSV)

1. (Daniel 7:7,19 and 23) History and Bible scholars agree that this fourth beast was the Roman Empire.
2. (Daniel 7:8,20 and 24) Out of the Roman Empire would emerge ten horns or a group of prominent countries. "Horn" and "king" as used by Daniel have a prophetic meaning of a country or nation with a significant amount of worldly power and influence. (See Daniel 7:17 and 23.)
3. (Daniel 7:8, 20 and 24) Out of these ten countries a new country will rise up, made up mostly of people and cultures from the others in the European or old Roman Empire area. "Little horn" means it will be a new country. It originates from the people of the old Roman Empire, but Daniel states it would be distinct (separate). That is the Hebrew meaning of the word translated "among" in verse eight.
4. (Daniel 7:8,20 and 24) The new country that emerges out of these countries will have to defeat three as it gains stature. The United States of America is the new nation that has risen from the countries, peoples, races and cultures that once made up the geographical area of the Roman Empire (Europe). And our history records a fulfillment of the prophecy of conquering three countries in Europe. America had to overcome England, France and Spain in different wars as our forefathers fought to establish our country as a nation. In our development as a nation, these wars (fought from the late 1700s through the early 1900s) established our form of government and our geographical boundaries.
5. (Daniel 7:20) This horn or new country grows in stature and power, becoming greater than any of the countries from which its people came.
6. (Daniel 7:21) After reaching the stature of a fully developed world superpower, which was at the end of World War II for the United States, Daniel prophesies the society of this

new country makes war on the saints and prevails over them until the Ancient of Days (Jesus) comes.

7. (Daniel 7:25) The government of this new country will make war on the saints after it becomes the top world power, by wearing them out as it changes the laws of its society.

We discuss throughout this book the power of worldliness and its deceiving philosophy which develops the "self desires of our flesh" now prevalent in our society—the area which is the center of the saints. This is readily seen when we review the impact of the teaching now coming from our mass communication media, materialistic ways, selfishness, greed, immorality, dishonesty and corruption, along with a complete breakdown of control by law and order. Remember, these conditions were not prominent in our society before World War II.

8. (Daniel 7:25) The saints are adversely influenced by the way our government changes the controlling laws of the land for a span of time which is a time, two times, and a half a time—a phrase used by Hebrew writers to indicate an unknown period of time. That is why the phrase they used includes all facets of how one would designate an unknown period of time: a time, two times, and a half a time.

Prophecy Fulfilled

We have fulfilled all of these prophecies in Daniel that help to identify the end time world power. No other country has fulfilled even one of the prophecies.

Some may wonder why I associate the beast in Revelation 13:1 with the new country or empire that rises up, consisting of the people from the countries mentioned in Daniel. **First,** we should notice that both John and Daniel bring forth the association of ten countries with this world power. **Second,** and probably more important, is the realization that Daniel is prophesying of those world empires in existence from his time until the end of time that greatly influenced Israel as a nation. Israel was destroyed in 70 A.D. Therefore, Daniel did not prophesy of those empires after 70 A.D. until the year that Israel once again became a nation, in 1948. It is essential to understand that Daniel's prophecies were centered around his people, their nation and those world powers in control while Israel is a nation. We then see that the little horn he introduces in chapter 7, which becomes greater than its fellows and rises out of the countries from the Roman Empire, will be that major "world power" influencing Israel after she regains her position as a nation near the end of time.

The United States of America has been the ruling influential power over Israel since this historical event took place in 1948. Our nation has fulfilled other prophetic predictions about this end-time power in that we have maintained treaties with Israel. However, the Scriptures state this will not always be, and at some future date we will break our alliance with Israel.

John is also describing this last great "world power" in Revelation 13. He calls it a beast, but it is in reference to its influence on the church, the Body of Christ. (Revelation 12:17) This last great power is the same one, and it has an impact on both the church and on Israel. This is why John and Daniel have prophesied of this last government power, and why their approach is similar but with different emphases. Daniel's prophecy is centered primarily around Israel, while John's prophecy is centered around the church.

Another concept that should be mentioned as we look back is that more than 35 years after the end of World War II, we still maintain that our primary objective is peace, and that we are going to bring peace to the world.

I believe that when we check the Scriptures, this particular characteristic of proclaiming to maintain peace while we hold the superpower position in the world, is one that was prophesied. It is characteristic of the beast or the antichrist. Our government has been proclaiming to be the protectors of peace throughout the world ever since World War II, yet it has let the deterioration of our own moral standards in society develop so that society can now seriously attack and harm many of our country's people and families along with many of the spiritual truths of Christianity. This spiritual attack has caused many of the saints to be overcome by the worldly pressures and standards which are now nationally accepted and approved.

The facts we have mentioned are to help support the true identity of what John saw our government become, emerging as the greatest in history—a worldly government that was prophesied by Daniel and one of the great empires to rule during the time Israel was to be a nation. After the Roman Empire, there was to be only one more empire, made up of the people from the countries of the Roman Empire—the one which promoted itself to be from God, and the one used by Satan to attack the saints of the central area of Christianity as it thought to change the laws of a normal civilized society.

I believe this is one of the reasons Paul instructs us to be sure to pray for the leaders of our country or anyone in authority over us, "that we may lead a quiet and peaceable life, godly and respectful in every way." (I Timothy 2:2)

Roman Empire Revived

The beast John prophesies about in Revelation 13:1 is without a doubt the ancient Roman Empire reappearing upon the prophetic scene. It is an empire that was developed by those people whose origin for the most part goes back to the old geographic area of the Roman Empire. However, as John gives us an indication in Revelation 12:17 (RSV), this reappearance will be across the ocean as John saw Satan waiting "on the sand of the sea."

Many scholars and historians have compared in detail the historical resemblance of the old Roman Empire and the ways of our modern day American society. This includes areas of life such as the government system, commerce, military strength, emphasis on things of the world such as food, pleasure, mundane cares of this world, athletics, mass building programs, deterioration of morality and a general acceptance of the standards of the times.*

Similarities of the Roman society and ours are so great that a recent President commissioned a committee to study their problems so that we might avoid making the same mistakes!

Satan has deceived us as to the method of his development of the beast, often referred to as the antichrist, which the Scriptures imply will happen. However, because the identity of the beast as given by the Lord is our own empire and society, we should not let it overwhelm us. If we apply some of the biblical principles concerning Satan, we would conclude that the deceptive spirit of Satan in the last days as he attacks the saints is here in our country. Actually his development of our world society in such a way as to get us to become so strongly self-willed (dependent on self), and so strongly "serving self" (the spirit of antichrist) is a testimony that our country is the center of Christianity—the target center of the end time spiritual warfare.

We need to remember that it has always been God and His children that Satan has fought the hardest and in the most deceiving ways. Simply review the Scriptures on that point. Recall how Satan caused Israel to fall away. Even logically it makes sense that Satan would develop the beast system here in the United States to war against the saints because of our country's Christian heritage. We must keep in mind that Satan is a most powerful spiritual enemy, and that our source of power for victory is only through Jesus. This lesson can be seen as we study the lives of the early Chris-

---

*Scripture says that the personality and character (spirit) of John the Baptist fulfills the prophecy on the reappearance of Elijah. (Matthew 11:14, Luke 1:17) In like manner, history is confirming that our country's present character is fulfilling the prophecy of the reappearance of the Roman Empire.

tians. Only Christ overcame the world and all that it threw at Him. By His life, He was able to show to the world God's great power and love.

Perhaps some who read this may not think I'm giving Christians much credit. It is not my purpose to discredit Christians but to open the eyes of believers to recognize the satanic power behind these various worldly positions. If it were not important for us to be separated from the influence of the world and the men of the world, God's Word would not tell us so. The fact that we have failed to recognize the effects of this influence does not deny this scriptural truth. As we understand our spiritual heritage and the church's spiritual warfare, we will soon realize it is not strange that Satan has used the tactics of presenting our worldly government and its ways as being from God. Satan knows this is what Christians want to hear. And, if we accept this, we will be open to many lies.

Obedience to Government Ordinances

Because I am discussing the recent political influence of our government I don't want to leave the impression that we should not respect the civil authority of our governing officials. It is most important that we do just as Paul teaches on this subject in Romans 13:1-7. As Paul writes to those Christians in Rome directly under the authority of the Roman Empire, he tells them that even the government of Rome was instituted by God for the purpose of maintaining law and order, and in that respect they were to be subject to its authorities even though the authorities didn't agree with Christian principles.

Paul is teaching us in these verses that it is through government authorities that God controls man and his actions. This teaching applies to all government authorities throughout the world. Each government has a God-given responsibility to keep under control the natural selfish desires of man. We believe that when a government fails to fulfill this, its most important God-given responsibility, it has deteriorated to the extent that God will not allow it to exist in its present form much longer.

As citizens of the United States it's important to note to what extent our government is carrying out this God-given responsibility of maintaining law and order. When the Lord laid it on my heart to examine this area, I was shocked and hurt because the facts reveal that our government has turned against the greatest of its God-given responsibilities. It has fallen apart in this most important government function, and is now the most irresponsible of all governments in the world in carrying out its number one responsibility as instituted by God.

In 1980 over 13 million crimes were committed in our society. It is heartbreaking to say, but in other countries—even those atheistic in belief such as Red China—the maintenance of law and order is being carried out far more effectively than in the United States. American reporters visiting Red China commented that consumer goods in that country are left out in the open on the sidewalks at night, yet no theft occurs.

The poltical influence of our society has kept us from realizing how Satan controls the ways of our society. Since World War II our government has allowed a breakdown in the laws of its society. This has opened the way for the rise of "man of lawlessness" attitude that Paul prophesied about in II Thessalonians 2:1-4—an attitude which now prevails in nearly all areas of American life, including a lack of respect for many of the biblical principles Christians are to follow.

Satan has tempted us by offering a worldly kingdom in which to put our faith, just as he tempted Christ. (Matthew 4:8-10) Christ did not give in to Satan's strategy as most of us have. In so doing we have become friends of the world— spotted by its system. Most of us have a stronger commitment to our worldly standards—the self-serving ways of our society—than to the Kingdom of God and to our Savior, Jesus

Christ.

In this chapter we have shared prophetic verses which identifies America's *world* position in end-time events. In no way does this take away from the *spiritual* history of our country.

Chapter 8

SATAN'S MODERN DAY POWER SOURCE

Satan has always tried to get Christians to doubt truths about God and His Word. His power to accomplish this under the recent spiritual influence of our society is far-reaching. This power has affected the majority of us in our society who name Christianity as our religious belief. In this chapter we want to share our understanding from the Lord on John's prophetic statement which describes the beast's power system used by Satan for the spreading of false teaching in the last days. Prophetically John describes Satan's power system with these words:

> Then I saw another beast which rose out of the earth. It had two horns like a lamb, and it spoke like dragon. It exercises all the authority of the first beast in its presence, and makes the earth and its inhabitants worship the first beast, whose mortal wound was healed. It works great signs, even making fire come down from heaven to earth in the sight of men; and by the signs, which it is allowed to work in the presence of the beast, it deceives those who dwell on earth, bidding them make an image for the beast which was wounded by the sword and yet lived. (Revelation 13:11-14)

John describes this second beast differently than the way he described the first beast of Revelation 13:1. The second beast, which "rose out of the earth," is the society ruled by the first beast. A society consists of those things—economic systems, industrial output, businesses, services, religious systems, educational systems, etc.—developed by the wisdom of man. Recall that prophetically the word "beast" means something with awesome power. John was so awestruck by our society's power to produce goods and services (gross national product) that he speaks of it as another beast. John is referring to our society since the time the first beast gained the throne of the world, which for our government was after World War II.

John was also overwhelmed by the ability or power our society had to teach and influence its people. He describes its speaking authority with the phrase "it had two horns like a lamb and it spoke like a dragon." Remember that the word "horn" in prophecy means something with power.

John goes on to say the teaching influence of our society will appear like a lamb. This means that it will appear harmless to most people, even though since World War II, it has had the power to speak or teach many character traits of Satan's nature. This is reflected in the deterioration of many of our moral and civil standards. There are two key principles to remember about Satan: (1) his power system to teach would be something from the world, his kingdom, or what we call society and (2) this false teaching influence from society would develop an "independent, self-seeking attitude" in the inner being of the people under its influence. That is the most dominant character trait of Satan.

Power Source Revealed

The initial revelation that was seared into my brother's heart revealed the wound of the first beast to be the bombing of Pearl Harbor. That truth opened the door to understanding the identity of the first beast, a governmental superpower.

My brother Charles received two revelations relating to the beast and its vast world system. The second dealt with the identity of the second beast with two horns that seemed harmless, yet spoke like a dragon—teaching the ways of Satan's world standards. Initially, I had trouble accepting what he had to say about the power source of the second beast. You, too, may find it difficult, but don't let that cause you to lay this book aside. Read through these next two chapters and I think you will find that current events overwhelmingly testify of the strong possibility that his revelation was true.

The Lord revealed to Charles that the two "horns" of the second beast (which John saw that seemed harmless yet spoke like a dragon) were the positive and negative power charges of electricity. With that I had to shake my head. *That's really way out,* I thought. When my brother had shared the first revelation about the first beast, there was an overpowering anointing from the Spirit of the Lord of its truth. That did not happen with this revelation about electricity. So I decided to let it rest for awhile.

I will share some comments made in a letter I received from my brother in 1971, about three weeks after our visit when he had first told me of his revelations.

> "I did not reason these out (speaking of the things the Holy Spirit had revealed) for I was not even studying Revelation and had accepted the fact that everything in it was some time in the future and would not be understood until that time came. . . ." He continues, "The beast in Revelation chapter 13, verse 11, is the outgrowth of electricity and electronics— now developing its own brain, the computer. He is doing unbelievable miracles today as long as the first beast (our government) is watching—space shots, etc.

> "It also required everyone to acquire a permit to do anything. The code refers to a computer standing for a man's name. Three sets of numbers with six numbers in each set. With a little reasoning, you can see that we are already becoming very dependent on this system to live as is most of the world.

If we must refuse to go along with it in the future to stay true to Christ, it will mean prison and death due to lack of medical care, etc. Or man in his great wisdom may make the decision to actually put to death those who refuse to go along with it.

"Man's wisdom has always been foolishness with God and will be used for his own destruction. It tends to be anti-Christ for it makes us depend on ourselves and the things of this world rather than Christ. It is very deceiving because most Christians hardly realize how much time, praise and affection they are giving these things, which takes away from worship and service to Christ.

"Today we are aware of tremendous suffering and needs all over the world. Yet the 'Christian Church' justifies itself in spending vast amounts of money, time and effort to build new buildings, spend much time in pleasure and live in luxury.

"Something has to be seriously wrong. God is not a respecter of persons. We are no better than anyone else. We will probably be judged by what we could have done for others and didn't, rather than what we are actually doing. Romans 12:1, 2 clearly states that the world around us should not set the pace for what we do or how we reason. Only God's Holy Spirit and Word should do that.

"Although heaven and earth shall pass away, God's Word never changes one little speck. What all Christians today need to do is to spend all our spare time and energy seeking God to be completely possessed by His Holy Spirit so that we may be guided through these deceiving times and not be ashamed at Christ's coming." (Quoted from a letter to me from my brother, Dr. Charles Fraley, dated July 10, 1971.)

My brother's revelation about electricity and the computer came in 1971. It is interesting that *Time* magazine, January 3, 1983, announced their man of the year for 1982 is not a man, but the computer.

My brother's revelation about electricity made some sense, but I had trouble putting it together. I could see where John, the writer of Revelation, could be coming from. To have a vision in the first century as he did, which revealed the power of electricity and its use in the period in which we now live, would make it seem that this power could perform great miracles. Just the use of an electric light, stove, iron or toaster would appear miraculous to John. And the way the use of electricity now controls so many areas of our life didn't happen until after World War II. However, I first had doubts that this was to what John was referring.

About three years later, in the spring of 1974, I was teaching a Bible class of high school students at my church. I don't remember now what the subject was, but I do remember there were 21 students in the class. All 21 professed to know Jesus as their personal Savior. Most of them stated they were Christians because they had been baptized and were a member of a Bible-teaching church.

I was interested in whether or not they really knew Jesus in their hearts. So Barbara, my wife, developed a test for me to give to these students. I don't recall the questions, but there were about 15 and she had structured them in such a way that I could pretty well determine by their answers if they really knew Jesus as their Savior. The results? It appeared that 18 out of the 21 did *not* know Jesus as their Savior, and did not comprehend what He had done for them.

Eighteen out of the 21 failed! These were high school students who attended church regularly and were involved in church activities. They believed they were Christians and were part of the Body of Christ. But the facts said they did not know Jesus in their hearts.

This caused me to share a lesson with them about true repentance and inviting Jesus into our hearts and lives. I wanted to explain to them what happens when we experience spiritual rebirth.

One of the best methods I had found to illustrate what happens in spiritual rebirth is through the use of a light bulb. Inside the bulb are many small wires and elements. It is similar to the human body in that we have many blood vessels, nerves, muscles, bones and other components which make up the active part of our physical being. All of the elements of the light bulb are wrapped in glass, similar to the way our physical elements are wrapped in skin.

When we empower the elements of a light bulb, it comes to life, lights up and gives off light. In a way, it has a personality through the glow of the light. It is not physical in that we can't touch the glow—we can only see it. This is accomplished by flipping a switch or plugging a cord into a socket. This allows the light bulb to make contact with an invisible power source we call electricity. We can't see the electricity; we can only see its effects. We see the light coming from the bulb.

In explaining spiritual rebirth, a similar thing happens. We have a physical body, and when we believe in and accept Jesus into our hearts, we are plugged into an invisible spiritual power source. We can't see it, but all who accept Jesus know through experience that it is true. This power source is the Holy Spirit, God Himself, who is a Spirit. He comes and indwells everyone who truly believes in and asks Jesus into his life.

> Yet to all who received him, to those who believe in his name, (speaking of Jesus), he gave the right (power) to become children of God—children born not of natural descent, nor of human decision or a husband's will, but born of God. (John 1:12,13. Words in parentheses are the author's.)

This new power source, the Holy Spirit, lights up our life. It changes our very nature, our character, our personality. Like electricity, it is something we can't see. We can only see the effects through the personality changes in people. Electricity and the Holy Spirit are similar in many ways. Both are invisible power sources which are able to bring about miraculous changes. Of course, we realize and understand that in many other ways they are not similar. Electricity is a physical power and the Holy Spirit is a spiritual power.

After explaining rebirth to my class, I walked back to the church auditorium. Suddenly I was overwhelmed by the Spirit of the Lord. I momentarily lost my stability and nearly went to my knees. The Spirit of the Lord revealed in that instant that the enemy is using electricity today as a counterfeit power source through the wisdom of man, and it is doing many things in ways similar to the Holy Spirit.

The Holy Spirit is referred to in Scripture as a teacher, a counselor, a comforter and one who is able to perform many miracles. In a similar manner, it was revealed that Satan, working through the mind and wisdom of man, has devised many ways to use the power system of electricity to teach, comfort and perform many miracles.

The Spirit of the Lord allowed me to see that these two horns which John prophetically describes are the power source he saw Satan using in our society to teach and deceive Christians in bringing about their involvement with the standards of the world. Prophetically, the word "horn" is used to describe something with power, and in Revelation 13:11 John uses this word to describe the teaching power of the society that rises up out of the first beast, after the first beast becomes the greatest governmental system in the world.

The positive and negative power charges of electricity that make possible the use of electrical power in the field of electronics is the power system which appears like a lamb (harmless), but is now able to teach, influence, mold and greatly control our mind and conscience and develop our attitudes in the ways of our society. This will be hard for some to accept, and that is certainly understandable. But I believe in time this truth will be confirmed in the hearts of many because I know the strong confirmation the Spirit of the Lord has given to me.

Does that mean there is something intrinsically wrong with electricity? Of course not! Electricity is a part of God's creation. It can be used for many wonderful purposes. But we also know that Satan uses all that he can from God's creation for evil purposes in this world. Look at the way he used an object of God's creation in the Garden to tempt and deceive Adam and Eve. Man himself is a part of God's creation, yet consider all the cruel things Satan has caused man to do throughout the history of civilization. The sun and moon are a part of God's creation, yet Satan has caused man to worship them as gods through the centuries. Mary, the mother of Jesus, was honored by God, yet Satan has caused her name and symbolism to be used in a pagan way as though she were a part of the Godhead. There are countless other examples of how Satan has used things from God's creation for evil purposes. The awesome power of the use of electricity to teach and control people fits into this realm, and John prophesies of its use under the direction of the beast system.

Satan has used this power source because of the resemblance between the operation of the Spirit and electricity. Our life spirit is that power which is breathed into us from God at conception (Numbers 27:16). It is an invisible force which gives us power for life. It denotes action. Likewise, the Holy Spirit of God which comes and dwells in us when we are reborn spiritually is also an invisible power force. He is the source of power which enables us to obey God's Word and live a holy life. He motivates the holy activities and attitudes of our lives as we yield to His control.

When we become a Christian, the Spirit of God takes up His residence in our being. We become the temple of the Holy Spirit, which is a power source strong enough to conquer and overcome our attachments to the ways of the world and the desires of our sinful nature.

> You, dear children, are from God and have overcome them, because the one (referring to the Holy Spirit) who is in you is greater than the one who is in the world. (1 John 4:4, Words in parentheses are the author's.)

As Satan has seen his time drawing near, he has set out to do as much spiritual harm to Christianity as he can. And as prophesied in Revelation 13:7, the beast will have the power to overcome the way many Christians live by destroying their walk in their power source, the reliance upon the indwelling Holy Spirit.

Paul speaks of this same problem when talking about the last days. He says in II Timothy 3:5 that men will have a form of godliness, Christianity, but will deny its power. In verses one through four of this chapter he describes the characteristic traits that will be displayed in the last days when we deny the power of the Holy Spirit. People (including Christians) will love themselves, love money, be proud, disobedient to parents and authorities, unholy, immoral, unforgiving, without self-control, lovers of pleasure rather than God. In other words, this will be the nature our last-day society will develop in us if we deny by our lifestyle the indwelling power of the Holy Spirit. Paul says many of God's people will deny the use of this power and will develop these characteristics. The fruits of many in the Christian community now bear testimony to Paul's prophecy.

For Satan's spiritual attack in these last days to have the most success, it had to be very subtle and very deceiving. Yet it had to be able to teach, influence and dominate our minds and hearts. Therefore, Satan has taken something that is a part of God's creation and which resembles (in nature and in effect) a Christian's power source, the Holy Spirit. He has taken the invisible power source of electricity which has been perfected to the extent that its effects are now capable of influencing us during most of our waking hours.

Never in the history of man has there been a means to do so much teaching to so many at one time as through our present electronic media — a device by which we are continuously bombarded by false standards of the world. Just as the Holy Spirit is our invisible power source to motivate and empower our actions for holy living standards, Satan is using the effects of the invisible power source of electricity to motivate us and teach us the ways of a world society, thus implanting its standards in our minds.

The results of his attack on the Christian community are obvious. It is heartbreaking to see so many Christians with troubled marriages, going through divorce and having serious problems with children. Emotional stress and depression are at record levels. Business ethics have never been worse among Christians. And it appears the desire to hunger and thirst for righteousness is found in only a few. This should not be our testimony according to Jesus' words in Scripture:

> I have told you these things so that in me you may have peace. In this world you will have trouble. But take heart! I have overcome the world (the influence and pressures of society). (John 16:33)

> Everyone who believes that Jesus is the Christ is born of God, and everyone who loves the father loves his child as well. This is how we know that we love the children of God: by loving God and carrying out his commands. This is love for God: to obey his commands. And his commands are not burdensome, for everyone born of God has overcome the world. This is the victory that has overcome the world, even our faith. Who is it that overcomes the world (its standards and way of life)? Only he who believes that Jesus is the Son of God. (I John 5:1-5. Words in parentheses are the author's.)

God's commands are not burdensome because He supplies the power through His Holy Spirit for us to keep them. This is what it means to live under grace rather than by law, where we would have to try to keep God's commands through our own strength.

> For sin shall not be your master because you are not under law, but under grace. What then? Shall we sin because we are not under law but under grace? By no means! Don't you know that when you offer yourselves to someone to obey him as slaves, you are slaves to the one whom you obey – whether you are slaves to sin, which leads to death, or to obedience, which leads to righteousness? (Romans 6:14-16)

Law means that we try to do something for God. Grace is God doing something for us. To live the Christian life under law requires that we try to keep God's commands. When we do and we are honest, we soon discover we fail miserably— especially in those areas that deal with our inner nature, such as exhibiting love, patience, kindness and self-control. To live the Christian life under grace is to discover how to let God's power—the Holy Spirit—living in us supply the power to keep His commands and perfect His nature in us.

It is Satan's objective to keep us from walking in the power of the Holy Spirit, which not only makes God's commands difficult, but impossible—especially those that relate to our inner nature and character. Paul discovered this and discusses it in Romans chapter 7:

> For I have the desire to do what is good, but I cannot carry it out. For what I do is not the good I want to do; no, the evil I do not want to do—this I keep on doing. (Romans 7:18,19)

Paul discovered that even though he was a Christian and wanted to keep God's commands to be kind, patient, self-controlled, not easily angered, not self-seeking, never boastful (proud) and never keeping a record of the wrongs in others, he found he could not be that way in his inner being, even though it was his desire.

He said:

> I find this law at work: when I want to do good, evil is right there with me. For in my inner being I delight in God's law, but I see another law at work in the members of my body waging war against the law of my mind and making me a prisoner of the law of sin at work within my members. (Romans 7:21-23)

Then Paul found that the life in the Spirit was the secret of being able to carry out the commands of God, because the power of the indwelling Holy Spirit is greater than the power of our own self-seeking sinful nature—that power which keeps us from God's commands.

Romans chapter 8 is where Paul shares this discovery and teaching. When walking in the power of the Holy Spirit he says:

> That the righteous requirements of the law might be fully met in us, who do not live according to the sinful nature but according to the Spirit.

> Those who live according to the sinful nature (our own inner character) have their *minds* set on what that nature desires; but those who live in accordance with the Spirit have their *minds* set on what the Spirit desires. The *mind* of sinful man is death, but the *mind* controlled by the Spirit is life and peace, because the sinful *mind* is hostile to God. It does not submit to God's law (it is self-centered) nor can it do so. Those controlled by the sinful nature cannot please God. (Romans 8:4-8. Words in parentheses are the author's.)

Our Mind is the Spiritual Battleground

Notice how often Paul makes reference to our mind when talking about this subject of living in victory over sin. Control of the mind is the key to warfare in the spiritual realm. Satan knows this, and this is why he has grabbed at the chance to make use of electronics to control the minds of Christians. He wants us to walk with our minds set on the things of the world and what our own natural desires would be. When we do, we will not walk according to God's nature, keeping His commands, but as Paul says, we will walk according to the dictates of our sinful mind which is hostile to God. It does not submit to God's law, nor can it do so. Satan knows if he can get the attention of our mind and keep it on our own desires and pleasures, then we will not walk in the Spirit and live in accordance with God's plan for us. We will live wanting to please ourselves.

God's Word has much to say about the importance of our *mind* in the battle of living for God or for ourselves because that is where the spiritual battles are fought.

Paul says:

> I beg you that when I come I may not have to be as bold as I expect to be toward some people who think that we live by the standards of this world. For though we live in the world, we do not wage war as the world does. The weapons we war with are not the weapons of the world. On the contrary, they have divine power to demolish strongholds. We demolish arguments and every pretension that sets itself up against the knowledge of God, and we take captive every *thought* to make it obedient to Christ. (II Corinthians 10:2-5)

This is a difficult passage, and may seem hard to comprehend. But it helps us to understand how serious our spiritual warfare is, and why Satan is using all of the elements from the world system to control our mind.

That is why Paul says we do not wage war as the world thinks of waging war. Our weapons are not physical in nature. We are concerned with the spiritual warfare that is taking place in our inner being with the mind as the center of activity. Our weapons, which include God's Word, prayer and the indwelling Holy Spirit, have the power to stand against every worldly teaching Satan's world system might implant in our mind that is contrary to God's standards.

The thought life . . . this is where the battles take place. Satan wants to control our thoughts. That is why there are many Scriptures that teach the importance of the mind in spiritual warfare. Though we are Christians, our mind is not liberated. It suffers constant onslaughts from the enemy, many coming through our modern electronic media. In spiritual warfare, it is critical that we do not provide ground for the enemy in our mind, being influenced and accepting teachings from the standards of the world.

Eve was sinless in her heart, yet she received Satan's suggested thought in her mind and was deceived about God's Word. Paul, speaking to the Corinthians, said:

> But I am afraid that just as Eve was deceived by the serpent's cunning, your *minds* may somehow be led astray from your sincere and pure devotion to Christ. (II Corinthians 11:3)

The mind of our *old* nature cannot submit to God's will because as Romans 8;7 states, it can't. Our mind must, therefore, be renewed in order to know the will of God—to know God's direction for our life.

> Therefore, I urge you, brothers, in view of God's mercy, to offer your bodies as living sacrifices, holy and pleasing to God, which is your spiritual worship. Do not conform any longer to the pattern of this world, but be transformed by the renewing of your *mind.* Then you will be able to test and approve what God's will is—his good, pleasing and perfect will. (Romans 12:1,2)

It is Satan's objective to prevent a renewing of our mind, using all possible worldly means to distract and occupy our mind. Today he is able to implant many thoughts and ideas through the use of electronics from the world system which tempts us to step out and become independent of God's Word and direction. We are to be aware of the purpose of these temptations.

> When tempted, no one should say, "God is tempting me." For God cannot be tempted by evil, nor does he tempt anyone; but each one is tempted when, by his own evil desire, he is dragged away and enticed. Then after desire has conceived, it gives birth to sin. And sin, when it is full grown, gives birth to death. Don't be deceived, my dear brothers. (James 1:13-16)

> So I say, live by the Spirit, and you will not gratify the desires of the sinful nature. For the sinful nature desires what is contrary to the Spirit and the Spirit what is contrary to the sinful nature. They are in conflict with each other, so that you do not do what you want. But if you are led by the Spirit, you are not under law. (Galatians 5:16-18)

Paul is teaching just as he taught in Romans 7 and 8 that the key is to live in the power of the Holy Spirit. It is only this power that can equip us to keep the true commands of God. When we are *not* led by the Spirit we are apt to put ourselves under a law-keeping religious system. These laws and doctrines that we establish will always be physical in nature so that we can keep them in the strength of our own will. Then, as we keep these doctrinal laws, the enemy will cause us to think we are living and walking in the Spirit because we are adhering to certain physical requirements.

Satan constantly tries to tempt Christians to yield to our own desires, our own strength, even in religious activities. When we yield to just our wishes, that stops the flow of God's power and we cannot obey God's Word—at least that part that controls our character. The result is that we fall and commit sin. The sin may be in the realm of pride, covetousness, or lack of self-control, jealousy, or it may be something more obvious. Regardless, we will act just like many people who are of the world, and we will experience their same problems. Divorce is a good example. It is now as widespread among Christians as those who are of the world. This should not be. Scripture says God hates divorce. He knows the inner pain it causes to those involved, and the sin of adultery that is often associated with divorce.

We are accountable to and equipped by God to wage warfare against the temptations in our thought life, not allowing the enemy to operate and cause us to fall.

> No temptation has seized you except what is common to man. And God is faithful; he will not let you be tempted beyond what you can bear. But when you are tempted, he will also provide a way out so that you can stand up under it. (I Corinthians 10:13)

However, Pauls says in II Timothy 3:1-5 that it is going to be difficult to live the committed Christian life in the last days, and many will deny the power of the Holy Spirit given by God to wage spiritual warfare and win the temptation battles over sin. He says this will be evident by the characteristics expressed through Christians. They will be lovers of them-selves, lovers of money, boastful, proud, disobedient to parents, unholy (immoral), ungrateful, without self-control, conceited, lovers of pleasure rather than God. Jesus gave similar prophetic warnings in Matthew 24:36-38 and Luke 21:34.

John prophesies that Satan will develop this condition, attacking the testimony of Christians through the system of the beast. (Revelation 12:17 through chapter 13) The beast system will have the power to overcome (conquer the tes-timony of Christians) by using the things of its society to cause us to quench the power of God's Holy Spirit in our life—our power to battle against the temptations Satan is throwing at our sinful nature. Both Revelation 13:7 and Daniel 7:21,25 tell us this will occur in the last days.

We need constant reminders that the main purpose for the power of the Holy Spirit in our lives, in addition to lifting up the name of Jesus, is to empower us to overcome the power of our inner sinful nature.

Perhaps you think I dwell a great deal on our sinful nature. So does the Bible—not in a condemning way, but in a truth-ful, helpful way. We are by nature self-centered, even in the good things we do. I believe the best way to deal with a weakness is to expose it. This will cause us to realize our dependence on God's power. Paul discovered this after he became a Christian and cried out, "What a wretched man I am." (Romans 7:24) He wasn't talking about condemnation, because he knew there was no condemnation for those who belonged to Christ Jesus. (Romans 8:1) But when he saw his true inner nature and the work of the law of sin, it drove him to seek God's way of walking in the power of His Spirit. (Ro-mans 7:14-8:8).

Let there be no mistake: The Bible focuses its emphasis on being filled with the Spirit so we may overcome the power of our self-centered desires. The evidence of being Spirit-filled will be demonstrated through our inner character and outer actions having victory over sin. That is what it means to be Christ-like.

> My dear children, I write this to you so that you will not sin. But if anybody does sin, we have one who speaks to the Father in our defense—Jesus Christ, the Righteous One. He is the atoning sacrifice for our sins, and not only for ours but also for the sins of the whole world.

> We know that we have come to know him if we obey his commands. The man who says, "I know him," but does not do what he commands is a liar, and the truth is not in him. But if anyone obeys his word, God's love is truly made complete in him. This is how we know we are in him: Whoever claims to live in him must walk as Jesus did. (I John 2:1-6)

John says it is he who has a desire to keep God's Word in whom true love for God is perfected. He states that anyone who says he abides in Christ ought to walk in the same way that He walked, which was in the indwelling power of the Holy Spirit of God. That is what it means to be filled with the Spirit—to walk as Jesus did.

We will not be sinless, however, as Jesus was. We are not that spiritual, and we won't let go of all our sinful self-serving desires. But I believe the Scriptures teach that our desire will be to obey the whole Word of God as we learn it. We will not rebel against any of its teachings. We will not set ourselves up in the temple of God saying what is important and what is not, but we will gladly follow God in yielding to His Word and direction as He gives us understanding. We will walk as Jesus walked in that we will rest our faith in the power and direction of the indwelling Holy Spirit, denying our own understanding and self-will as we grow, and learning not to depend on the power of our own self-will. If we really know Him, we will know that these attitudes will continually grow in us because the same Spirit that lived in Jesus is now living in us.

Many Christians today, I feel, are focusing too much on spiritual gifts as indication of being filled with the Spirit. I know the value of these gifts to the Body of Christ. I have certain spiritual gifts myself and believe any gift from God is good. However, the Scriptures do not teach that gifts are a sign of spirituality or that we are walking in the Spirit. Only fruits, which reveal the nature of God's character dwelling in us, give evidence of our being filled and walking in the power of the Holy Spirit. The emphasis in God's Word of walking in the Spirit and living the victorious Christian life will be evidenced by our victory over sin. That was true in the life of Jesus, the Apostles and Christians throughout the centuries. God's Word has not changed.

John saw that the beast system, working primarily through man's use of electronics, was able to attack and keep Christians from yielding to the power of the Holy Spirit as did Jesus and others.

The Counterfeiter

We can learn much about the methods of Satan by examining the teaching methods of the Holy Spirit. Satan is the great counterfeiter so as he attempts to teach and influence Christians, he will be trying to copy those techniques used by the Holy Spirit. Both the Holy Spirit of God and unholy spirit of Satan want to train, teach, mold and control our attitudes, thoughts, conscience and spiritual position. The Holy Spirit of God teaches us by giving enlightenment on God's Word which He inspired men to write. The various experiences through which He guides us teach us to depend on the power of His indwelling presence. We learn, too, through the trials and testimonies of other Christians. The unholy spirit of Satan doesn't have to dwell within us to control us. All he has to do is cause us to yield to "self" or our old nature of the flesh. (Ephesians 2:1-3) Satan will attempt to control us and keep us walking in the strength of our own will power through the attractions of his world system.

As children of God and members of the spiritual Body of Christ, we must constantly be aware of the teaching methods

of these two spiritual beings. We must realize that each pos-
sesses tremendous spiritual power to influence us. Each
desires to exercise over us whatever dominion we will allow.
Do we have a desire to yield by faith to the power of the
indwelling Spirit of God, or do we have a desire to yield to
the "self-will power" of our old nature? Each of us must
choose to whom we will yield. (Romans 6:13,16,19)

Our minds are at work continuously, feeding the spiritual
part of our beings. If we yield ourselves to the teaching and
influence of the Spirit of God so that He can feed our hearts
with thoughts of the Lord Jesus Christ and the understanding
of God's precious Word, then our hearts will develop His
image to the extent of our faith and complete dependence
upon Him. If on the other hand we let our minds feed our
spirits with the thoughts and standards of the world, serving
ourselves, then our hearts will cause us to act like poeple of
the world. If Satan can influence us to think about "self," we
will soon forget about Jesus. Satan's influence develops in us
an "independent attitude" which prevents us from realizing
the need to a deep commitment to Jesus as Lord. And this
prohibits us from walking in the power of the Spirit of God.

Most of us don't suspect that many of the ideas taking
root in our minds are often inspired by Satan. They come
from the spiritual influence of his world. This is especially
true today because of the multiplicity of methods available
which so strongly influence and teach us the ways of our
society. Satan is making a strong attack on our minds because
he knows that to have the most influence on our spiritual
being, our minds must be his prime target. This spiritual truth
is taught by Solomon when he states this about mankind:

For as he thinketh in his heart, so is he. (Proverbs 23:7, KJV)

Satan has developed a society in the United States which
has great power to deceive, influence and control our thinking. Of course, this satanic plot has been developed in a very
subtle way.

Satan is not allowed to violate our will. He is limited strictly to suggestions. However, the power of suggestion is one of the greatest forces that can motivate us. Satan is masterful in using this power. His knowledge of human weakness has enabled him to design a way to present his deceiving suggestions so we'll use "self-will power" to get things done, regardless of the area of endeavor. This has been a great part of his strategy for attacking the saints in these last days. He has tried to prevent us from understanding the true spiritual walk—that of denying self-will. This denial is the necessary ingredient for spiritual victory.

If we understand that to spiritually influence and control man Satan must control his mind, or thought life, we will be in a better position to understand the teaching power system of the "second beast" or "false prophet." John prophetically describes this teaching power of the "second beast" (the false spiritual influence of society) when he says, "It had two horns like a lamb and spoke like a dragon." Satan draws this power out of something God put into the world. The Spirit of the Lord has revealed John is prophesying about the power of electricity as he saw its ability to teach and control our minds, and therefore, to spiritually influence our standards.

Our Exposure

Handling our exposure to the electronic media—TV, radio, movies, video, music, etc., is crucial in our spiritual walk and development because these devices communicate to our mind.

We should think of the media as a "teacher." Anything that has the capability of implanting thoughts or ideas into our mind should be thought of as a potential teacher. We must ask, "What spiritual principles of life am I or my children being taught? How do they compare to the counsel of God's Word?"

God's Word has many good directives that pertain to this subject. For example:

Blessed is the man who *does not walk in the counsel* of the wicked or stand in the way of sinners or sit in the seat of mockers. But his delight is in the law of the Lord, and on his law he meditates day and night. For the Lord watches over the way of the righteous, but the way of the wicked will perish. (Psalm 1:1,2,6)

I will sing of your love and justice; to you, O Lord, I will sing praise. I will be careful to lead a blameless life—when will you come to me? I will walk in my house with blameless heart. *I will set before my eyes no vile thing.* The deeds of faithless men I hate; they will not cling to me. Men of perverse heart shall be far from me; I will have nothing to do with evil. (Psalm 101:1-4)

The key to spiritual victory or defeat is determined by how we set our minds.

John saw the electronic media's power to teach worldly ideas as a vital element in the end-time spiritual warfare. (Revelation 13:11) It is an element which God's people never had to contend with before. There has never been a means with which to teach so many at one time—exposing our minds to the standards of the world.

Most Effective Electronic Media

Satan's most effective use of this electronic media is television. Its impact is both audible and visual. This subtle educational tool of Satan is in nearly every American home — over 170 million sets throughout the country—and has literally commanded the time and attention of almost everyone. An average child in our society will have watched from 18,000 to 22,000 hours of television by the time he or she is 18 years old. It is also estimated that by the time an individual is 65 years old they will have been under the influence of this false teaching device for a total time equal to ten years. By contrast, if the same person went to church every Sunday until age 65, they would have spent an equivalent of only four months studying the Bible.

The National Commission on the Causes and Prevention of Violence reported as early as October of 1969 that "The preponderance of the available evidence strongly suggests that violence in TV programs can and does have adverse effects upon audiences." This report explains how powerful television is in the learning processes of children. "Television is teaching moral and social values about violence which are inconsistent with the standards of a civilized society." Please note: this report compares the commission's findings with the norm for what is considered to be a civilized society. The norm for a society which claims to follow biblical standards should be much higher.

This report reveals how violence is promoted on television as an acceptable standard of achieving ends and handling difficult situations. Even more devastating is the fact that TV, with its accessibility, now has a much greater influence on standards and the general teaching of children than a child's own parents. The report comments: "The TV set is never too busy to talk to them, and it never has to brush them aside while it does household chores. Unlike their preoccupied parents, TV seems to want their attention at any time and goes to considerable lengths to attract it. Indeed, parents too often use the TV set as an abdication of their parental responsibility to instill proper values into their children."

Paul A. Witty of Northwestern University has commented on this subject, stating, "Children gradually come to accept violence, hate, and destruction as normal ways of life. Their sensitivity to human suffering gradually becomes affronted by frequent exposure to anti-social behavior."

Notice how Satan is using this teaching weapon as well as other teaching outlets in our society (including many schools in our society) to cause our minds to be clouded to the basic issues which personalize man as a human being. Such characteristics as love, concern for others, mercy, compassion, patience, self-control and kindness have been greatly de-emphasized in recent years. Many Christians actually serve and, therefore, worship the self-seeking life style society has created, while that society is destroying the very nature of God, which includes those characteristics just listed.

John Killackey, a deputy superintendent of police in Chicago states, "If you ask a young person today whether he knows it is a sin to kill somebody, he is likely to ask you, 'What is sin?' Boys and girls don't go to church anymore, and more and more of them are living in broken homes. Add to this the fact that they are subjected to a steady diet of stabbing, maiming, strangling, shooting, burning and boiling on television and in movies, and you can see why young people are not likely to care or know about law and order."

Former Federal Communications Commissioner Nicholas Johnson says, "Children get more verbal impact from radio and television than from parents, teachers, neighbors and church combined." He further indicates that the songs they usually sing are commercials, their heroes have been created in Hollywood, and the possessions they crave are those of the sponsors.

Even the advertising on television has become an influential giant. It is being used by Satan to draw the masses to desire worldly things and develop worldly lust. The next time you watch television, run a spiritual test on advertisements. Observe how advertisements are directed at the three areas which comprise our sin nature: the lust of the flesh, the lust of the eyes and the pride of life (being somebody). Notice how many advertisements fit into the same pattern of selling a product that Satan used in tempting and deceiving Eve (Genesis 3:1-6) and in tempting and trying to deceive Jesus. (Matthew 4:1-10)

In addition to the problem of accepting violence as a proper norm, we're also being taught through this convincing worldly media to accept an ever-increasing emphasis on sex and the lowering of moral standards. The deterioration of our moral standards is one of the most influential educational tasks now being accomplished by this electronic media. Many have now adopted a licentious attitude toward sex and under the guise of freedom, everyone is permitted his sexual preference.

Today many of the programs and movies being shown on television are considered charmingly modest, and yet a few years ago, they would have been considered the bottom of the barrel in permissiveness. And it's all presented to appear both attractive and proper.

Satan is attacking Christians today by trying to cause as many as he can to break and rebel against the teachings in God's Word. He is causing tremendous pressures through his world teaching system. We can see this by the rapid increase in heart trouble, mental illness, suicide, violence, divorce and other social problems. We are allowing ourselves to be taught and influenced by this false teaching prophet of the world — the media of mass communication which is capturing our time and our minds daily.

Most Christians spend a great deal of time watching television, listening to the radio or stereo, reading books, newspapers or magazines — continuously involving themselves in worldly pursuits. God instructs us to meditate upon His Word or things of His Spirit. To which spirit do we give the most time? Satan has deceived us to the point that our worldly teacher (false prophet), the mass communication media, has become so much a part of our environment we hardly question its existence, much less its main purpose. It has almost become another sense and a part of our natural way of life as the "world now comes into our livings rooms." We no longer have to go out into the streets to find it.

This point is illustrated very well by a poem I came across, entitled "The Devil's Vision."

The devil once said to his demons below,
"Our work is progressing entirely too slow.
The holiness people stand in our way
Since they do not believe in the show or the play.
They teach that the carnival, circus and dance

The tavern and honky-tonk with game of chance,
Drinking and smoking, these things are all wrong;
That Christians don't mess with the ungodly throng;
They are quick to condemn everything that we do
To cause unbelievers to be not a few.
They claim that these things are all of the devil;
That Christian folks live on a much higher level.
Now, fellows, their theology, while perfectly true
Is blocking the work we are trying to do.
We will have to get busy and figure a plan
That will change their standards as fast as we can.
Now I have a vision of just what we can do,
Harken, I'll tell this deception to you;
Then find ye a wise, but degenerate man
Whom I can use to help work out this plan.
There's nothing so real as the things that you see;
The eyes and the mind and the heart will agree;
So what can be better than an object to view?
I say, it will work and convince not a few.
The home is the place for this sinful device,
The people deceived will think it quite nice.
The world will possess it, most Christians can't tell
That it is all of the devil and plotted in hell!
We'll sell them with pictures of the latest news
And while they're still looking, we'll advertise booze.
At first it will shock them; they'll seem in a daze,
But soon they'll be hardened and continue to gaze.
We'll give them some gospel that isn't too strong
And a few sacred songs to string them along.
They'll take in the ads, with the latest of fashions
And soon watch the shows that will stir evil passions.
Murder and love-making scenes they'll behold
Until their souls will be utterly cold.
The old family altar which once held such charm
Will soon lose its place without much alarm.
Praying in secret will also be lost
As they look at the screen without counting the cost.
The compromise preachers, who don't take their stand,
Will embrace this new vision and think it is grand.

They'll help fool the people and cause them to sin
By seeking this evil and taking it in.
Influence is great and this you can see;
Just look at my fall and you'll have to agree.
It won't take too long, my demons, to tell
That the vision of Satan will populate hell!
Divorce will increase, sex crimes will abound;
Much innocent blood will be spilled on the ground.
The home will be damned in short order I say,
When this vision of mine comes in to stay.
Get busy, my cohorts, and put this thing out;
We'll see if the church can continue to shout.
The holiness people who stand in our way
Will soon hush their crying against show and play.
We'll cover the earth with this devil vision
Then we'll camouflage it with the name television.
The people will think they are getting a treat
Till the antichrist comes and takes over his seat.
He'll rule the world while the viewers behold
The face of the beast, to whom they were sold.
We'll win through deception, this cannot fail;
Though some holiness preachers against it will rail."

(Author Unknown)

We know that man's technological use of electronics is the power source of the second beast which John saw, and is being used to develop and perform its great miracles and signs.

It has been because of man's technological advancements in the field of electronics that the "things of the world" have been able to both teach us and supply us with many of our needs. This has created in us a strong independent attitude. It is actually impossible to properly evaluate how much the advancement of modern technology has clouded man's basic existence. Human concerns for others such as mercy, love and compassion (characteristics of God) now take a back seat to the pursuit of more and better things in the world, with the use of faster methods and machines. Our confidence and dependence on God has been replaced by confidence in modern day technology because we have let it become the ultimate cure for our ills. American technology has become the theology of a system that promises salvation by materialism. Senator Mark Hatfield observed this and stated, "In many ways, God has been replaced by technology and we worship at the altar of materialism. When we are in trouble, we rely on the technological fix, instead of faith."

As recorded in Revelation, John saw miracles, wonders and signs happening every day as he observed what was taking place through this invisible power source of electronics, even though we may consider them commonplace. The field of electronics includes our total communications media and much more. In fact, if we pause for a moment of contemplation, we soon realize how dependent man has become on the technology of electricity in all avenues of life. This is not evil within itself, but Satan is using it wherever he can for an evil purpose to cause us to develop our own independence. Even though this is a prevalent philosophy, it is contrary to the teachings of the Lord Jesus Christ.

Test of a False Teacher

John saw the method used by Satan's world and its ability to teach stating, "It had two horns like a lamb and it spoke like a dragon." (Revelation 13:11) Jesus gave us a test to use on anything that has the ability to teach and affect our mind so that we can determine whether it has a spirit of a false teacher.

Watch out for false prophets. They come to you in sheep's clothing, but inwardly they are ferocious wolves. By their fruit you will recognize them. Do people pick grapes from thornbushes, or figs from thistles? Likewise every good tree bears good fruit, but a bad tree bears bad fruit. A good tree cannot bear bad fruit, and a bad tree cannot bear good fruit. Every tree that does not bear good fruit is cut down and thrown into the fire. Thus, by their fruit you will recognize them. (Matthew 7:15-20)

There are several considerations in the test from Jesus to determine whether or not the teaching influence coming out of our society is that of a false prophet. Here are some of them:

1. It comes in sheep's clothing; it appears to be harmless.

2. Inwardly it is like a ravenous wolf; its spiritual influence may appear to be harmless, but it is trying to destroy our spiritual relationship with God, His power in our life and our commitment to the teachings of His Word.

3. Therefore, examine its fruits because you will know it by its fruits.

4. A true prophet bears good fruit. It can't bear evil fruit. This would be reflected in a growing dependence on the power of God in our life which brings victory over sin.

5. Likewise, a false spiritual influence will bear evil fruit and develop a growing spiritual attitude in the people of being "independent," wanting no accountability and seeking to satisfy their own desires, even in Christian activities.

6. The evil prophet may use the name of God or Lord, and promote many mighty works in His name to gain our acceptance, but it will not result in obedience to the will and Word of God.

To test the spiritual influence of our society, we should do as Jesus instructed and examine the fruits of our society, not our works. This test should be from the time we began to reign on the throne of the world at the end of World War II. An examination of our fruits helps to broaden our understanding of the reality of Satan's attack and the power he has released in our society. Some of the areas to examine would include crime and violence, racism, drugs and narcotics, the sex revolution, gambling, greed, alcohol, pleasure seeking, failures in the home, business ethics, and open blasphemy against God.

Other Societies

Some might ask, "Haven't these fruits been evident in other societies?" Of course, the answer is "yes." But never has a single society experienced such a breakdown in so short a period of time! Never has the attitude of a society changed so drastically as ours since we took over the throne of the world at the end of World War II. This is an even greater realization when we take into account that our forefathers established our Constitution on Christian principles. This has not been the case in other societies.

The satanic power being displayed by our society's spiritual influence and pressure is beyond man's ability to cope with or understand. This is reflected in the fact that over 50 percent of the hospital beds in America are now filled with mental patients.

It seems that most of us in America no longer seem to know what the standards of a civilized society should be. We have been influenced thoroughly by a satanic power behind the scenes. The spiritual fruits of a godly influence in any society will be characterized by love for one another, the existence of peace among its people, the presence of joy, and the growth of an attitude of patience, kindness, goodness, faithfulness, gentleness and self-control! These are characteristics of God that are manifested when we yield to Him and truly follow His ways.

Jesus Christ said, "You shall know them by their fruits." We have been under the power of a false prophet so deceptive that we have not been able to detect its spiritual influence — an influence which has developed an attitude in its people that has caused them to be the most self-centered, independent and haughty society in existence. It would deceive even the elect, if God would allow it. (Matthew 24:24) Whether we like to accept this truth or not, fruits reveal true identity, and Jesus says that we shall know a false spiritual influence by its fruits, not by its name or by its mighty works.

Chapter 9

LATEST DEVELOPMENTS ON THE MARK OF THE BEAST

I begin this chapter knowing its title is not totally correct. Regardless of my recent research, there could be new developments in electronics technology announced within weeks after I finish. It's a constantly changing field.

I am not an electronics expert. However, there are events we need to be aware of which make use of the electronic power system John saw Satan using to his advantage. We need to understand the potential of giving the "beast system" control over our lives, which is closing in on us at a rapid pace.

John, the writer of Revelation, describes some conditions that will be accomplished in our society through the use of electronics at the end of the Gentile Age in which we now live. He begins with a reference to the "second beast," or our present society:

> It exercises all the authority of the first beast in its presence, and makes the earth and its inhabitants worship the first beast whose mortal wound was healed. It works great signs, even making fire come down from heaven to earth in the

sight of men; and by the signs which it is allowed to work in the presence of the beast, it deceives those who dwell on earth, bidding them make an image for the beast which was wounded by the sword and yet lived; and it was allowed to give breath to the image of the beast so that the image of the beast should even speak, and to cause those who would not worship the image of the beast to be slain. Also it causes all, both small and great, both rich and poor, both free and slave, to be marked on the right hand or the forehead so that no one can buy or sell unless he has the mark, that is, the name of the beast or the number of its name. This calls for wisdom; let him who has understanding reckon the number of the beast, for it is a human number, its number is six hundred and sixty-six. (Revelation 13:12-18)

John, inspired by the Holy Spirit, wrote these words nearly 1900 years ago. As we review what he saw then, pay attention to how specifically he defines certain "numbers" and "marks." Until recent years these verses baffled Bible scholars. Now that we have a clearer understanding of the meaning of these verses, there is perhaps no passage of Scripture which better proves the accuracy and inspiration of God's Word. You may agree after our discussion of how these truths are coming to pass in our lifetime. (In the following verses, words in parentheses are inserted by the author for clarity.)

It exercises all the authority of the first beast in its presence, and makes the earth and its inhabitants worship the first beast whose mortal wound was healed. (Revelation 13:12)

The second beast (our society), through the capability of its power source, causes people to have awesome respect for the world position of our government. That is how the word "worship" is used by John. By strict definition it means to hold in awe. Since World War II, the attitude of people throughout the world has been one of high regard for our political, military and economic strength. This has been made possible through our society's tremendous output of goods and services. John foresaw that this was how the second beast would cause people to worship (hold in high esteem) the power and position of the first beast (our government).

Stating that the second beast (our society) is what has caused the world to hold our government's world position in awe is a unique description. In the past, world governments that became so powerful to be described as "beast" because of their power were developed primarily through the strong leadership of dictators or rulers. This is not the case with our government's world position. John prophesies it will be because of the strength of the second beast, our society, that our government will become so prominent. Historical facts prove this to be true.

The industrial, economic, agricultural and professional output of goods and services in our society is what has made our government's political and military position so strong. The establishment of empires in the past came about through military conquest. Then the victors would tax the people they conquered and/or confiscate their natural resources, goods and services. This has not been true in our country's development. And we are the only system which has fulfilled this unique prophetic description.

Working Great Signs

> It (the output of our society) works great signs, even making fire come down from heaven to earth in the sight of men; and by the signs which it is allowed to work in the presence of the beast, it deceives those who dwell on earth. (Revelation 13:13,14)

John saw miracles taking place through the use of electronics, though today we consider them commonplace. Throughout our present society men are beginning to ponder if we are not in danger of seeing electronic technology become the theology of our society. It is a known fact that we have become increasingly dependent upon electronics.

John states many will be deceived through the use of electronics. The technology to implant worldly temptations and to teach and deceive our minds through the use of the electronic media is overwhelming today. We can clearly see John's prophecy of Revelation 13:7 being fulfilled where he said, "It (the beast) will have the power to overcome the saints." Most of us are "overcome" today in living the victorious Christian life, due to the power of the beast system to tempt our sinful nature. One can hardly question that the living standards of many Christians have changed dramatically due to the teaching of worldly standards coming through our electronic media.

Many Christians seem oblivious to the spiritual dangers and their effects when we openly expose ourselves to the teaching influence of Satan's world system. Eve listened to Satan's temptation. Though she had been commanded not to eat of the tree of the knowledge of good and evil, she was deceived, and fell. She experienced spiritual defeat, which then caused other trials.

The fruits being revealed through the lives of Christians today tell us our spiritual walk is more like the experience of Eve, rather than that of Christ, who won victory over sin and the temptations of the world.

An Image

> It deceives those who dwell on earth, bidding them make an image for the beast which was wounded by the sword and yet lived; and it was allowed to give breath to the image of the beast so that the image of the beast should even speak, and to cause those who would not worship (serve) the image of the beast to be slain. (Revelation 13:14,15)

John saw the power of the second beast (man's technical knowledge developed through the resources of our society) make an image for the first beast. This image will be an electronic image created out of the wisdom of man, symbolic of the philosophy of our world governmental power. The Greek word John uses for "image" in these Scriptures is "eikon." This word involves the two ideas of "representation" and "manifestation."

An image that best represents and manifests the United States today would be a technological tool that would make people dependent on its use. And all the while this technological image will enable the first beast (our government) to control the people living under its rule because we become so dependent on it for our material and pleasure desires. I do not have any direct revelation from the Lord as to the identity of this image, but knowing that its power source is electricity, all indications tie it to the electronic computer. I'll give you a few reasons why. You may already be aware of some of them.

Our society has become almost totally dependent upon the computer. It has been evolving since the end of World War II when the first beast (our empire) began to reign over Satan's kingdom, the world.

The computer has had more impact in creating our materialistic independent attitudes than any other device man has invented. Through-out present day technology the growth of computers has been phenomenal. In 1965 computers were a six billion dollar business. Today that figure is close to 100 billion dollars.

The entire world of commerce and industry now functions by the use of computers. Our country's space program was able to out-perform Russia in going to the moon because of our advanced state of computerization.

Computers make airline and motel reservations, monitor cardiac care patients in hospitals, figure our payrolls, check our credit, control scientific experiments, forecast trends in the economy, and even help to educate our children. Computers are the most amazing machines ever built by man. They come in all shapes and sizes. They are used by department stores, hospitals, banks, airlines, utilities, government agencies, credit card organizations, industrial plants, post offices, schools, universities, publishing companies and hundreds of other organizations that affect and, perhaps, control our daily lives. Without computers, hardly an industry or large organization could remain the same; there would be disorder—even chaos.

Our alarming dependency on computers seems bound to increase. If we decide to take a plane trip, we might use a computer-checked credit card or a bank check, also handled by a computer, to pay for our computer-recorded ticket. We may drive to the airport in our computer-designed car over computer-designed roads through computer-controlled intersections. We would ride a computer-designed airplane, sit in our seat wearing clothing made of cloth cut by a computer, and read a newpaper set in type by a computer.

Computers can solve in tenths of a second scientific problems which took hours to solve in 1950. In a few seconds, a medium-sized computer can calculate the answer to a problem that would take someone a hundred days to solve if that person did not eat, sleep or do anything but add. In ten seconds a human can add two four digit numbers, while a computer can balance 10,000 checking accounts without making a mistake. The computer is providing knowledge at an unbelievable rate even though considered to be still in its "age of infancy."

In Daniel 12:4, we find the following statement: "But Daniel, keep this prophecy a secret; seal it up so that it will not be understood until the end times, when travel and education shall be vastly increased!" (Living Bible) It is incredible how this prophecy describes the technology of our day. The "knowledge explosion" we now see has been made possible through the use of the electronic computer.

The computer is only about 35 years old, yet it can now accomplish the thinking of millions of human brains. For example, there are single computers that can perform nearly one billion transactions in one second, easily capable of storing records concerning every person on earth. And Control Data Corporation recently announced plans to manufacture the "world's fastest" computers. Its initial product mission will be to develop a 10-gigaflop (10 billion calculations per second) machine for delivery by the of 1986. Their end-use is almost all to the government. The Apollo 13 flight which ran into trouble 205,000 miles from earth had its flight problems solved by scientists who worked out the corrections on a computer in 84 minutes. To accomplish the same amount of work before the computer, it would have taken one man with pencil and paper 1,040,256 years.

It has been approximated that human knowledge doubled only once up until the year 1800 A.D. Between 1800 and 1900 human knowledge doubled again. Today it is estimated that our knowledge is now doubling every ten to 15 years, and some experts say it is doubling every six years.

Words are inadequate to describe the advances now taking place in computer and interactive technology of recent years. A tiny ten-dollar microprocessor, which fits on the tip of a finger, is equivalent to a computer which filled a room and cost $500,000 a few years ago. And even these developments will soon be eclipsed by more powerful microcomputers— computers that according to a computer scientist "can be commanded rather than programmed." Computers costing nine million dollars today will be held in our hand within three to five years.

The C2E2 Computer was called "one of the most advanced of its type" by *Apple* magazine. "It turns on and off lights, radios or TV sets, types letters, answers the telephone, composes music, etc. . . . all by voice command."

It has been said by those in the know that "Had the automobile developed at a pace equivalent to that of the computer during the past 20 years, today a Rolls Royce would cost less than $3.00, get three million miles to the gallon, deliver enough power to propel the ocean liner Queen Elizabeth II, and six of them would fit on the head of a pin. If the airlines had progressed as rapidly as this technology, the Concorde would be carrying half a million passengers at 20 million miles an hour for less than a penny apiece!"

Words to explain the technological revolution which will drastically change the structure of society are understatements before they are written. One thing is clear: before the end of this decade, electronic voices will be squawking at people from all manner of everyday objects including vacuum cleaners, washing machines, alarm clocks and car dashboards.

A new microwave oven can "respond to your verbal instructions, and announce in its own voice when the meal is completed." New television sets in Japan now turn on and off and change channels by voice command. Electronic "talking" devices are now mass produced by Texas Instruments, an American company. Bell Telephone is projecting cordless phones and a national telephone number for each individual. Hitachi produces a "voice response system which lets a computer speak with a natural human voice." These voices are now being heard through various service media. For example, computer voices are making phone calls, conducting pre-programmed surveys.

Mark of the Beast

According to John's prophecies, "the image" or computer will have the electronic capabilities of controlling man through a marking system of numbers.

> Also it causes all, both small and great, both rich and poor, both free and slave, to be marked on the right hand or the forehead, so that no one can buy or sell unless he has the mark, that is, the name of the beast or the number of its name. This calls for wisdom: let him who has understanding

reckon the number of the beast, for it is a human number, its number is six hundred and sixty-six. (Revelation 13:16-18)

It is important to review how certain numbers are used in the Scriptures and note their symbolic significance. For example, the numeral seven denotes something that is complete or full. In the Bible, the numeral six refers to man, and this is why John says that 666 is a human number. For example, man was created on the sixth day, man's appointed days of labor and toil are six, the Hebrew slave was to serve for six years, and for six years the land was to be sown.

In Revelation 13:18 John combines six with six and another six, spiritually indicating the increase in man's own self development that takes place in the period near the end. John uses a trinity of this number to show that man becomes obsessed with his own self sufficiency through the deception of the beast and his commitment to his own technological powers. The triad of man's being—spirit, soul and body (I Thessalonians 5:23)—becomes committed in placing "himself" above all other gods. As Paul says in II Thessalonians 2:4, he "opposes and exalts himself against every so-called god or object of worship so that he takes his seat in the temple (his own body) of God proclaiming himself to be God" (by the faith he places in his own technical advancements).

The spiritual significance of this number, John says, is a "human number" and is important for our overall understanding of the cause of the rebellion, or falling away, that will take place in the geographical center of Christianity near the end times. We have learned from John's prophecies that man sets himself up in the temple of God because he is influenced by today's technological power to become too self-sufficient, too independent. These developments have caused us to serve ourselves like a god.

It appears that because we become so dependent on the

"image" of the beast, the computer, John tells us the beast system will be able to implement control of the people by regulating buying and selling through a marking system which uses numbers. It has only been possible in recent years to imagine how these prophetic Scriptures would be fulfilled.

The use of computers, credit cards, bank cards and numbering systems now cause our economic affairs to be handled through electronics, and is a confirmation that the power system of the beast could be electricity, as was revealed to my brother in 1971. That could be what John saw and described with the prophetic words which he wrote.

In 1980 a radical change occurred in credit cards, making them debit cards. The debit card eliminates credit, moving us closer to "electronic money" and a cashless society.

Computer systems are available now that will eliminate the need for money. Buying and selling transactions are handled by a computer number through an individual's bank. Pilot cities are already operating on this system. John prophesies that the time will come when it will be necessary to have the mark of the beast or we will not be able to buy and sell. He mentions this mark as being a number. Satan is steadily working on the consciences of people in our society, conditioning them to accept the use of a numbering system as a means of control. For example, our Social Security numbering system is set up to record personal data, including age, name, number of children, salary, credit rating and many personal habits. It is now used to control many of the things we need to obtain to live in our society—drivers licenses, checking accounts and credit. We can't be employed, and in some places can't obtain public utilities, without a Social Security number.

There's a growing fear that the computer is setting the stage for a "Big Brother" society. Until the computer, the concept of a controlled society in our land was fictional to the majority of people.

We are all tied to a computer through our Social Security number, driver's license number, birth certificate and credit card numbers. Every geographical move we have made, every penny that we have paid to the Internal Revenue Service each year, is all on computer record.

A key to identifying the numbering system of the beast is the number "666." (Revelation 13:18) The number six throughout Scripture relates to man and his developments. It is through our own electronic achievement that man will set up the system which will allow the beast to control our buying and selling. It will be done through a numbering system encoded with the number "666." The number "666" has gained prominence in recent years due to its computer application.

The world bank code number is "666." It has been reported that Sears, Penney's, Montgomery Ward and others use "666" as a transaction prefix number. IBM's supermarket equipment is prefixed with the number 3-"666."

The three digit international card code number is "666" and banking officials report all new banking cards have the prefix "666" encoded on the magnetic tape on the back of the card, invisible to the naked eye. The same is true with various charge and debit cards such as Visa and Mastercard. If you have one of these cards, look on the back. There is a brown magnetic tape about one-half inch wide by three inches long. Up to 100,000 characters of information can be micro-encoded on this magnetic strip. There are new micro-chips the size of a fingernail that are capable of recording 250,000 characters. The key for entry into these memory systems are the numbers "666." There is a long list of "666" code numbers now in use, including several government agencies.

Why all the sixes? Computer technicians say, "6" is the perfect computer number. Apple Computer, Inc., celebrated the reality of this when it introduced its first 200 Apple I units to be retailed for $666.66. (*Wall Street Journal,* November 11, 1981) Prophecy students know that "sixes" are among the secrets of the economy destined to close out this, the Gentile Age.

"666" and Bar Marks

John made an astounding prophecy in Revelation 13:16 when he said that "no one can buy or sell unless he has the mark." He tied in a marking system with the numbering system of the beast society as the method used for control. Did you know that a computer reads "marks," not numbers? Only by the wisdom of God could John have known this.

> "The grocery industry has developed what it calls the Universal Product Code (UPC), which to the consumer looks like a series of vertical lines covering an area about the size of a large postage stamp." (*Los Angeles Times*, August 25, 1974)

The UPC is a means to identify the food manufacturer, the product including size and flavor, price information, taxability, food stamp eligibility and other related information which may be stored in the computer. The purpose of the Universal Product Code is to standardize an identification system.

The interpretation of the Universal Product Code marks is most revealing in that the three numbers "666" are the key working numbers for every designed Universal Product Code. Every group of Universal Product Code marks has in it three unidentified numbers. All three of these numbers are 6, making the use of the numbers "666" the key to using this identifying marking system. There are three sets of numerical marks:

Sets

Set #1 is designated by the number 1
Set #2 is designated by the number 2
Set #3 is designated by the number 3

The Universal Product Code uses a mark design and each design stands for a number. The numbers 0 through 9 each have mark designs. It is these mark designs that a computer reads. The number 0 has three different mark designs, the number 1 has two different designs. The number 2 has two different designs, the number 3 has two different designs, the number 4 has three different designs, the number 5 has three different designs, the number 6 has three different designs, the number 7 has two different designs, the number eight has two different designs, and the number 9 has three different designs.

The preceding illustration shows the exact mark design for each number. There are three different sets of mark designs. Sets 1 and 2 have a mark design for each of the numbers 0 through 9, and set 3 has a mark design for only the numbers 0, 4, 5, 6 and 9.

On almost any item you purchase in a grocery store, you will find a series of marks somewhere on the outside package. It will look something like this:

All of the marks, or bars, in the symbol are identified by numbers at the bottom of the code except for three marks. The mark at the far right, in the middle and at the far left are not identified.

FIGURE 1

In Figure #2, I have isolated the three marks that are unidentified in Figure #1.

FIGURE 2

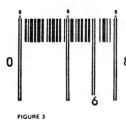

FIGURE 3

A visual inspection of the three unidentified marks compared to the mark designs for each number indicates that these marks are always the number "6" (Figure #3), and there are always three of them uncovering the coded use of the number "666" in all bar codes.

Following are some examples of Universal Product Code designs and the number "666."

UPC Design #1, and "666"

This is the most common design, showing the numerical value "6" at the top of the bar on the left, in the center and on the right. However, these three are unidentified on the package of your product. Check some articles and you will discover it to be true in every case.

Side A   Side B   Side C

UPC Design #1 Extended

This UPC symbol is found on magazines and books. The extension has nothing to do with the coded use of "666" in the body of the symbol. Again, the three "6" marks will not be identified on your product.

This Universal Product Code design is the second most commonly seen. As in the first design, there are three marks that are not identified.

When we isolate the three unidentified marks, we discover each bar is a design for the number "6". The code "666" is in a different configuration of this design.

There is no deviation. Every Universal Product Code has three unidentified marks whose number equivalent is "6" encoding it with the code number "666." The reason is that computers work on a series of 6 cores like the supermarket Model 304 produced by National Cash Register. It allows changing direction of current to performing switching operations. The 6 cores work in conjunction with 60 displacements X 6—one character—one bit of information. The formula for this system is 6 60 6. To number a card, person or item, the transaction must be prefixed "six hundred, threescore and six." That is an amazing correlation with what John saw and wrote concerning the electronic image that will someday be used to control buying and selling.

At the heart of the "'marking" system is this: If a national or international system can identify every little article with a bar code, it will be an adequately tested system when the government calls on it to identify every individual with a bar code.

Credit and bank cards already make use of bar codes, micro-encoded on the magnetic strip on the back of the card. When these marks are scanned by a laser, the optical pattern is converted to an electrical signal (analog), which is converted to a digital signal; then decoded by a microprocessor.

It is stated that 100,000 characters can be micro-encoded on the ½" X 3" magnetic strip found on the back of bank and credit cards.

The deadline for converting all U.S. bank cards to the magnetic tape type was March 1982 (*Business Week*, February 23, 1981, p. 107). After this date, all information pertinent to financial transactions can be micro-encoded in the discretionary data track of the magnetic strip. If we could look at the micro-encodations on the magnetic strip of our bank cards under magnification they would appear similar to the encodations of the Universal Product Codes.

Identification Card

We might expect bar codes on final cards to be assigned by the government, and the responsibility for issuing them given over to the Federal Reserve Banks. Government officials are seriously talking of the need to link people to an identification card because of the ease with which a false I.D. may be obtained. A bill is already before Congress for approval of such a pesonal identification card.

U.S. News & World Report, September 15, 1980, contained an article entitled: "A National Identity Card?" The article indicated the U.S. Government was contemplating issuing this all-purpose identity card without which a person would not be able to work or transact business of any kind.

It is ironic to recall that when the Social Security number was originally assigned, it was a "very personal number." It was to be used only by the Social Security Administrator, and information about it was to be kept confidential. Obviously that confidentiality did not last long.

Navy Times, August 4, 1980, reports the Department of Defense had received a bid to manufacture I.D. cards for the military personnel which would "use optical stripes (marks) such as those used in the Universal Product Code seen on grocery packages" . . . and that these "will be hooked into a worldwide computer system."

Military personnel report they are now being assigned bar codes. The important thing for all of us to realize is that we are already in the age of the mark, the age of John's prophecy.

Bar code marks have been designed to identify every manufactured item. Through the use of the marks there is the card with the personal identification number which permits the exact identity of every person. There is also the "electronic chip" for intramuscular injection which could be the final means of personal identification. Or it could be the use of a laser tattoo gun which can painlessly place a laser mark on the right hand or forehead in one thirty-billionth of a second. An IBM #3666 scanner not only reads the Universal Product Codes, but it can also read the invisible laser tattoo put on by an IBM laser gun. Scanners for registering laser-tattooed computer marks for identification already are built into checkout stand units in many stores.

Through the use of credit cards we have been conditioned to accept the necessity of owning a card. It appears whatever card we now have will one day become a debit card with a personal identification number. Then one card will perform all of our identity functions. It will also be the means of operating the electronic funds transfer—cashless—marking system now on present course. And it will have all systems set in proper working order, if and when the laser tattoo marking system is the system that must be enforced.

The use of a card has subtly, quietly been transitioned— first with the magentic strip, then with a bar code, into a debit card, which makes possible the elimination of all credit; a personal identification card which will include our life history; a Social Security card, without which we cannot be employed; and a money card, without which one cannot buy or sell. The means is being established for an I.D. mark which could someday be used to control our economics (buying and selling) through a marking system as John stated. And there will be adequate computer facilities (the electronic image John saw) to effect a "1984" style Big Brother System with follow-up.

Even U.S. Government officials share in this concern. An article entitled "Uncle Sam's Computer Has Got You"[1] uncovers a reason for this fear. Excerpts from this article read.

> Aroused by the increasing fears of government snooping, Americans are taking a hard look at the spread of electronic computers throughout the federal bureaucracy. Scattered throughout the bureaucracy are about 11,000 computers of all sizes and types—twice as many as there were five years ago. It takes some 150,000 people to operate and maintain these machines, at a cost of about 10 billion dollars a year. The government currently is buying or leasing new systems at a rate of better than 1,500 a year.

> With some 3.9 billion records on persons stored in thousands of federal data systems, there is mounting concern that computers could be manipulated with equal efficiency to control, intimidate or harass the citizenry. Available in government computers is a vast array of data on virtually every American, including personal finances, health, family status and employment.

> Jerome B. Wiesner, president of the Massachusetts Institute of Technology, has warned that in its pursuit of a more efficient society, the government could wind up "creating an information tyranny" with complex electronic-surveillance systems to identify and keep track of individuals and subgroups of the population with special characteristics. (Editor's note: This could include all Christian activities.)

> David F. Linowes, who headed the Privacy Protection Study Commission, asks: "What happens if the data that is being collected gets into the wrong hands? There is no reason to believe that someone won't come along at some point to abuse it."

> Many experts believe that the problems raised by the rapid growth of electronic technology can only grow larger.

New machines are being developed that are smaller, faster and cheaper than anything now being used. Some will be able to understand verbal commands, and perhaps will be adaptable to eavesdropping on private conversations. Looking further ahead, scientists are pondering machines that can predict an individual's behavior and that can secretly interpret a person's brainwaves.

Privacy Commission Chairman Linowes issues this warning: "At some point in the not-so-distant future, data collection, maintenance and dissemination may no longer be merely a tool of society, but will instead become an end in itself—a force with awesome powers of surveillance and control over the lives of individuals."

"666" is here! The mechanics for total economic control are rapidly coming into existence. Satan is establishing the means, methods and atmosphere so that this electronic "image" will give complete control of our people to the first beast. We can expect Satan to maneuver his world governments and our economy to bring about a condition where this control will have to be enforced. This may be a complete devaluation of the dollar, bankruptcy of the government through heavy deficits, uncontrollable inflation, or a combination of these and other conditions. However, we who are in the Body of Christ need only to commit our faith to the strength of our Lord, knowing that He will provide the way for us to overcome and conquer this world, regardless of how strong its pressures may become.

The Lord has a purpose in allowing the development of a marking system which will eventually bring about "the mark of the beast" in our society. We will share in the next chapter prophetic Scriptures which give enlightenment on "God's Next Move In America," and what may bring about conditions that would require the implementation of a marking system.

Chapter 10

GOD'S NEXT MOVE IN AMERICA

I do not believe God's next move in dealing with the church in America—His bride—the Body of Christ—will be the Rapture.

I have no desire to go into a lengthy discussion on the Rapture. I am familiar with all three different views as to the timing of this occurrence (pre-tribulation, mid-tribulation and post-tribulation) and the Scriptures to support each one. Regardless of what I might say on any one view, that is not the crucial issue at hand. The important fact for each of us is that we be ready.

I believe God's next move in our society will be to prepare the bride—all true born-again Christians—for the coming of Jesus. According to biblical teaching I am of the opinion most of us are not ready for His coming.

Then I heard what sounded like a great multitude, like the roar of rushing waters and like loud peals of thunder, shouting: "Hallelujah!" For the Lord God Almighty reigns. Let us rejoice and be glad and give him glory! For the wedding of the Lamb has come, and his bride has made herself ready. Fine linen,

bright and clean, was given her to wear. (Fine linen stands
for the righteous acts of the saints.) (Revelation 19:6-9)

Is the church in America ready for the coming of Jesus?
Are we full of righteousness, walking in the Spirit, overcoming
sin? Are we the church triumphant? Or are we covetous,
divorcing, depressed, worldly-minded, rebellious, grasping for
materialism and success, competitive, lukewarm, permissive,
adulterous, immoral, rich and increased with goods, unaware
of spiritual blindness and poverty, pleasure-loving, filled with
fear and anxiety, satisfied only to seek for good health and
happiness?

What kind of church (bride) is Jesus coming to claim? An
overcoming church! A church without spot or wrinkle! A
people whose affections are set on things above! A people
with clean hands and pure hearts! When I speak about the
church, I refer to the overall state of the Christian community
in our country. That is not to say there are none walking in
victory over the power of the world system, but the majority
of us are not.

These things are not said in a condemning way, to cause
anyone to feel guilty, or to show a critical spirit. But I do
want to be open and honest about the spiritual condition of
many Christians in our country. The power of the "beast"
system has extinguished our light. In this past generation we
have become guilty of measuring spiritual progress by what
we know, not by how we *live*. This is why in recent years the
world has begun to shout, "God is dead!" No longer does
the fruit of our testimony bear witness that we are overcoming
the influence of the world. We are suffering many of the same
personal problems and turmoils as do the people of the
world.

How many churches are you aware of that are flooded
with the awesome presence of Jesus Christ? Where believers
are so awed and reverent, they gather in holy silence? Where
no one dares be flippant or silly? Where the singing is so
filled with Christ's presence that sinners weep? Where the

backslider and the wicked sinners become
either run to the altar, or out the door? W
is so anointed his face seems to shine, and his words ..
aflame with convicting power?

How many Christians do you know who live in glorious victory over the power of their inner selfish sin nature that only comes from spending much time in the presence of Jesus? How many Christians do you know who are exciting to be around because you can sense victory and peace in them? Where are those who rejoice in their victories over worldly lust and passions—who have found and appropriated the strong arm of the Lord on which to place their hurts, problems, temptations and anxieties?

Mixing with the World

We are the last-day generation of Christians Paul spoke of in II Timothy 3:1-5—Christians guilty of the "sin of mixture."* This condition has come about through the wordly teaching power of the beast society. We have been shutting out the actual presence of Christ because we no longer want to be a separated people. We want to mix with the world and its standards. We do not want to be different.

"Mixture" means to "combine or blend into one mass so that individual characteristics are gone." It is the intermingling of two elements, causing them to lose their separate uniqueness, and take on a new, singular character.

That is one of the greatest harms the influence of our electronic media has caused in Christianity today. God's people want to blend and intermingle, and soon we lose our unique, different, special character. We lose our godly, right-eous qualities and take on many characteristics of the world society in which we live.

---

*I wish to acknowledge that many of the concepts I share on this subject of "sin of mixture" are from an article written by David Wilkerson by the same title. A copy can be obtained by writing David Wilkerson Crusades, P.O. Box 260, Lindale, Texas 75771.

From the very beginning, God chose to reveal His presence *only* through a special, separate people. He chose to reveal Himself through Israel — but only if they would avoid the sin of mixture with the world:

> For you are a people holy to the Lord your God. The Lord your God has chosen you out of all the peoples on the face of the earth to be his people. (Deuteronomy 7:6)

Moses knew there was only one thing that made them special, or different, from all other people on earth. It was not because they were in themselves worthy or holy. It was the presence of God revealed in their midst! They alone had the actual presence of Almighty God!

> The Lord replied, "My presence will go with you." Then Moses said to him, "If your presence does not go with us, do not send us up from here. How will anyone know that you are pleased with me and with your people unless you go with us? What else will distinguish me and your people from all the other people on the face of the earth?" (Exodus 33:14-16)

Here is conclusive proof that God's people are special and different because of the actual presence of the Lord in their midst! Take away His presence, and there is no difference from the rest of the world. That is what we mean when we refer to Christians walking in the power of the Holy Spirit. God's presence within us is what makes the difference. When we as Christians do not walk in God's power, but in the power of our own strength, our character will not be much different than that of other people. We will not be a separated people and, therefore, we will experience a nature similar to those people of the world. And our problems will be the same as theirs.

Any congregation or group of people can boast that they are Spirit-filled, but if there is no overwhelming presence of Christ and victory over sin at work in their midst, they are just as ordinary as everyone else. Satan's modern day schemes to deceive have worked. We are unique only when Christ's presence is in full revelation among us. And that will be manifested by having victory over the power of sin in our lives.

God warned Israel that any mixing with the world would cause Him to withdraw His presence, and He would reject them as the special channel of His revelation.

But Israel loved to mix! God's people were determined to do away with everything that made them different from the rest of the world. They despised the reproach of being separated. They wanted kings, like the rest of the world. They wanted sexual freedom like the rest of the world. They wanted to flirt and indulge in adultery and still cover the altar with tears; they wanted the lust, the passion, the immortality, the fornication and the idols of the rest of the world. So they rejected His commandment to be separated and special to Himself. They sinned and became proud and vain, and made themselves images and worshipped all the host of heaven—to do evil in the sight of God "as did the wicked."

> So the Lord was very angry with Israel and removed them from his presence . . . even Judah did not keep the commands of the Lord their God. They followed the practices Israel had introduced. Therefore the Lord rejected all the people of Israel; he afflicted them and gave them into the hands of plunderers until he thrust them from his presence. (II Kings 17:18-20)

There was no need for Israel to seek after counselors or spiritual advisors or prophets—to find out why they were so harassed and filled with despair. They knew why troubles were piling up on them—the presence of the Lord was gone!

The predominant message of the prophets was, "Your iniquities, or sins, have turned away the presence of God." God spoke to His people through His prophet, Jeremiah, saying:

> "Should you not fear me?" declares the Lord. "Should you not tremble in my presence? . . . But these people have stubborn and rebellious hearts . . . Your sins have deprived you of good. Among my people are wicked men . . . Their houses are

full of deceit; they have become rich and powerful...They do not plead the case of the fatherless to win it, they do not defend the rights of the poor...Should I not avenge myself on such a nation as this?" declares the Lord. A horrible and shocking thing has happened in the land...and my people love it this way. (Jeremiah 5:22-31)

Israel had mixed with the world around it, lost its unique character, and had taken on the character and identity of the world. So God hid His face from them, rejected their new character and withdrew His presence.

Have we missed that major point God is making in the Old Testament? How much clearer could it be that God will not put up with our mingling with the unholy, the unclean? Why was there such an emphasis on a separated priesthood in the Old Testament? To give us an example of God's firm commitment to reveal Himself through a holy, clean, separated people.

> You and your sons are not to drink wine or other fermented drink whenever you go into the Tent of Meeting, or you will die. This is a lasting ordinance for the generations to come. You must distinguish between the holy and the profane, between the unclean and the clean. (Leviticus 10:9, 10)

> You are to be holy to me because I, the Lord, am holy, and I have set you apart from the nations to be my own. (Leviticus 20:26)

That is the special message of the Old Testament—the story of a unique severed, separated, different people who would maintain God's cause on the earth, through a manifestation of His presence.

The New Testament is even stronger in condemning the sin of mixing with the standards of the world. There is nothing in the Old Testament quite as strong as the warnings of Paul against affinity with the world:

> Do not be yoked together with unbelievers. For what do righteousness and wickedness have in common? Or what fel-

lowship can light have with darkness? What harmony is there between Christ and Belial? What does a believer have in common with an unbeliever? What agreement is there between the temple of God and idols? For we are the temple of the living God. As God has said: "I will live with them and walk among them, and I will be their God and they will be my people."

"Therefore come out from them and be separate, says the Lord. Touch no unclean thing and I will receive you."

" I will be a Father to you, and you will be my sons and daughters, says the Lord Almighty." (II Corinthinans 6:14-18)

Satan knows that is the key required for walking in the power of God's presence—in His Holy Spirit. That is why as his time is drawing short, he has raised up the "beast" system to attack the standards and life of those who bear testimony of Jesus. (Revelation 12:17)

God wants the world to see the difference between His people who love Him and the rest of the unbelieving world. He wants us to be examples of a delivered and victorious people trusting in His mighty arm to deliver us from all harm and evil.

The reasons for separation from walking in the ways of the world are the same today as in the past. God wants to draw a line between His people and this wicked age so that the unbeliever can know there is none like Him in all the earth to deliver them. The wicked people of this age must have an even greater manifestation of the Lord's presence; nothing else will get their attention.

Whatever is mixed with the world can never be of God. It can never be a channel of Christ's actual presence. Our Lord is going to expose and either write off or change every ministry that is leavened with the spirit and methods of this age. He is going to withdraw His presence from every confessed believer who yearns for the pleasures and seductions of this world. They will be left dry, empty and confused. He cannot

—He *will* not—trust His holy presence to those who are not wholly separated in their hearts from the world, and yielded only to Him.

Disobedient servants will not be able to stand against the attacks of the devil, the moral landslide, the economic ruin and other chaotic conditions that are coming in this, the final years of the Gentile Age. They will once and for all lose the touch of God, and though some will be saved, they will be counted unworthy of the anointing. If you are of "this world," you are not of His! Jesus said, "I am not of this world..." (John 8:23)

Speaking of His true disciples, He said,

They are not of this world, even as I am not of it. (John 17:16) But I have chosen you out of this world. That is why the world hates you. (John 15:19)

Do we really understand what Jesus is saying to us? "I have put a difference between you and the world. They will hate you because of the presence of my character in you."

If that is true, why are we trying to gain the approval of the world? Why do we mix their music with ours? Why do we seek their good will? Why do we bend our morals to accommodate them? Why do we seek their applause or blessing? We are not of this world! We ought to accept this difference as taught in Scripture and quit trying to be like the people of the world.

The world loves its own—but we are not of it. God help us to joyfully accept His special holy character of separation and difference, and give up on the world. It will only be those who are truly separated unto Christ who will have any power to save the world.

Do not love the world or anything in the world. If anyone loves the world, the love of the Father is not in him. (I John 2:15)

The Christian who tries to live in both worlds shows dishonor to the very cross of Christ, for Jesus gave Himself that He might deliver us from this present evil world. How can we have any part of its standards?

Paul understood this:

> May I never boast except in the cross of our Lord Jesus Christ through which the world has been crucified to me, and I to the world. (Galatians 6:14)

The Holy Spirit will soon be calling out the true followers of Jesus Christ, separating them, purging them and getting them prepared as a special people to bring back His glorious presence to shake the earth. We are to be a people crucified to the world!

Most all of us are guilty to some degree of mixing too much with the world. That is society's power John speaks of in his prophecy. I acknowledge its power and know it has had an effect on my overall spiritual commitment—not because that is my heart's desire or because I want to be spotted by the world—but because of the beast's power, it is difficult to totally escape the influence of our society.

Preparing the Bride

Knowing we are living in the last days and can expect the imminent coming of Jesus, God is going to prepare the bride, His Church. But Satan has caused the bride in our country to become adulterous.

> You adulterous people, don't you know that friendship with the world is hatred toward God? Anyone who chooses to be a friend of the world becomes an enemy of God. (James 4:4)

The battle is the Lord's! We know the bridegroom (Jesus) is ready. But when there is a marriage, both parties must be ready and committed to one another. Jesus has proven His commitment by sacrificing His all for His bride, the church.

God's next move in America is going to be to prepare the bride for a worthy King.

God's preparation of the bride is going to require the endurance and faith of the saints. (Revelation 13:10) God will see to it that when Jesus comes, the bride will be a committed church, not a church living in adultery with Satan's kingdom, the world.

God is going to shake everything that can be shaken! He is going to shake, and scrub, and burn, and purge and purify to get the bride ready.

No man or woman of God will escape the purging. God will accomplish His task of getting all the worldly dross and filth out of us. He will expose all sin, all adultery and all foolishness. The Holy Spirit will reprove us of sin, righteousness and judgment.

> Jesus said: "Those whom I love, I rebuke and discipline. So be earnest and repent. To him who overcomes, I will give the right to sit with me on my throne, just as I overcame and sat down with my Father on his throne." (Revelation 3:19, 21)

Through shaking, purging, purifying and disciplining us, God is going to let the devil and the world know who has the power. It is important to allow the Lord to develop in us a heavenly vision of holiness and humility, and that we not hold on to our worldly vision so many of us have developed due to Satan's deceitful schemes.

During the coming time of testing, we will have a need to know the Lord in all of His fullness, with our eyes focused on eternal values. The Lord's preparation will cause us to anxiously await our coming marriage. All of our false values will tumble, and earthly dreams and plans will lose their meaning.

That is the way it should be! I believe anyone who has experienced marriage can identify with anxiously awaiting for that day. A wedding is something that requires a great deal of planning and preparation. It's going to be the same when

Jesus comes. I believe that will be the condition of the bride. But first we need to be refined as gold, to be the finest, purest bride ever. Don't you think Jesus deserves this?

As we have shared throughout this book, and as Scripture has warned us, Satan has flooded us in this, the end of the Gentile Age, with many new worldly doctrines that have deceived the saints, causing covetousness, adultery, immorality and self-seeking lifestyles. He has done harm to the bride of Christ, trying to cause the bride to be an adulterous one when Jesus comes. But God won't allow that.

Satan has come as an angel of light! (II Corinthians 11:13-15) One popular example of that, which is attractive to many because it fits our modern way of wanting to live, is the new gospel that says, "Gain is godliness." Paul says:

> If anyone teaches false doctrines and does not agree to the sound instruction of our Lord Jesus Christ and to godly teaching, he is conceited and understands nothing. He has an unhealthy interest in controversies and arguments that result in envy, quarreling, malicious talk, evil suspicions, constant friction between men of corrupt mind, who have been robbed of the truth, and who think that *godliness is a means to financial gain.* But godliness with contentment is great gain. For we brought nothing into the world, and we can take nothing out of it. But if we have food and clothing, we will be content with that . . . some people, eager for money, have wandered from the faith and pierced themselves with many griefs. But you, man of God, flee from all this, and pursue righteousness, godliness, faith, love, endurance and gentleness. (I Timothy 6:3-11)

Yes, we in the American Church, as a whole, have become adulterers with the world. Though we may not have done so on purpose, the enemy has deceived us through the power of the society in which we live—the beast system.

Satan has caused us to become prostitutes, committing fornication with the world. He has caused the church institution to become the mother of prostitutes in Babylon, which is riding on the beast system.

John describes the woman on the beast in Revelation 17:

Then the angel carried me away in the spirit into a desert. There I saw a woman sitting on a scarlet beast that was covered with blasphemous names and had seven heads and ten horns. The woman was dressed in purple and scarlet, and was glittering with gold, precious stones and pearls. She held a golden cup in her hand, filled with abominable things and the filth of her adulteries. This title was written on her forehead:

MYSTERY
BABYLON THE GREAT
THE MOTHER OF PROSTITUTES
AND OF THE ABOMINATIONS OF THE EARTH.
(Revelation 17:3-5)

We know the beast with seven heads and ten horns represents our governmental superpower system. The woman is a vivid picture of the sensual, rich church of today which is sitting on the beast — a famous, influential woman in possession of great wealth and prestige, but naked, poor and spiritually blind committing adultery with Babylon, the spirit of worldliness.

It is the very description of the Laodicean Church mentioned in Revelation 3:17 which says:

"I am rich; I have acquired wealth and do not need a thing." But you do not realize that you are wretched, pitiful, poor, blind and naked.

When John saw a woman supported by a beast, he was seeing into our day — viewing a carnal church infiltrated by the world. You and I know it's true. The world has crept into the church! It is deceiving and seducing the children of God, trying to turn God's people to spiritual harlotry with the world.

We are trying to do God's work with worldly methods. It has become fashionable to copy the world in our churches by using ungodly singers with the world's style of music, style of dress and even its choreography! Some religious television programs are being directed and produced by men who have nothing at all to do with Christ.

Can you imagine an uncircumcised Philistine being called into the holy place by a priest of Israel to choreograph the ministry before the ark of the covenant? That priest would have been slain by God right on the spot.

Jeremiah was shocked that the people of his day were being willingly led away by such deception. He lamented, "...My people love it this way." (Jeremiah 5:31)

God is getting ready to do a new thing! The Holy Spirit is going to woo the children of the Lord away from the bigness, brightness and sensationalism. He is going to revive and sanctify His people to discern between the clean and unclean. No longer will Babylon be able to seduce God's people away from the altars, to play with their toys, to get them preoccupied with ease, prosperity and pleasure—robbing them of their faith. Babylon is going to fall and with it God is going to purge and shake all that can be shaken. We will be refined by God and anxiously waiting for our Bridegroom when He comes.

The economic power of our society is the center of Babylon as we close out this age. We have over 50 percent of the world's wealth, while we have only 7 percent of the world's population. This is not consistent with the teachings of Christ or the lives of the early Christians. When we try to determine what our god truly is—whether we are serving ourselves or the true and living God—we must examine the facts as they are, not necessarily what we have been led to believe. The word "god" is defined as any person or thing that is made the chief object of one's love, interest, aspirations, service and life. The god of most people in our nation has become "self."

We have become independent, haughty and self-sufficient. We seek the self-satisfying lifestyle. That is the spirit of Babylon, the spirit of the world.

The next move God is going to make in America will cause the collapse of our economic power. Babylon is going to fall. That will begin God's purging and refining process in our country.

Babylon in Scripture

Babylonism is a satanic willfulness which seeks to solve its own problems and to build its own arrangement of things. The "great society" theme we promote in America is a current expression illustrative of this present attitude. The popular religion of humanism, which has swept through our country, is the religion of Babylon.

Babylon is a system whose beginnings are found in Genesis 11. Nimrod was the ruler of the original Babylonian empire after the great flood. The people were totally self-centered, seeking to be independent. The Babylonian material system has long been in the world. At the close of the Gentile Age, the great materialistic system of Babylon is going to fall.

> Fallen! Fallen is Babylon the Great! She has become a home for demons and a haunt for every evil spirit; a haunt for every unclean and destestable bird. For all the nations have drunk the maddening wine of her adulteries. The kings of the earth committed adultery with her, and the merchants of the earth grew rich from her excessive luxuries. (Revelation 18:2,3)

At the end of the Gentile Age, the spirit of Babylon is centered in a nation. Jeremiah 50 and 51 presents Babylon as a nation. Revelation 18 presents it as a city. This is not a contradiction, because in Scripture nations are often referred to by the king or capitol city. Our modern press does the same thing, using the name of Washington for the U.S.A., Moscow for the Soviet Union or Paris for France. Using the name of a country's leader is also common.

The Spirit of God goes to almost unprecedented pains in describing the Babylonian nation in the last days. One prominent, powerful and God-blessed Gentile nation is singled out and is referred to as Babylon.

Revelation chapter 18, Jeremiah 50, verses 12, 23, 31, 37, 38 and Jeremiah 51, verses 7, 13 and 53, list the identifying characteristics of this end-time nation. There is an overwhelming resemblance to that of our own nation's character. Note some of the characteristics given in Scripture:

"The youngest of the nations" (Jeremiah 50:12)

"Born from a mother country," which was Britain for the United States (50:12)

"A mighty military and political power" (50:23)

"An arrogant, proud and haughty nation" (50:31)

"People of foreign descent" (50:37)

"Covetousness reigns as the people live sumptuously, but want more while many in the world are starving" (50:38)

"Nation with Godly heritage" (51:7)

"A nation of great wealth and prosperity" (51:13)

"Great attainments" (51:53)

"Space travelers" (51:53)

"A home for the cults and occult practices" (Revelation 18:2)

"Worldwide immorality" (18:2)

"Large in foreign aid" (18:3)

"Large importer to satisfy the lust of the people" (18:3)

"Center of Christianity" (18:4)

"Excessive crime, sexual permissiveness, homosexual freedom, decadence of marriage vows, etc." (18:5)

"Proud and boastful people" (18:7)

"Other countries' economic strength depends on her economic strength" (18:9-19)

"World trade center" (18:11-13)

"Extravagant tastes" (18:14)

"Nation of influential cities" (18:18)

"Nation known for her music" (18:22)

"Nation known for her crafts" [manufacturing capabilities]
(18:22)
"Nation known for her food production" (18:22)
"Her businessmen and great corporations are known
worldwide" (18:23)

The prophet Malachi told the people of Israel ,that God
would tear down what they had built in their wickedness.
The people quickly reacted in a self-justifying manner, wanting
to know when they had polluted the name of the Lord. And
they did not change their conduct. They simply did not
believe God meant them. Throughout Scripture God requests
us to hear His counsel that He has taken against a certain
Babylon at the close of the Gentile Age, which appears to be
the economic lifestyle of our country. This counsel is
recorded in Revelation 18 and parts of Jeremiah 50 and 51.

I have listed several of the characteristics of this end-time
Babylonian society because it is important that we identify
this nation, not only for the sake of seeing God's counsel
toward her; but in Revelation 14 we are told the fall of Babylon, or this nations's economic system, is a part of the time
sequence as to when the "mark of the beast" will be
implemented.

Sequence of Events that Close Out the Gentile Age

The Three Angels
First Angel: Time sequence Number 1:
                Revelation 14:6, 7

> Then I saw another angel flying in midair, and he had the
> eternal gospel to proclaim to those who live on the earth—to
> every nation, tribe, language and people. He said in a loud
> voice, "Fear God and give him glory, because the hour of his
> judgment has come. Worship him who made the heavens, the
> earth, the sea and the springs of water." (Revelation 14:6,7)

We are currently living in the time zone of sequence
Number 1. In recent years, as never before, the gospel of

Jesus Christ has been poured out and made available, both here in our country and around the world. Though sin has greatly increased grace has increased, all the more to fulfill God's promise. I will not examine all of the resources and ministries involved in completing the fulfillment of this event. With some investigation on your part, I am sure they are evident.

Second Angel: Time Sequence Number 2: Revelation 14:8

A second angel followed and said, "Fallen! Fallen is Babylon the Great, which made all the nations drink the maddening wine of her adulteries." (Revelation 14:8)

The next major sequence to occur will be the collapse of our materialistic economic system. "How could such a thing happen?" you may ask. I don't know how it will come about, but I can see that our economic structure is at a boiling point now and professional economists across the land over-whelmingly agree it will soon have to explode. Why? As a nation, our government cannot continue to build up the huge deficits we now have so the populace can continue to live in luxury as we have become accustomed. It has been our greed for things and our self-seeking lifestyle that has driven us so deeply into debt. It has been the power of economics, this materialistic influence, that has caused us in the Body of Christ to commit adultery with Babylon and become spotted with and accept so many worldly standards in our lives and in our churches. That is why God is going to allow our economic bubble to burst. Babylon is going to fall.

Our national federal debt has reached the point of no return! In 1976, there were about 650 billion dollars in funded debt compared to $1.4 trillion by the end of 1983. If all government debt is taken into consideration (such as pensions, entitlements, loan guarantees, etc) the real federal debt is 10 trillion.

In 1976, there were $190 billion in government guarantees to insure private lenders such as the Housing Guarantee Fund, Foreign Military Sales Funds, the Overseas Private Investment Corporation, Agricultural Credit Insurance Fund, etc. That $190 billion had grown to $346.7 billion in 1982. In 1976 the Rural Electrification Administration alone guaranteed $4 billion of credit. That is now $30.6 billion.

The maritime industry, through their Federal Ship Financing Fund, insured about $5 billion in 1976. That figure is now $7.9 billion—up 58 percent.

The big ones, such as insurance for banks, savings and loans institutions and student loans, were 1.6 trillion dollars in 1976. Congress has now passed a resolution putting the "full faith and credit of the United States" behind all insured FDIC and FSLIC insured deposits. That is now $2.4 trillion, up 50 percent.

If you don't think Uncle Sam will ever have to make good on this one, keep in mind that many of our major banks have hundreds of billions of dollars loaned to Brazil, Mexico and other countries who are defaulting on their loans, and have no prospects of ever having the money to pay them off. Already the third world debt is over $800 billion, with at least 25 percent of it owed to U.S. banks. These loans were made partly from the funds put into our banks by the people of this country. What if there were a run on the banks? Where would the money come from to pay everyone back?

A recent *San Francisco Chronicle* article gives us another great lesson on our vulnerability. It reported a bank industry study concluding that if an earthquake destroyed the banks in California, losing their records, or just putting them out of commission for as little as two weeks, the repercussions to the national banking system would be awesome. The whole banking system could come crashing down around us. This is an incredible network of interrelated, interdependent institutions often lending or borrowing hundreds of millions overnight. There would be all kinds of problems with checks clearing and banks becoming insolvent because of California banks not meeting their obligations to other banks.

God's Word says:

"O, Babylon, city of power! In one hour your doom has come! In one hour such great wealth has been brought to ruin!" (Revelation 18:10,17)

What move God will use to cause the fall of our economic system, I don't know. But when it happens it will be sudden and quick, without warning — other than what we have recorded in Scripture.

The financial obligation of our federal government is nearly 20 times more than the total money supply. The total obligation of $10 trillion is more than the value of everything that everyone in America owns. Our nation is in hock up to its ears, and Uncle Sam has promised to cover everybody.

The defenders of bigger government argue that not all of these obligations will ever come due. That's probably true of about $3 trillion out of the $10 trillion. However, 20 percent of our debt is in the hands of other countries — the Germans, the Japanese and the Arabs.

In the final analysis it all breaks down to these numbers: our national debt is $5,285.00 for every American man, woman and child. This does not include our nation's "off the books" debt such as Social Security and other federal obligations. That number is $10 trillion, which means every man, woman and child has a total financial obligation of $43,478.00. There is a strong possibility that $26,000 of that will come due. In 1990, if the present trend can continue that long before it falls, each of us will be on the hook for at least $82,400.00 — a total financial obligation of $20.6 trillion. On most days, our huge and growing government deficit is advancing at a phenomenal rate of over half-a-billion dollars per day. The U.S. government outspent its income by $195.4 billion in the fiscal year 1983. It was the 14th year in a row that our government operated in the red.

Third Angel: Time Sequence Number 3: Revelation 14:9,12

And another angel, a third, followed them, saying with a loud voice, "If anyone worships the beast and its image, and receives a mark on his forehead or on his hand, he also shall drink the wine of God's wrath, poured unmixed into the cup of his anger." (Revelation 14:9, Revised Standard Version)

This calls for patient endurance on the part of the saints who obey God's commandments and remain faithful to Jesus. (Revelation 14:12)

After the fall of Babylon or the fall of our economy, which has provided so many things for most of us from the world in recent decades, there is going to be terrible chaos. We have become conditioned to so many luxuries that when they are gone, I doubt if any of us can predict the problems this will cause. There will be severe crime, bloodshed and more chaotic conditions than we can imagine. Things will immediately get out of control, not because people don't have what they need in order to live, but because people will be fighting to get the things they are now so conditioned to having. It won't be as it was in the earlier days of our country or as in most cultures throughout the centuries where people have always lived with only the necessities.

Government will have no choice. It will be forced to move quickly to implement a control system of buying and selling. It will make use of a system that has already been developed and known to work—the marking system described in a previous chapter.

John foretold this condition:

Also it (the beast) causes all, both small and great, both rich and poor, both free and slave, to be marked on the right hand or the forehead so that no one can buy or sell unless he has the mark, that is, the name of the beast or the number of its name. (Revelation 13:16,17 RSV. Words in parentheses are the author's.)

Obviously there will be a great deal of opposition from the Christian community. We know we cannot submit to a marking system which uses numbers as a means of controlling buying and selling. But economic conditions will get so bad the majority of the people will demand action, and the beast system will have to carry out what has been recorded in Scripture. Most of the population will welcome the new law.

God's Word, speaking about that time when the mark of the beast occurs, addressed the subject:

> This calls for patient endurance on the part of the saints who obey God's commandments and remain faithful to Jesus. (Revelation 14:12)

Initially, I doubt if refusal to take the mark will create any major difficulties. But as the months pass, then a year or two, the thirst for power in the governmental system will begin to emerge. Christians will come under greater pressure to bow down to the system.

It may be possible, and many hold this belief, that one man, an extremely strong leader, will become prominent and hold tight reins on our governmental system. He will become an adversary, and strongly oppose the position of Christians and what are now our constitutional freedoms. He will oppose our country having strong ties with Israel. I don't know that pointing to one particular man is that significant. There were many Caesars during the rule of the beast, the Roman Empire. Overall, it is the power of the "beast system" which carries out Satan's attacks, not just one individual.

The Purification Process

The mark of the beast which will control buying and selling will be allowed by God as a part of His purification process.

It has been the deception of the materialistic influence in the world that has caused us to become so spiritually soft. A part of God's way of separating us from Satan's deceptive worldly schemes will come about by taking us out of the buying and selling process. We will be forced to become totally dependent on our God for wisdom on how to provide our needs.

As John states, speaking of the end-time Babylon:

Then I heard another voice from heaven say: "Come out of her, my people, so that you will not share in her sins, so that you will not receive any of her plagues; for her sins are piled up to heaven, and God has remembered her crimes." (Revelation 18:4,5)

Spiritually, we are to come out of the spirit of this world. The purging, shaking, scrubbing and burning most of us desperately need if we are honest, will soon begin and change our present conquered condition. And we will be the better for it, because only in the power of Jesus are the true values of life realized.

The promised purging of the Lord to take place will cause us to become totally dependent on Christ. Then, as a bride adorned for her husband, we will be ready for His coming. The degree of purging and breaking and shaking we each need to prepare us for the coming of the Lord will depend on how strongly our heart is attached to self and the world.

How long will it take God to get the church ready? Only He knows that. Those things are in the hands of our God and we can trust Him.

In your struggle against sin, you have not yet resisted to the point of shedding your blood. And you have forgotten that word of encouragement that addresses you as sons:

"My son, do not make light of the Lord's discipline, and do not lose heart when he rebukes you, because the Lord disciplines those he loves, and he punishes everyone he accepts as a son."

Endure hardship as discipline; God is treating you as sons. God disciplines us for our good that we may share in his holiness. No discipline seems pleasant at the time, but painful.

Later on, however, it produces a harvest of righteousness and peace for those who have been trained by it. (Hebrews 12:4-7, 10, 11)

God has said, "Never will I leave you; never will I forsake you." So say with confidence, "The Lord is my helper, I will not be afraid. What can man do to me?" (Hebrews 13, 5,6)

Chapter 11

THE ONLY ROAD TO SAFETY

Darkness will soon cover the earth; the ocean waters quiver with the oncoming storm. Many ships will drift aimlessly in the troubled waters; many will appear secure and sturdy, but they will be following a false light and the wrong direction. Do not chart your course by ships on your left or your right—look only to me (Jesus) for your direction. Many will follow the assuredness of those ill-fated ships, but they will meet with the same destiny.

Your ship will be tossed, rocked and battered by the wind and rains, but I will be with you in the same manner as I was with my apostles—ready to command your rough seas to "Be still!"

Just as in the days of Noah did I make my plans known, so I am doing now also. Only I can tell you how to build your ark...only I can tell you what provisions need to be taken aboard for your survival. Others would say to you, "this is your need," or "that is your need," but I alone know your true needs: And when the storm begins, your safety and comfort will come in knowing that I am in control of your life.

250

Many bright beacons will tempt your path with "Here, over here you will find quiet waters!", or "this is your way to safety", but do not be deceived, these beacons would lead you astray.

Your course has been set by the hand of the Living God— stand firm and do not waver. Be not moved by what goes on around you, but affix your eyes on me and do not remove them. Trust in my ways, and cast your fears to the wind. I will never leave you nor forsake you. (Written by Angie Clarkson, a sister in the Lord who is now deceased)

An Overview

In a way, all the teaching we've done and the Scriptures we have reviewed concerning the period of the Gentile Age, lead us to the subject of this last chapter. An overview of the material will help to introduce this final chapter.

Chapter 1—"God's Prophetic Timetable"

We reviewed the Jewish people beginning with Abraham to the present day, and the fulfillment of events foretold by the Old Testament prophets. Through this historical and scriptural analysis we were able to establish God's prophetic time period in which we now live. We are at the close of the age of the Gentiles—the Church Age.

Chapter 2—"The Church in Review"

How the Church Age will be closed out can better be understood if we are somewhat aware of its history. We reviewed several key historical events. The Holy Spirit poured out and Satan cast down to earth to set up the battle condition in the spiritual realm depicts the history of the church. Historical events were analyzed in this chapter, revealing how Satan uses both persecution and deception in spiritual warfare, often working through key worldly authorities and governments to attack God's people.

Chapter 3—
"America, America, God Shed His Grace On Thee"

This chapter was a continuation of the church's history and revealed the unique way God moved to develop an unknown land. The discovery of America and its spiritual development were reviewed. History reveals God moved with a special anointing on men to establish America as the spiritual center of the church for the last days of the Gentile Age.

Chapter 4—"Knowing Our Enemy"

America, the spiritual center of the church, has also become the center of spiritual warfare. Satan has always waged his most severe warfare against God's people. We explored the tactics Satan uses to wage warfare against Christians, especially in the realm of deception. All Scripture relating to the period in which we now live warns that Satan will not use persecution but deception against the central area of the church. We saw that here in America, many of those last day deceptive devices and techniques the Bible warns about are coming to pass.

Chapter 5—"Satan's Attack Vehicle"

Satan has a primary vehicle which he uses to wage his spiritual warfare against God's people. A biblical study on the identity of this vehicle showed that it is called "the world." It refers to those things which have been developed by the efforts of man, not the things created by God. Today we use the word "society" in the same manner the Bible uses the word "world." Satan uses the things of society as his attack vehicle because, as Scripture says, they are under his control.

Chapter 7—"Satan's World Vehicle—*The Beast*"

In the book of Revelation, John, the prophet, sees the development of an ultimate vehicle to attack the testimony of Christians at the end of the church age. He calls this world system a "beast," because prophetically any governmental superpower is known as a beast among the systems of the world, due to its awesome power. Both the United States and Russia would qualify as beast systems in the world today. In this lesson we discussed in detail the meaning of those Scriptures in which John describes and identifies the beast system he saw that would carry out Satan's deceptive warfare against the church in these last days. Every descriptive characteristic given in Scripture has been fulfilled or is being developed (such as the means to implement the mark) by our governmental system, whereas no other system has fulfilled even one. Since America is the center of Christianity, we should expect Satan to develop his ultimate world system here.

Chapter 8—"Satan's Modern Day Power System"

In his vision, John saw that the society under this great government would develop a system of power that to him was unique. It was able to perform all sorts of miraculous things and had tremendous ability to teach and influence the minds of the people based on the standards of the world. Not knowing what this power was, he used biblical prophetic terminology to describe it. We shared the Lord's revelation which identified this power system as electricity. Through the use of this power system Satan is currently carrying out his battle for the mind, influencing many Christians, causing them to submit to world standards.

Most Christians are unaware of Satan's use of this power system. However, we are seeing its devastating effects through much spiritual defeat in the lives of Christians. One example of this is the breakdown in many Christian homes.

Chapter 9—
"The Latest Developments on the Mark of the Beast"

John saw man develop an "image" which represented the

first "beast" and its power system. Through this image, which is the electronic computer, John says the beast governmental system will be able to control buying and selling through the use of a mark, which is associated with a number. John gives an identifying clue to the working of this mark and numbering system in that the number "666" is a key to its use. We discussed the progress of this numbering system John prophetically described nearly 1900 years ago, and we looked at some of its current applications.

Chapter 10—"God's Next Move in America"

The stage is being set for closing out the Gentile Age, which will be climaxed by the coming of Jesus for His bride—the church. We shared why God's next move in America will be to prepare the bride. Satan, working through the deception of the end-time beast's power system has caused us, the church, to become idolatrous—"a harlot sitting on a beast." We have become dependent on the world's economic system, the spirit of Babylon. The fruits of our individual lives and policies controlling our churches too often prove this to be true. However, Satan will not always experience so much victory in the lives of Christians, causing us to commit adultery with the world. God is soon going to allow conditions to develop that will shake, purge and purify the church in America, getting the bride ready for Jesus' coming. Since the church's commitment to economics (materialism and pleasure) has been one of the strongest deceptive tools our enemy has used to conquer the spiritual testimonies of the saints, God in His purging and purification process, will allow the marking system of the beast to come about. It will be required that Christians refuse to participate. This will be one of the means God will use to purify the church to deliver us from committing adultery with the world. Jesus deserves better than an adulterous bride. God will see that we are a committed bride.

Commitment

Some who will read this book may justifiably ask, "What can I do about it? If this is where we are at, so what?"

I would not suggest that anyone go out and attempt to change anything to suit their own will, and through their will-power. The battle is the Lord's. But He wages His battles through His people. And to do so, He needs a committed people. So, seeing where we are in the realm of prophecy, demands a call for all Christians to consider their commitment.

When the subject of total commitment is discussed in Christian circles, the question that most often arises is, "What exactly does it mean?" Our first reaction will normally center around wanting to be involved in some activity. We are trained in our society to place our confidence in something we can do through our own "self-willpower." We will go to extremes carrying out tasks of a physical nature, making up rules and regulations, believing that this must be total commitment.

Yet with all our physical efforts we still do not experience true spiritual victory, which means overcoming our sin nature and the self-centered ways of the world. Too much of the time we are left longing for the characteristics of God's sacrificial love for our fellow man, His joy and abiding peace, patience, kindness, gentleness and self-control.

We experience defeat because we try to understand and commit in activities of the flesh that which is of a spiritual nature. Total commitment to the Lord Jesus Christ is not something of the flesh, but of the Spirit ... of the heart. Therefore, we can't apply our normal approach of using human wisdom or human understanding in this area. That which is of the flesh is flesh, and that which is of the Spirit is Spirit. We cannot combine the two. (John 3:6)

If we can recognize this principle and accept it, we can begin to approach the subject of "commitment." God is a Spirit; therefore, what we commit must be of a spiritual nature.

It must come from our inner being. The position of our physical nature will become quite different in our thinking than what is common to man. It becomes simply that of a vehicle. We yield it only as a vessel for God to work in and through.

> For it is God who works in you to will and to act according to his good purpose. (Philippians 2:13)

Commitment Versus Involvement

Commitment means the giving of ourselves—our total being—as a living sacrifice to God so He and His indwelling power are in control. It means a willingness to change. *Today, many Christians are involved; few of us are committed.* There is a vast difference.

It is very easy to be involved. Involvement means activity. We can be active in our church in doing many works in the name of Jesus, but that does not mean we are committed to Him and His teachings. "Commitment" is where our activity requires sacrificing all that is for our benefit for the benefit of others and the glory of God. Paul says:

> I appeal to you therefore, brethren, and beg of you in view of (all) the mercies of God, to make a decisive dedication of your bodies—presenting all your members and faculties—as a living sacrifice, holy (devoted, consecrated) and well pleasing to God, which is your reasonable (rational, intelligent) service and spiritual worship. Do not be conformed to this world—this age, fashioned after and adapted to its external, superficial customs. But be transformed (changed) by the (entire) renewal of your mind—by its new ideals and its new attitude—so that you may prove (for yourselves) what is the good and acceptable and perfect will of God. (Romans 12:1,2 Amplified Bible)

You may recognize that the giving of ourselves as a living sacrifice for our Father to control is a fulfillment of the first commandment. Jesus stated that we are to love God with all of our heart, mind, body and soul. To love is to give. (John

3:16) So for us to love God with all of our being is to give all of our being, or wholeheartedly desire to sacrifice all of our self-will.

The coming wedding of the bride (the church) to the bridegroom (Jesus) will require a committed bride. The Christian community in America, as a whole, is not presently a sacrificing body, but a self-seeking body similar to the church described at Laodicea. (Revelation 3:14-22)

Refinement is in order. In His love, God knows the only road to safety that will stand the test of these last days is the development of our commitment to the bridegroom—the Lord Jesus.

God must purge us of our self-willed, self-seeking lifestyles that the enemy has developed through the beast society.

Even our religious commitment to "things," "doctrines," "ordinances," "traditions," "structures" and "personalities" must fall—they will not stand the testing. Only Jesus overcame the world.

> I have told you these things so that in me you may have peace. In this world you will have trouble, but take heart! I have overcome the world. (John 16:33)

Recent history reveals that we have been repeating many of the same mistakes Israel made when Christ walked the earth. The Jewish people established a tradition of interpretation which made keeping God's laws merely an external matter. (Mark 7:1-15) When Jesus came He emphasized the error of this false interpretation by the religious leaders. He told them what God really intended. Jesus was clear in explaining that God looks at the heart—not merely the outward performance. Most Jewish leaders had developed from their own human wisdom an idea of what God was like; therefore, Satan was able to deceive them with religious independence and spiritual pride so they could not even recognize God when He came in the flesh in the person of Jesus Christ.

We should learn this lesson well, because the Jews knew the Scriptures and they honored the name of God. They were zealous in wanting to serve God, but it was by the wisdom of man. They were not willing to commit—sacrifice—themselves to the spirit of the law or the Lordship and character of God in directing their lives.

Like them, we often reject the total surrendered life because of our indifference to our spiritual needs. We are too busy with worldly activities and pursuits because we have become caught in the treadmill of daily existence. Our inner spiritual being has become secondary. Like the Jews, we often know the Scriptures intellectually and we honor the name of God. We are zealous in wanting to serve, to be involved, but it is often by human wisdom and willpower. The true Spirit of Christ and His glory is often lost in our involvement because our heart is really seeking to satisfy our self-life.

This condition exists because we don't know how to detach ourselves from the world. We aren't even sure this is necessary. Our society system now controls the minds of most of us under its continuous influence from the media—radio, television, newspapers, magazines—as well as eduction and materialistic success. The self-centered spirit of our land and its influences have brainwashed us. It is a bombardment of the ways of the world that John referred to in I John 2:16 —"the lust of the flesh," the "lust of the eyes" and "the pride of life." The power of this worldly influence has become so intense that most of us can barely help but love and be attached to some of the things and self-seeking ways of this world. This plan of attack against Christians has happened, as prophesied in the Bible, through the spiritual influence and direction of what John calls the beast system in Revelation. Satan has perfected in our society one of the principles Jesus teaches in "the parable of the sower," when He said, "What was sown among the thorns is the man who hears the word, but the worries of this life and the deceitfulness of wealth choke it, making it unfruitful." (Matthew 13:22)

It is up to each of us to determine in our own will, in our own heart, if we have a desire to commit completely to Jesus. This does not mean surrendering to a church or a church system of doctrine. Such limited surrender does not give us the strength for spiritual victory, even though the church is vital. Church systems are powerless to correct the spiritual defeat which is now plaguing so many Christians. Systems cannot give Christians personal victory over their inner conflicts, bias and bigotry, emotional disturbances, poverty, hunger, hate, lack of brotherly affection and sinful actions of the flesh. The church has not given victory over adultery with the world. Our church systems are not solving the breakdown of the biblical home structure.

Newspapers are filled with reports of violence and brutality. Unwanted children roam the streets of our cities and child abuse and molestation have become a national horror story. Our society is going backward instead of forward in human relations. We have continuous war, and people seem unable to learn how to live together. The facts increasingly reveal that a contagious spiritual disease has infested our country. This has been brought about by a super deceptive power in our society which has trained and influenced us to get hung up on seeking for and gratifying our self, being self-sufficient and independent.

The following is from a Christian Children's Home of Ohio:

CABBAGE PATCH DILEMMA (An American Tragedy)

Isn't is amazing (and sad) that we in America have our priorities so mixed up that hundreds of people will wait outside a store in the cold for over 8 hours just to buy a doll? What drives folk to riot and destroy property in city after city as they stampede through store aisles grabbing and pushing to buy a doll? People have been injured in these incidents, some trampled. Guards are on duty to provide security for would-be customers. Sales clerks are armed with ball bats to control the crowds.

A local radio station in the midwest reported that a plane would fly over a local stadium with a load of these dolls. People were told to go to the stadium with a catcher's mitt in one hand and to hold their charge cards above their head so they could be photographed in order to bill them and the dolls would be dropped from the plane. Do you realize that over 2 dozen people showed up? What a sad sight to see grown adults (?) peering into the sky with a credit card in hand waiting for the plane.

A store in Akron had 10 dolls for sale this past weekend with prices ranging from $800 to $3,000. These were "originals." A lady had a mink coat made for her doll. Terrorists have kidnapped some dolls and are holding them for ransom.

The creator of these dolls said that he wanted each child to make a commitment to care for these dolls forever and thus the idea of adoption papers. These young people make a pledge to be good parents and the papers are signed. Some children interviewed said that they like these dolls best because they have real "belly buttons."

OUR KIDS HAVE REAL BELLY BUTTONS TOO. THEY ENTERED THIS WORLD MADE IN THE IMAGE OF GOD. THEY HAD PARENTS. SOME WERE ADOPTED. THEY WERE CUTE AND CUDDLY. THEY WERE PURE AND NEW. THEY WORE DIAPERS. THEY WERE GIVEN A NAME. THEY NEEDED TO BE CARED FOR FOREVER TOO. BUT, THE REAL WORLD IS DIFFERENT.

In a country where a child (A REAL ONE) is abused every 2 minutes of every day; where sexual abuse and incest are multiplying each year; where we have more children locked up than ever in the history of this nation; and where teenage suicide is the leading cause of death among our children, it seems silly, maybe even a little vulgar, to be so concerned about dolls.

SURPRISE. Children do not come from the cabbage patch. They are a gift from God to be loved, nurtured, and protected. There are plenty of REAL KIDS who need our help.

One half of all children in our nation do not live in a home according to God's plan, which is to have their original mother and father.

A Christian commitment that does not require going to the cross for death of the self-seeking lifestyle does not work. It does not bring victory. Our society is going backward in human relations because too many people are trying to be Christians without Christ. Satan doesn't mind if we are involved in what society calls Christianity if he can keep us making our own plans and running our own lives independent of God.

Christ, and Christ alone, must be the center of our life, our commitment and worship.

> He is before all things, and in him all things hold together. And he is the head of the body, the church; he is the beginning and the firstborn from among the dead, so that in everything he might have the supremacy. For God was pleased to have all his fullness dwell in him, and through him to reconcile to himself all things, whether things on earth or things in heaven, by making peace through his blood, shed on the cross. (Colossians 1:17-20)

Our self-seeking lifestyles have caused us to no longer want Christ as much as we want what He can do for us. We seek His healing power, His promises, His happiness, more of this earth's goods—but would we be satisfied with just Him alone?

David Wilkerson wrote:

> "How many of us would serve Him if He offered nothing but Himself? No healing, no success, no prosperity, no worldly blessings, no miracles, signs or wonders. **What if**—once again we had to take joyfully the spoiling of our goods? **What if**—instead of clear sailing and problem-free living, we faced shipwreck, fears within and fightings without? **What if**—instead of painless living, we suffered cruel mockings, stoning, bloodshed, being sawn asunder? **What if**—instead of our

beautiful homes and cars, we had to wander about in deserts
in sheepskins, hiding in dens and caves? **What if**—instead of
prosperity, we were destitute, afflicted, and tormented?"

Do you realize that the majority of Christians down through
the centuries have lived their lives under these conditions?
Review the history of the early years in the church under
Roman rule, the Dark Ages, the Reformation wars. Study what
is happening in Russia today where, if you are a Christian,
provisions of life are sacred. In many places of the world
today, Christians only have one thing—Jesus. They have
Jesus.

The only road to safety is our commitment to Jesus. The
reason we see so much spiritual defeat over the power of sin
among Christians is because we lack commitment to Jesus.
We talk about Him, we sing to Him, wave our hands to
Him—but are we satisfied with only Him and nothing or no
one else?

The church once confessed its sins. Now we are more
concerned with confessing what we believe to be our rights.
Because we in the body of Christ are not surrendering ourselves to Jesus our society is in chaos. America has become
infested with drugs. Drug traffic is the largest business in our
country—over 80 billion dollars a year. Many of our people
are infected with the spiritual diseases of homosexuality and
sexual permissiveness. Homes are being destroyed because
of selfishness. We are dishonest and greedy—we are the "give
me" generation. Spiritual infection has touched every avenue
of the lives of our people and too often we in the church
have gone right along. No longer are we the "salt of the
earth" that preserves the good. No longer does our light of
purity shine so brightly in a dark, sick world that we offer
hope for a wayward society. People of the world see we have
many of the same inner personal problems they do.

Our spiritual ointment to deliver our society from the power
of sin which is hurting so many of our people has lost its

effect. It's true! Look around. Many think Christianity has become popular and that may be true in name, but we have lost our power. No longer do we seek first His righteousness. We seek for our own benefits and position.

Sacrifice

Commitment means *sacrifice*. What are we to sacrifice? Spiritual sacrifice is taking all our self-life, our rights, to the cross.

> Then he (Jesus) said to them all: "If anyone would come after me, he must deny himself and take up his cross daily and follow me. For whoever wants to save his life will lose it, but whoever loses his life for me will save it." (Luke 9:23,24)

The spiritual power which gives us this kind of purity is what the church needs — not the power that develops worldly prestige and popularity.

To sacrifice all that is our self-life is what God wants. This means giving up personal rights. This is not popular in Christian circles, but that is where the power lies. The true teachings of Jesus will develop in Christians the characteristics He gave us in the greatest sermon ever preached, "The Sermon on The Mount." Jesus outlined in this sermon those inner characteristics that will be developed in us as we learn to take up our cross daily and follow Him. Jesus listed the characteristics of a Christian in Matthew 5:3-10.

> Blessed (happy) are the *poor in spirit* ...
> Blessed (happy) are those who *mourn* ...
> Blessed (happy) are the *meek* ...
> Blessed (happy) are those who *hunger and thirst for righteousness* ...
> Blessed (happy) are the *merciful* ...
> Blessed (happy) are the *pure in heart* ...
> Blessed (happy) are the *peacemakers* ...
> Blessed (happy) are those who are *persecuted because of righteousness* ...

Spiritual Characteristic No. 1— *Poor in Spirit* (emptied of self interest)

This is the key to all that follows in the development of our Christian walk. It deals with the process of emptying us of our old nature so we can be filled with the power of God's nature, His Holy Spirit. As a spiritual vessel, we cannot be filled with the new until the old is emptied. The world system despises the quality of "poor in spirit," and Satan uses all the tools available from the world system to promote self-confidence, self-assertion, self satisfaction, self-exaltation, self-glorification, self-dependence and self-reliance. Satan's character is self-centered and Jesus says that characteristic in each of us must go to the cross and be put to death (made inactive). Jesus shocks the wisdom of the world with His teachings that are in direct conflict with all that is of the world.

This characteristic isn't popular in the Christian community either. Because it isn't we cannot be filled with the power of God. This is why Christians are experiencing much defeat in their personal lives. We as people want to look at other humans—their personalities, business success, natural abilities, personal appearance—all the worldly characteristics. We even promote these characteristics in the church.

Only Jesus' quality of humility stands the test of many storms. Scripture says Jesus was not someone to simply look at. (Isaiah 53:2,3). He is described as someone so unattractive that no one would be naturally drawn to Him.

To be "poor in spirit" means absence of pride in our abilities; an inner awareness that we live and breathe in the presence of God; placing no emphasis on family heritage, nationality, natural temperaments, worldly position and authority, wealth, academic training, personality, intelligence, or other special abilities.

To become "poor in spirit" requires a constant looking to Jesus and dependence on the power of the indwelling Holy

Spirit. We are not to try, and cannot within ourselves, develop this characteristic. It is a matter of commitment to Jesus who will then develop it in us. To try to do so ourselves would probably cause us to remove ourselves from society, endeavor to change our personality, purposely bring about personal hardships, etc. This type of activity actually brings a greater awareness of "self," which causes us to end up being less "poor in spirit." Jesus is talking about our inner nature. Only the Lord can change that, and only to the degree we in our heart are willing to commit and sacrifice our being to Him.

Spiritual Characteristic No. 2 — *Mourning*

The characteristic of mourning means we see sin in our self and sin in the world as it really is. We do not try to escape from reality.

Again, we experience a characteristic given by Jesus which is totally contrary to the teachings of society. It is a spiritual attitude Satan wants us to avoid. He tries to develop in us the desire to escape from reality, seeing the world as it really is.

As a whole, the major theme of worldly pleasure—money, the energy and enthusiasm expended in the entertainment world—is an expression of Satan's great aim in using the world system to move us away from this spiritual characteristic—"the spirit of mourning."

Mourning is that characteristic which allows us to see and have a deep inner pain and concern for the sin in the world. It allows us to see our own natural sinful self. It allows us to recognize the sin principle at war within us.

Jesus mourned because He saw the horrid, ugly and foul thing called sin in the world. He saw its terrible results of pain, sickness, grief, unhappiness and death. He saw it sending many people to the grave on their way to hell. That is why it brings mourning; we see what it does to people. We see what a sacrifice sin caused God to make. Sin stabs God right in the heart. It caused God deep pain to send Jesus to the cross.

The characteristic of mourning opens us to see our needs and the needs of the world, and how these needs have been totally met in Jesus alone. The degree to which we possess this characteristic plays heavily in the appreciation we have of God's deep love, our Christianity and our commitment.

Spiritual Characteristic No. 3—*Meekness* (having a true view of oneself)

Again Jesus brings us face to face with a characteristic completely opposed to the nature of man.

To control and influence the world we normally rely on the strength and power of military and material goods, our abilities, intellect and aggressiveness. Yet, Jesus says, "The meek shall inherit the earth." (Matthew 5:5) This baffles the wisdom of the natural man of the world.

However, we in the organized church often depend on the world's ways, and trust in our abilities and means of power found through men. We do not identify with God's way, the spiritual way of meekness.

Meekness was the lifestyle of Jesus, Moses, David, Abraham, the prophets, Paul, Peter and many others throughout the history of God's people. They became servants to others, regardless of the cost. And they did not rely on their abilities, taking the things of God into their hands to accomplish, but submitted their self-will to God, becoming totally dependent on Him.

One of the greatest leaders of all time was Moses, and Scripture describes him as a meek man. (Numbers 12:3) He was to be head of all Egypt, and through his position and natural power of authority, he could have accomplished the Israelites' return to Palestine. Yet God chose to strip and purge Moses of all his self-power, position and abilities and only allowed his mission to be accomplished by the character and power of God.

The same is true of Jesus. He took on the form of a servant. He did not try to use the political systems of His day to accomplish God's mission. Instead he sacrificed Himself, giving His all for others in meekness—a power contrary to the world's ways. But it is the way that works. Examine His long-lasting results.

Meekness is that characteristic which centers on our relationships. But it does not mean we are to be flabby, lacking in strength, firmness, vigor or force. We are not to be simply easy-going, "nice," weak in personality, or exhibiting a compromising spirit of peace at any price. Examine how Jesus lived. He knew His mission.

It is the quality of meekness which causes us not to demand anything for *ourselves*. When people talk about us, scorn us, state untruths about us, we are not to fight back. We won't even want to. We are not sensitive about ourselves. No longer are we concerned about our own interests. We are not concerned about our rights. Nor do we make demands for our position, privileges, possessions or status in life. We no longer go on the defensive trying to protect ourselves and our opinions, or having to be right. Our self-life has gone to the cross. It has been crucified. Meekness is that characteristic which allows us to truly see ourselves and realize that in our natural state, there is nothing worth defending. We are only vessels for God to live in and through.

Spiritual Characteristic No. 4—
To Hunger and Thirst for Righteousness

As we develop the first three Christian characteristics we've discussed, we see the Lord's perfect sequence in our being emptied of all that is of "self"—our old nature. To the degree we are emptied of our self-seeking nature, we will desire to be filled with God's righteousness. The Lord will develop that desire into a thirst and hunger.

Righteousness is the way to real peace. It is the Christian characteristic which gives a definite sign of our Christianity. It is that nature which distinguished Jesus from all other men who ever lived. If we welcome and desire righteousness, God's Spirit is truly transforming us into His image.

To hunger and thirst is to have an awareness, a consciousness of a deep and desperate need, to the point where we experience pain in our soul. It stays until satisfied. It is like the feeling one has if he longs to be with the one he or she loves . . . the way we long to be home if away and homesick. It is like the inner drive men and women have as they commit themselves for training to be a sports champion. The drive is so desperate, it hurts. It brings pain, suffering and agony because it is an all-out commitment to sacrifice. Jesus' commitment against sin caused Him to resist to the point of shedding blood. (Hebrews 12:4)

It is important to note that Jesus did not tell us to hunger and thirst after happiness or blessings. You see, they are a *result* of seeking righteousness. To make the mistake of having the wrong thing as our object is like a doctor treating the pain and ignoring the cause. Jesus directs us to righteousness because only it treats and fills a man who has been emptied of "self."

Satan is using all the many elements in our world society with great deception to prevent our self-emptying process— dying to self interest. This in turn eliminates our inner hungering and thirsting for righteousness. It affects our being filled with God's spiritual power to conquer sin and minister through love to our world.

Jesus promises that if we hunger and thirst for righteousness, we will be filled—not by our efforts, but through God's grace. We will be filled with the anointing and power of the Holy Spirit. If one is emptied of his self-seeking nature and is filled with God's nature, the next three characteristics given by Jesus—being "merciful, pure in heart and a peacemaker" —describe the nature that will control our personalities and actions.

Spiritual Characteristic No. 5 — *Merciful* (to have pity, compassion and sorrow plus action)

The principle of mercy looks at the miserable consequences of sin. It is a character quality to have both a deep sense of pity and a desire to act and relieve the suffering of sin.

Mercy is the characteristic which allows us to see others with a different eye. It is a Christ-like eye. Our attitude toward others changes because we begin to see people as creatures to be pitied; creatures that are slaves to sin; creatures that have been trapped and engulfed in Satan's world; creatures that are slaves of hell as we once were; creatures that need forgiveness as we need forgiveness.

Mercy differentiates between the sinner and sin. It moved Jesus to say, "Forgive them for they know not what they do." Because of His characteristic of mercy, Jesus could see through those who persecuted Him to be victims of Satan and his world system. It was God's characteristic of mercy that had pity on mankind and caused Him to make salvation available to all through the sacrifice of His Son, Jesus, as an atonement for our sins.

Spiritual Characteristic No. 6 — *To Be Pure in Heart* (to have singleness of mind that is void of self-interest)

To be pure in heart is for us to be single-minded in bringing glory to God in all things, rather than seeking for our own interest.

The whole principle of the Christian doctrine emphasizes the heart. Jesus baffled the scholars of His day because He bypassed the intellectual mechanics of the Scriptures and zeroed in on their effect on the heart. He made it clear we must be changed from the inside out. We must receive a new heart.

Through this characteristic, Jesus takes us to the seat of all of our problems. It is out of our heart, Jesus says, that evil thoughts, false witness, blasphemies, immorality, etc., proceed. The cause of any problem in life, any unworthy desire we may have, Jesus says, comes from the heart.

To allow the Lord to develop in us a new heart will bring freedom from any hypocrisy. We will have a singleness of mind in life to know God, to glorify God, to love Him and to serve Him in His kingdom. In every respect, this becomes our supreme desire in life—to seek only God, in nature, in events in history and in events in our own lives.

Spiritual Characteristic No. 7— *To Be a Peacemaker* (to no longer look at the effect of things upon ourselves, so that we are not sensitive, touchy or defensive)

This is the greatest of all Christian characteristics—the one we should cry out for God to burn into our lives. We should desire that He change our lives, through the other characteristics, so we can reach a position of spiritual maturity. Then this quality can become a reality in our lives. Of all things in the history of mankind, whatever his endeavors, inner peace is the one thing he most strives to possess. It is God's greatest desire that His children be the vessels that will bring peace on earth and goodwill to men.

To be a peacemaker does not necessarily mean being an easy-going person who will seek peace at any price—who will say nothing to avoid trouble, try to appear nice or simply be an appeaser.

A peacemaker has a different view of himself than other people because he has been delivered from concern for "self."

The characteristic of meekness enables him to be absolutely neutral in a conflict—not sensitive, touchy, or on the defensive. His interest is focused on bringing inner peace to mankind regardless of personal sacrifice. He sees a much bigger and more important purpose in life than gaining his own rights. Our supreme example is Jesus who sacrificed His rights and went to the cross to bring a hope of peace to our hearts and to this earth.

Like Jesus, a peacemaker's primary concern is that God be glorified among people. He looks at all disputes, whether individual, national or international, as a distraction from bringing glory to God, rather than being concerned with how it may be affecting himself or his interests.

In practice, a peacemaker does not stand on his own dignity. God did not stand on "His dignity." He did something to bring peace on earth. He humbled Himself through His Son to make peace.

A peacemaker is selfless, lovable and approachable, endeavoring to diffuse peace wherever he goes. Other people sense a peacemaker, and approach him freely, knowing they will receive understanding and direction to find peace in their hearts. This is why people are drawn to Jesus.

The blessing promised to a peacemaker is a tribute to us all. Jesus says, "They will be called the sons of God." In essence, Jesus is saying, "Like Father, like son." For when we repeat this characteristic of being a peacemaker, Jesus says, "This is truly being like a son of God."

Spiritual Characteristic No. 8—
Persecuted for Righteousness' Sake

Persecution is an action often taken against those who possess the inner characteristics of a Christian.

People wanted to persecute Jesus because His nature was so different. His righteousness, illustrated in the characteristics just described made the righteousness of those around Him look cheap, second class, tasteless and showy. His light was so bright it showed up the darkness of evil in the hearts of men who did not want to believe they were evil. His light had to be extinguished, so they persecuted and killed Him. The same has happened to other Christians. As these characteristics became the dominant nature of their inner being, people around them could not accept the power of that individual's light.

These spiritual characteristics of a Christian are contrary to the wisdom and natural ways of man. They are even considered foolish, but in them we find the true secret that brings happiness: joy, peace and love.

They tell us what a Christian professes. They are a mirror for us to use, not a window through which we look at others. They point out what our nature as Christians should be. They show us that *being* is more important than *doing*. Actions or works are a result of *being*. These characteristics tell us we are not to control our Christianity; our Christianity is meant to control us. The Apostle Paul says,

> I have been crucified with Christ and I no longer live, but Christ lives in me. The life I live in the body, I live by faith in the Son of God, who loved me and gave himself for me. (Galatians 2:20)

Jesus should be allowed to develop all of these characteristics in each of us. As members of God's family they are to become our new nature—not by the power of self-will (which is impossible) but through the power of the indwelling Holy Spirit. Even a brief examination of these spiritual character qualities tells me it is impossible for me to achieve them on my own. This new nature is totally opposite to that of the world and the way we normally function. Yet I know these character qualities given by our Lord Jesus should develop so they flow naturally, just as our old self-centered character qualities flow naturally.

Having this new nature requires commitment on my part. It demands that I sacrifice all of my old nature so God can bring death to (make inactive) my old nature and mold me into a new person. It is this type of commitment and sacrifice that the power of the beast system has virtually eliminated. Yet Paul says it is this kind of sacrifice which should be our spiritual worship. (Romans 12:1)

A personal examination of these characteristics* and con-tinual growth in them helps us realize our true spiritual commitment and sacrifice. A careful look at God's true char-acter, however, is often painful because it will usually crush us.

Note, also, that the purpose of this self-examination is not to impose condemnation of our souls, for there is no con-demnation of those who are in Christ Jesus. (Romans 8:1) Rather, the purpose is to help each of us realize that total and complete dependence on God will enable us to live an exemplary Christian life in a world that so totally opposes us, and constantly tries to develop in us characteristics which are the very opposite of those we have just discussed. This is what John saw and described in prophetic terms in Reve-lation 13, stating what would happen at the close of the Gentile age. With man's technological knowledge, most of which is used for worldly purposes, John saw that Satan's world system would have an overwhelming teaching power to oppose the growth of these spiritual characteristics of poor in spirit, mourning, meekness, to hunger and thirst for right-eousness, merciful, pure in heart and to be a peacemaker.

By stating these true spiritual characteristics, Jesus gave us the only formula for true happiness. They serve as a checklist to help us see why so many people in our society —Christians included—are unhappy, and are experiencing severe problems. The world is successful in developing its counter-characteristics—those which oppose God's nature.

The difference is in whether we are *committed* to Jesus and His teaching or are just busy with religious activity. We can be involved all the way in religion, or what society might call Christianity, but if we do not possess the characteristics

---

*I have given only a brief review of these Christian characteristics. There has been much written about each one. For further study I would rec-ommend the book "Studies In The Sermon On The Mount" by D. Martyn Lloyd-Jones, published by Wm. B. Eerdmans, Grand Rapids, Michigan.

of God, we are simply doing our own thing—making our own plans and running our own lives independent of God. If we are not growing in our dependence upon Him, letting these spiritual characteristics of God be so developed in us that they dominate all of our activities, then we have missed the most important teaching of the Bible.

We must express the nature of Jesus in all we do. We are to be holy and pure, the salt of the earth, as Christ lives in us and through us. We must let the love of God flow out to others, drawing them to Jesus. Let us examine what Paul says in I Corinthians 6:19: "Do you not know that your body is a temple of the Holy Spirit within you, which you have from God? You are not your own; you were bought with a price. So glorify God in your body." Too often we act and think as though we belong to ourselves. We don't like to think that we belong only to God, to serve His purposes on this earth. It is amazing how Satan has deceived us and developed in us such a strong attitude of self-seeking.

Upon learning that a believer must be totally committed to Christ and sacrifice all that there is of himself, some people may say, "I can't yield to that type of Christianity. I can't buy that kind of commitment where I have to give up all my desires to follow Christ. That's fanatical. You're asking me to do the impossible."

Jesus asked for this kind of commitment because He alone knows what is best for us. Only He can direct our lives so we will have the inner victory he intended His followers to have behind the enemy lines of this world. Jesus defeated the deceiving tactics of our enemy, Satan. So in His love, Jesus says, "Let go and let me take over. Yield all to me and I will do the impossible." All He wants is for us to acknowledge that we truly want to surrender our self-will to Him. And even though we do not know all of the inner spiritual changes that might be necessary for such a commitment, we need only to tell Him that we will trust His power and authority— not our own.

Paul teaches that only Jesus can really change any of us. "Therefore, if anyone is in Christ, he is a new creature; the old has passed away, behold, the new has come." (II Corinthians 5:17) Please notice Paul says that "he is a new creature," and that Jesus Christ is the one who creates in us this new nature. It's not religion, a church system or personal willpower. These can change only the symptoms, not the inner being of a man. And it is only when our inner character is changed on the inside that true spiritual victory is fully realized and the fruits of the Spirit begin to become our normal Christian way of life. Only Jesus can set us free from the power of our sinful self-serving character.

Let us examine Paul's list of personal credentials and his zealous devotion to a religious system. It will help us determine proper direction and true success in fully committing our all to Jesus. Referring to His religious life when He was totally involved, Paul says:

> Yet, if anyone ever had reason to hope that he could save himself, it would be I. If others could be saved by what they are, certainly I could! For I went through the Jewish initiation ceremony when I was eight days old, having been born into a pure-blooded Jewish home that was a branch of the old original Benjamin family. So I was a real Jew if there ever was one! What's more, I was a member of the Pharisees who demand the strictest obedience to every Jewish law and custom. And sincere? Yes, so much so that I greatly persecuted the church; and I tried to obey every Jewish rule and regulation right down to the very last point. But all these things that I once thought worthwhile—now I've thrown them all away so that I can put my trust and hope in Christ alone. Yes, everything else is worthless when compared with the priceless gain of knowing Christ Jesus my Lord. I have put aside all else, counting it worth less than nothing, in order that I can have Christ, and become one with him, no longer counting on being saved by being good enough or by obeying God's laws, but by trusting Christ to save me; for God's way of making us right with himself depends on faith—counting

on Christ alone. Now I have given up everything else—I have
found it to be the only way to really know Christ and to
experience the mighty power that brought him back to life
again and to find out what it means to suffer and die with
him. So, whatever it takes, I will be one who lives in the fresh
newness of life of those who are alive from the dead. I don't
mean to say I am perfect. I haven't learned all I should even
yet, but I keep working toward that day when I will finally be
all that Christ saved me for and wants me to be. (Phillipians
3:4-11, Living Bible)

Paul studied under one of the greatest philosophers of his
day, Gamaliel. If Paul were alive today, he would probably
hold a Ph.D. in philosophy and theology. He would have an
understanding knowledge of economics, political science,
history and the languages; he spoke both Greek and Hebrew.
Paul was also very religious. He was a member of the Pharisee
sect. He was involved.

Paul fasted a couple of times a week, prayed three times a
day, gave ten percent of his earnings, and we are sure that
he seldom missed attending the assembly. Paul had social
status, born from the people of Israel in the tribe of Benjamin,
and able to trace his family heritage back to Abraham. Paul
had reason to take great personal pride in who he was. But
with all of his religion, political authority, economic position,
educational background and intellectual ability, he says, "All
things which were gain to me, those I count lost for Christ; in
fact I count everything loss that I might know Christ better."
He had experienced that there is only one power that has
any force at all to deal with the influences and pressures of
the world and its systems. It is Jesus, only Jesus.

Spiritual surgery is necessary for all of us to put to death
the self-life which will allow our full commitment to Jesus.
Only God can perform this surgery; it is not within the power
of man to change his inner nature.

The teachings of our society lead us to dependence on
the things Paul says he counted loss. We are taught to be

concerned about our heritage, family name, our rights, personal fame or importance, social status and accomplishments. Paul says it is all garbage. It is all of this world!

Christ did not become influenced by the system or society. He said, "I have overcome the world." (John 16:33) He did not yield to the inner pressures and worldly influences around Him. That is what spiritual victory is all about—true peace and joy. Christ offers the same spiritual strength to all of us. But Satan has used the overpowering influence of our society to keep many of us from realizing this kind of inner victory. In Revelation 13:7, John prophesied that this would happen to the saints living under the power and worldly authority of the beast.

> "It (the beast) was allowed to make war on the saints and to conquer (overcome) them." (Revelation 13:7. Words in parentheses are the author's.)

We might better understand how the effects of the influence of our society have overcome the spiritual power of the saints if we closely examine what Paul says in Philippians 3:10. In this verse he gives us the insight that becoming spiritually detached from the "things" of the world is the only way to really know Christ.

It is the only way to experience the mighty power that brought Christ back to life again—the power of the Holy Spirit. (Romans 8:11) To experience the mighty power which will give us spiritual victory over our self-seeking nature, and thereby experience the peace that Christ promised, we must be willing to allow God to perform spiritual circumcision on our inner being. We must get rid of our attachments to the "things" of Satan's world. God will go into spiritual battle on our behalf, but only if our hearts truly desire it.

God Is Spirit

Since surrendering to the power of Jesus is the only key to inner peace and joy, and living the victorious Christian life, we must find the means by which we can surrender our self willpower and become "poor in spirit" as our Lord Jesus taught in Matthew 5:3.

Paul said, "I have been crucified with Christ and I no longer live, but Christ lives in me." (Galatians 2:20) Most of us do not know how to make this spiritual principle a reality in our Christian life. The spiritual process necessary for its development is especially difficult in the present self-gratifying atmosphere of our society.

The surrendering of our self-will is difficult for us to understand because we have a fleshly nature. Therefore, our first reaction is usually to try and accomplish our commitment of self-will to Jesus in the power of the flesh. Paul had this same problem. (Romans 7:14-25) It was not until after he knew he was now under the law (rule) of the Spirit that he was able to obtain spiritual victory. (Romans 8) When we "know" that total commitment to Jesus is not of the flesh, but of the Spirit, and therefore we can't apply human strength or understanding to this task, then our position to spiritual commitment will begin to grow.

Spiritual Work

To spiritually commit our self-will to Jesus, we need to know that it is only God or Satan who can perform a work in the spiritual realm. It is not within man's power to do so. So if we have the desire to surrender, we must turn everything over to God, become completely dependent upon Him, and then by faith trust God to perform a work in our lives which will result in spiritual surrender. Only then can we stand with the power of Christ to overcome the spiritual influences of our society.

If you have a desire to fully surrender your all to Jesus, then I urge you to ask God, through prayer, to begin a new work in your life. Ask Him and trust Him to do whatever is required to bring about a complete commitment in your life. Tell the Lord that you want Him to work in your life—to enable you to surrender your all to Jesus as Lord, and know His power in overcoming the world. All that our loving Father needs and wants from us is to see a sincere desire to fully surrender.

The reason we must ask God to do this work in our lives is because we do not have the spiritual power or the spiritual know-how to surrender ourselves. "Self" will never crucify "self." We are dependent on God to perform this work in us just as we are dependent on His power to bring about spiritual rebirth when we first become a Christian. We may not understand the spiritual mechanics, but we can have confidence that His work will be done with complete and total love. This is not to say that we won't have trials and tribulations, because at times these are necessary to break and bring death to our self-seeking willpower so that we can surrender. But you will find that these difficulties of discipline will turn into great joy and peace and produce the fruit of righteousness after spiritual surgery has been performed.

The purpose of this book is to challenge us to a deep commitment to Christ. The body of Christ is to prepare for the soon-to-come bridegroom.

This book has not centered on what it means to become a Christian, though that may be the spiritual condition of some readers. Instead, it has addressed itself to those in the Body of Christ who are willing to go before the Father and say, "God, I want you to do whatever is necessary to strip me of every attachment I have to the enemy's system. I want to experience the fullness of your character and power of the Holy Spirit."

"Wait a minute," you may be saying. "I'm just not there. I'm not about to start praying for God to do whatever He wants to do in my life." If that is your situation, please don't feel a heavy burden if you are not willing to pray in that way. It is not my desire to lay a guilt trip on anyone.

If you are not ready for that prayer, it is important that you be honest about it. Next, I would ask that you go to prayer choice No. 2, which is, "God, I want to be honest. I'm not ready to pray that first prayer, but I know it is right. I want to be in such a spiritual condition that I could pray such a prayer. Teach me and mold me until I can say, "I'm willing to sacrifice all that is necessary in my life. I want you to do anything and everything needed in my life to purge me, to strip me, to totally empty me of all that is of my inner self-nature. I want to make Jesus the Lord of my life. I want to possess His characteristics. Father, I am not at that point yet, but I know it is right to be there, so bring me to the place where I can pray such a prayer from my heart."

Commit Daily

We must have an attitude of prayer, wanting God to perform spiritual work in our lives daily. We need to yield to Him, asking Him to do whatever is necessary to teach, train and mold us spiritually. Then, we should thank Him for everything that happens, welcoming whatever spiritual lesson He may be teaching us. His spiritual teachings yield great and lasting blessings and bring us into a closer relationship and communion with Him.

Christ sacrificed His all in heaven for mankind. He became an atonement for our sins. He reestablished the close communion we can have with Him and our Father, as He died on the cross to do away with our independence. He shed His blood to forgive us of wrong acts and thoughts. He rose again from the dead so He could replace our sinful natures with His own life. Paul expresses the tremendous love God has manifested to mankind when he says, "Anyone who receives Christ into his life becomes a son of God." We become a member of the royal family of God.

By becoming a member of God's family, we develop a relationship with God that is greater than any other relationship we can possibly know on earth. We become His servants while we're on earth, and we have an eternal inheritance as His child.

Satan had to come up with a most deceptive scheme to throw us off track and adulterate the type of commitment referred to. It is Satan's goal to destroy that kind of attitude and the realization of God's beautiful love for us.

The Scriptures teach us that Christ alone gives us our security. Our dependence must be on Him alone, and we must trust only in His power and His love. Christ has not only set us free from the effects of sin, but He has also set us free from the power of the world and our sinful nature. Whoever the Son has set free is free indeed. (John 8:36) Accept and believe this truth. As Jesus conquered the effects of the world, we also can conquer the spiritual effects of the world, but it can be only through the power of Christ.

The words written in this book are to warn us of the way Satan has planned his attack against Christianity in America near the end of the church age. May these studies help motivate us, as God's people, to commit our all to Jesus Christ— our only means to safety to "avoid being marked by the beast" in the last days in America.

I believe nearly every Christian church or fellowship of believers has that core of people whose hearts' desire is to know the Lord with a deep commitment. Maybe you are one of these people or want to be. I believe God, in His love, will raise up each group of committed Christians to stand in the gap in prayer, steadfastness, love and concern on behalf of other believers in their church or fellowship who are wayward—those who will be tossed to and fro during the coming time of purging and refinement. There is a critical need for committed Christians to take such a stand.

STAND FIRM . . .

When the world around you crumbles,
and you're not sure what to do—
when those you love the very most
find it difficult to love you . . .
STAND FIRM . . . and trust in Jesus.

When the pressure seems unbearable
and you carry a burden so great,
roll back those cares on your Savior
and in His glorious presence do wait.

When you're swayed by the needs all around you
and you give—more and more, day by day,
recall that your own strength is limited
and God's Word only must you obey.

When well-meaning friends and acquaintances
want to tell you just what you should do,
Remember—only one God do you serve,
and He alone knows what's best for you.

So, whether in mountains or valleys,
only Jesus' voice must you follow;
for all others—no matter how loving,
are distracting, misleading and hollow.

STAND FIRM... and trust in Jesus.

—Angie Clarkson

Perhaps as you read this book you are not sure you truly know Jesus Christ, other than as a name in your religion. Don't be ashamed to admit this; be honest about it. Honesty of the heart is one of the truest virtues—one we can count on to bring us rewards. It is honesty that allows us to admit we have pride in our hearts, that we are selfish, that we are sinners. To admit this is not weakness, but the sign of an honest individual.

God has done something about our pride, our selfishness and our sins. This something is *someone*—Jesus Christ. But to benefit from what God has done you must know Jesus Christ as more than just a name. You must be willing to swallow that pride, be big enough to humble yourself before God and admit your true inner nature as a sinner. You must be willing to repent.

Next, you must ask the Lord Jesus to come into your heart as the Savior and Lord of your life. If you do this and are honest in your confession, you *will* receive Him into your heart. You may not immediately understand all that transpires, but you'll know it is true—you can have complete faith in that. Jesus will truly make you a new person on the inside, as He has done for millions throughout the history of Christianity. The evidence of this fact far outweighs any logic one may have against it. You can know this truth and begin to testify of a change that is taking place in your inner life. It's up to you. True wise men are not too proud to seek Him. Ask Jesus Christ into your heart.

Don't allow your pride and intellect to keep you from the LIFE that is available through salvation found in Jesus—God's greatest gift.

FOOTNOTES

Chapter 3

Most of the historical content prior to 1800 is based on the work of Peter Marshall and David Manuel as published in their book *The Light and the Glory,* published by Fleming H. Revell Company, Old Tappen, New Jersey—1977.

1. Marshall, Peter and Manual, David: *The Light and the Glory,* P.149—Old Tappan, New Jersey—Fleming H. Revell Company—1977.
2. Ibid., P.149
3. Ibid., P.216
4. Ibid., P.217
5. Ibid., P.217
6. Ibid., P.236
7. Ibid., P.237
8. Ibid., P.247
9. Ibid., P.247
10. Ibid., P.250

Chapter 7

1. Sanborn, Frederic R.: *Design for War,* Devin-Adair Co., Inc. N.Y.—1951. Swomley, John M. Jr.: *The American Empire,* The MacMillian Company N.Y., N.Y.—1970. Theobald, Admiral Robert A.: *The Final Secret of Pearl Harbor,* serialized in U.S. News and World Report, April 2, 1954, Pages 50 thru 93. Official Governemnt Documents: *Army's Pearl Harbor Report.* Official Government Document: *Foreign Relations of the United States and Japan.* Schuman, Frederick: *International Politics,* McGraw-Hill Inc., N.Y., N.Y.—1958. Historian Beard, Charles A.: *President Roosevelt and The Coming of the War,* New Haven, Conn., Yale University Press—1948.

Chapter 9

1. *U.S. News and World Report: THE COMPUTER, How It's Changing Our Lives,* Books by U.S. News and World Report, Washington, D.C., 1972.

A PERSONAL NOTE FROM THE AUTHOR

My heart's desire is that this book conveys the message that my primary interest is in serving our God and His Son, our Lord Jesus. Other significant interests in my life are:

FAMILY

My wife, Barbara and I have been married for twenty-seven years. We are the parents of nine children, three of our own and six guardian children and we make our home in Scottsdale, Arizona.

CHURCH

I serve as an elder of Trinity Church in Scottsdale where both my wife and I are presently teaching adult Sunday School classes.

HOME LIFE FELLOWSHIP

Our home is the Thursday night meeting place for our Christian friends. We meet weekly to share our burdens and our joys, join in intercessory prayer and fellowship in the Word.

WORK

I am employed as Vice President of Pimalco Corporation, Chandler, Arizona. Pimalco is a manufacturer of aerospace aluminum alloys for the aircraft industry.

CHRISTIAN EDUCATION

Barbara and I were instrumental in founding Paradise Valley Christian School (K-8) in 1974 and I serve as President. We are also active in Phoenix Christian High School, from where five of our nine children will soon have graduated.